To Maurice

Romanian Policy towards Germany, 1936–40

Rebecca Haynes
Lecturer in Romanian Studies
School of Slavonic and East European Studies
University College London

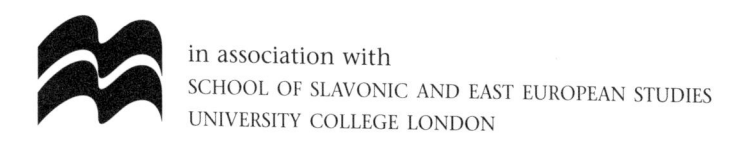

in association with
SCHOOL OF SLAVONIC AND EAST EUROPEAN STUDIES
UNIVERSITY COLLEGE LONDON

First published in Great Britain 2000 by
MACMILLAN PRESS LTD
Houndmills, Basingstoke, Hampshire RG21 6XS and London
Companies and representatives throughout the world

A catalogue record for this book is available from the British Library.
ISBN 0–333–74727–5

First published in the United States of America 2000 by
ST. MARTIN'S PRESS, INC.,
Scholarly and Reference Division,
175 Fifth Avenue, New York, N.Y. 10010

ISBN 0–312–23260–8

Library of Congress Cataloging-in-Publication Data
Haynes, Rebecca, 1962–
Romanian policy towards Germany, 1936–40 / Rebecca Haynes.
p. cm.
Includes bibliographical references and index.
ISBN 0–312–23260–8 (cloth)
1. Romania—Foreign relations—Germany. 2. Germany—Foreign relations–
–Romania. 3. Romania—Foreign relations—1914–1944. 4. Germany—Foreign
relations—1933–1945. I. Title.

DR229.G4 H49 2000
327.498043'09'043—dc21
                                                                99–089963

© Rebecca Haynes 2000

All rights reserved. No reproduction, copy or transmission of this publication may be made without written permission.

No paragraph of this publication may be reproduced, copied or transmitted save with written permission or in accordance with the provisions of the Copyright, Designs and Patents Act 1988, or under the terms of any licence permitting limited copying issued by the Copyright Licensing Agency, 90 Tottenham Court Road, London W1P 0LP.

Any person who does any unauthorised act in relation to this publication may be liable to criminal prosecution and civil claims for damages.

The author has asserted her right to be identified as the author of this work in accordance with the Copyright, Designs and Patents Act 1988.

This book is printed on paper suitable for recycling and made from fully managed and sustained forest sources.

10 9 8 7 6 5 4 3 2 1
09 08 07 06 05 04 03 02 01 00

Printed and bound in Great Britain by
Antony Rowe Ltd, Chippenham, Wiltshire

Contents

Acknowledgements vii

Abbreviations of Primary Sources viii

Introduction 1

1 Victor Antonescu and Romania's Foreign Policy Readjustment, September 1936 to December 1937 19

2 'Friendly with the Whole World': The Goga–Cuza Government and the Comnen Foreign Ministry, December 1937 to December 1938 43

3 Grigore Gafencu: The Persistence of 'Equilibrium' between the Great Powers, December 1938 to March 1939 67

4 From 'Equilibrium' to 'Hand in Hand with Germany', April to October 1939 99

5 Germany's Transformation to a 'Fairy Godmother', Autumn 1939 to June 1940 119

6 Carol and the Axis, June to September 1940 145

Conclusion 167

Bibliography 181

Index 201

Acknowledgements

This book is the product of doctoral research originally funded by the British Academy. There are many people in Britain and abroad who I must thank for helping me bring this research to publication. First, I would like to thank my doctoral supervisors, Professor Dennis Deletant and Dr Karen Schönwälder, and my examiners Dr Maurice Pearton and Professor Jeremy Noakes. My gratitude is due to the staff at the Nicolae Iorga Institute, in Bucharest. During research in Bucharest in 1994–95, I particularly appreciated Professor Ioan Chiper's support and generous help. Thanks are also due to the staff of the Foreign Ministry Archives in Bucharest, especially the director, Nicolae Dinu, and Ion Calafeteanu, and to the patient staff at the State Archives, Bucharest, the Foreign Ministry Archives in Bonn and the Bundesarchiv in Berlin and Koblenz. My weeks spent researching in Germany were funded by the Research Policy and Funding Committee of the School of Slavonic and East European Studies, to whom I am much indebted. My understanding of Romanian diplomacy also benefited from conversations held with, amongst others in Bucharest, Professors Florin Constantiniu, Dionisie Gherman, Dinu Giurescu, Andrei Pippidi, Șerban Rădulescu-Zoner and Nicolae Tanașoca, Dr Gheorghe Iancu, Dr Cristian Popișteanu and Dorin Matei. Special thanks are also due to Mrs Ileana Troiano, introduced to me by Nicolae Rațiu, who gave me valuable advice regarding the background to the 'Tilea affair'. She kindly allowed me to read and copy private papers relating to her father, V. V. Tilea. I am grateful also to my publisher, Mr Tim Farmiloe, and to the Director of the School of Slavonic and East European Studies, Professor Michael Branch. Thanks also to my mother, for her support during my period of research. Last, but by no means least, I am especially thankful to Dr Martyn Rady for giving so freely of his time and providing me with much-needed advice and suggestions.

REBECCA HAYNES

Abbreviations of Primary Sources

Arh. St.	Arhivele Statului (State Archives, Bucharest)
Arh. St., M.P.N.	Arhivele Statului, Fond Ministerul Propagandei Naționale
Arh. St., P.C.M.	Arhivele Statului, Fond Președinția Consiliului de Miniștri
Arh. St., S.U.A.	Arhivele Statului, Statele Unite ale Americii: microfilm of German diplomatic records microfilmed at Alexandria, VA and housed at the State Archives, Bucharest.
DBFP	*Documents on British Foreign Policy, 1919–1939*. Third Series: 1938–39, 9 vols, London, 1949–1955.
DGFP	*Documents on German Foreign Policy*, Series C: 1933–1937, 6 vols, Washington, D.C. and London, 1957–1983; Series D: 1937–45, 14 vols, Washington, D.C., London and Arlington, Virginia, 1949–1976.
MAE	Arhiva Ministerului Afacerilor Externe (Archive of the Ministry for Foreign Affairs, Bucharest).
PA	Politisches Archiv des Auswärtigen Amtes, Bonn
PRO	Public Record Office, London

Introduction

In June 1941 Romania invaded the Soviet Union as an ally of the Third Reich. Despite the importance of this event, there has been little attempt by either Romanian or western historians to explain how the Romanian–German alliance came about or to explore Romanian policy towards Germany in the years leading up to the outbreak of the Second World War. The general tendency of Romanian historians has been to depict Romania as the victim of Great Power intrigues. According to a widely-held interpretation, Romania remained loyal to the western powers throughout the 1930s and had strictly limited links with the Reich. It was only western perfidy in abnegating its political and economic responsibilities in South-East Europe and German pressure which forced Romania to enter the Axis camp in 1940. General Antonescu's pro-Axis foreign policy thus appears in stark contrast to King Carol II's allegedly pro-western orientation.[1] Such a depiction of Romanian interwar diplomatic history has remained largely unreconstructed, despite the opportunity for historical revision afforded by the changes in 1989. Indeed, the arguments used in the communist era are now often harnessed to the flag of Romanian nationalism.[2]

Western historians, on the other hand, have been largely restricted in their exploration of Romanian diplomacy by lack of access to Romanian primary sources. The only substantial work in a western language which looks in detail at the relationship between Romania and Germany is Andreas Hillgruber's *Hitler, König Carol und Marschall Antonescu*, originally published in 1954.[3] Hillgruber's account, however, relies exclusively on German documentary sources and is mainly concerned with General Antonescu's war-time alliance with the Reich. A substantial contribution to our knowledge of Romania's relationship with Germany is provided by Dov B. Lungu's *Romania and the Great Powers, 1933–1940*, which was published in 1989.[4] Lungu's account is concerned with Romania's policies towards all the European Great Powers and, as such, his account of the details of Romanian policy towards Germany is necessarily brief.

This study is an attempt to remedy the gap in our knowledge of Romanian policy towards Germany during the later part of the reign of King Carol II, from the fall of the pro-French foreign minister Nicolae Titulescu on 29 August 1936 to the abdication of the king on 6 September 1940. The fall of Titulescu signalled a shift in Romanian foreign policy away from Titulescu's emphasis on French-backed collective security, in which Germany was regarded with some hostility. The Romanian foreign ministry now sought a policy of friendship with, and unofficial neutrality towards, the Reich. The opening of the war in Europe in 1939 led to Romania's increasingly close alignment with Germany. By the summer of 1940 Carol had already set in motion the events which were to lead to Romania's alliance with Germany and entry into the Axis. General Antonescu's signing of the Tripartite Pact in November 1940 represented the culmination, and logical outcome, of Carol's policies since 1936.

*

Greater Romania was the product of the peace settlement which followed the First World War. The collapse of the Habsburg and Romanov empires provided the opportunity for the incorporation of a number of predominantly ethnically Romanian provinces into the Old Kingdom of Romania (the Regat). These included Transylvania (together with the Banat and Maramureş,) and the Bukovina from the Habsburg empire, and Bessarabia from the Russian empire. Southern Dobruja, which Romania had acquired in 1913, remained within Greater Romania despite its largely Bulgarian population. Greater Romania had now almost twice the size and population of the Old Kingdom. The Romanian economy continued to be overwhelmingly agricultural throughout the inter-war period. The country's industrial sector remained small and its infrastructure primitive. The resulting social and economic problems beset all of Romania's inter-war governments.[5]

The primary aim of all Romania's foreign-policy makers following the First World War was to maintain 'respect for the existing territorial order in Europe and defence of the country's frontiers'.[6] This factor was never forgotten and coloured all of Romania's relationships with neighbouring countries and Great Powers, including the relationship with Germany. In particular, the Romanian government feared potential territorial claims against their country by Bulgaria, Hungary and the Soviet Union, which continued to covet southern Dobruja, Transylvania and Bessarabia respectively.

During the 1920s and early 1930s, Romanian governments believed their country's territorial integrity could best be protected by integration into the League of Nations and the French-backed collective security system in Eastern Europe. A Treaty of Friendship was consequently signed with France in 1926. The Romanians also entered a number of regional alliances to protect their territorial integrity. Agreements concluded between Romania, Yugoslavia and Czechoslovakia in 1920–1921 formed the basis of the so-called Little Entente. This provided for mutual assistance in the event of attack by Hungary, from which country all three Little Entente members had received territory under the Paris treaties. In 1921 Romania signed an alliance with Poland which provided for mutual defence in the case of attack by the Soviet Union. In 1934 Romania, Yugoslavia, Greece and Turkey united to form the Balkan Entente which provided for mutual defence against revisionist Bulgaria.[7]

Until the First World War Romania had retained strong economic and political links with the German empire. In 1883 Romania had joined the Triple Alliance with Germany, Austria-Hungary and Italy. The Romanian government had entered the alliance largely in the hope of receiving German military support in the event of Russian incursions into the Balkans. Germany and Austria-Hungary had also been Romania's main trading partners and investors in the pre-First World War era.[8] The Paris peace treaties cut these links and the western powers acquired Germany's investments in Romania, including assets in the oil industry. It was now France which became the linchpin of Romania's alliance system and economy, becoming Romania's main creditor and one of her foremost investors, together with Great Britain and the United States. Germany was now ranged amongst the revisionist countries, giving moral support to Hungary in its calls for the restitution of Transylvania. During the 1920s, Romanian–German relations dwindled to an all-time low. Romanian diplomacy towards Germany was primarily concerned with enforcement of Romania's financial claims against Germany resulting from the Paris peace treaties, including reparations.[9]

Romania's adherence to the French-backed collective security system is particularly associated with the francophile foreign minister, Nicolae Titulescu. During his two ministries from 1927 to 1928 and again from 1932 to 1936, Titulescu sought to strengthen Romania's position within the collective security system. In 1933 he oversaw the Little Entente's Pact of Reorganisation. The pact sought to ensure that each Little Entente member would not enter into a political or economic agreement with another country without the consent of all the Entente countries. Titulescu was also instrumental in the creation of the Balkan Entente in 1934.[10] During the 1930s both Germany and the Soviet Union re-emerged as major actors in European affairs. Titulescu's diplomacy was concerned with bringing the Soviet Union into the collective security system as a counterweight to the growing power of Germany. Titulescu sought to prevent what he called a 'return to Bismarck's policy – that is to say, Russo–German friendship' which Titulescu believed would be at the expense of the smaller countries of Eastern Europe. Titulescu's overtures towards the Soviet Union in the early 1930s, however, foundered on the issue of Bessarabia. The Soviets refused to give unequivocal recognition to Romania's sovereignty over Bessarabia. In 1934 the Romanian government established full diplomatic relations with the Soviet Union but the Bessarabian issue remained unresolved.[11]

In May 1935, Romania's French and Czechoslovak allies signed separate treaties of mutual assistance with the Soviet Union. In the following year, Titulescu sought an alliance between France, the Little Entente and the Soviet Union. A mutual assistance pact between Romania and the Soviet Union was to be part of this alliance system, so that Romania would 'become a vital link in a reshaped French system exclusively against Germany'.[12] In July 1936 Titulescu and Soviet Foreign Minister Litvinov signed a preliminary agreement for a mutual assistance pact between the two countries. As before, however, the Soviets refused to recognise Romanian sovereignty over Bessarabia.[13]

Titulescu's single-minded pursuit of an alliance with the Soviet Union was a major factor in his downfall.[14] His proposed alliance went against the strongly anti-bolshevik sentiments of both King Carol and the Romanian ruling elite.[15] The Romanians feared that bolshevik infiltration of Romania would lead to the destruction of the monarchy and the country's social and economic structure. This remained a fear throughout the inter-war period and was aggravated by Romania's social and economic problems. In addition, neither the king nor Romanian politicians could countenance an alliance with the Soviets while the Bessarabian question remained unresolved. In 1935 King Carol had quarrelled with Titulescu, arguing in favour of closer relations with Germany rather than the Soviets. During the summer of that year King Carol forbade Titulescu from entering into negotiations with the Soviets.[16] By 1936 both King Carol and the vast majority of Romanian politicians had come to see friendship with Germany as the necessary counterweight to the Soviet Union. Such a diplomatic move was believed to be possible because, while Romania had a direct territorial conflict with the Soviet

Union, she had none with Germany. Thus, by the mid-1930s, the German Reich was beginning to be perceived by many Romanian politicians as a potential guarantor against Russian infiltration into the Balkans: the very role the Second Reich had played for Romania before the First World War.[17] Nevertheless, any political reconciliation between Romania and Germany remained impossible while Titulescu remained in power.[18]

Titulescu's attempts to bring the Soviet Union into the mainstream of Eastern Europe's collective security system also antagonised Romania's anti-Soviet Yugoslav and Polish allies. Both countries had already achieved closer relations with the recently revived German Great Power and had no wish to be incorporated into a Soviet-backed system which was clearly directed against Germany. In 1936 the Poles informed the Romanian government that in the event of a Soviet–Romanian alliance, their treaty with Romania would be abrogated. The Polish government began to campaign in Bucharest for the dismissal of Titulescu. King Carol and members of the Romanian government greatly valued the Polish alliance as the country's only defence against a Soviet attack. They were therefore disposed to take Polish complaints against Titulescu seriously.[19]

Unfortunately for Titulescu, his attempts to incorporate Romania into an enlarged Franco-Soviet security system also coincided with France's gradual loss of prestige among Eastern European governments. France's 1935 alliance with the Soviet Union was not appreciated even by the Romanian government's staunchest francophiles.[20] During the French political campaign which culminated in the election of Léon Blum's Popular Front government in May 1936, Romanian public opinion was easily whipped up by German antisemitic and anti-bolshevik propaganda.[21] Not only did France appear to the Romanians as ripe for 'bolshevisation', but the French government had also long been giving evidence of its unwillingness to curb the revival of German power. In March 1935 the French government had been unable to prevent Hitler's imposition of compulsory military service in Germany. It was Hitler's remilitarisation of the Rhineland in March 1936, however, which provided the decisive blow to French prestige in Eastern Europe. France's inability to act decisively in her own national interests made it unlikely that she would be willing to come to the aid of her far-flung Eastern European allies. Even Titulescu now came to doubt France's commitment to her allies.[22] Moreover, France's concrete obligations to give Romania military aid in the event of war were unclear. The 1926 Treaty of Friendship only laid down joint discussions between chiefs of staff in the event of aggression towards Romania.[23] For his part, King Carol had long doubted France's ability to help Romania in the event of attack. He continued to hope for rapprochement between France and Germany in order to protect Eastern Europe from Soviet attack.[24] Even after the outbreak of the war in 1939, this continued to be Carol's hope.

The decline in France's standing in Eastern Europe also coincided with Romania's loss of faith in the League of Nations. The League's failure to solve the 1932 Manchurian crisis weakened belief in the League's ability to resolve international conflicts.[25] The imposition of sanctions against Italy by the League following the Abyssinian invasion in 1935, with the full support of Titulescu who was Romania's permanent representative to the League, was greatly resented by King Carol and many Romanians. Italy was an important trading partner for Romania and King Carol was in favour of strengthening political links with her. Many in Romania came to see the League as a potential impediment to Romania's relations with other countries.[26]

By the summer of 1936 Titulescu's pro-French and pro-Soviet policies no longer seemed in keeping with the changing international situation, and in particular with the re-emergence of Germany as an active Great Power. Titulescu's policies had antagonised many within Romania as well as Romania's allies who sought good relations with Germany. Following the remilitarisation of the Rhineland in March, Titulescu had sent a message of support to France in the name of the Balkan Entente. Yugoslavia, Turkey and Greece subsequently contacted the German government, distancing themselves from Titulescu's message. The incident underlines the importance which Romania's allies already placed on accommodating themselves to Germany's growing influence in Eastern Europe.[27]

Titulescu's unpopularity at home and abroad was now such as to enable King Carol to remove him from power and take personal control of Romania's foreign policy. Carol had been unable to remove Titulescu earlier owing to his high-standing in western capitals.[28] Not only did Titulescu's foreign policy prevent the creation of stronger links with Germany, but Carol also had personal reasons for wanting Titulescu removed. Since his accession to the throne in 1930, Carol had wished to set up an authoritarian, personal regime. Titulescu was one of the politicians most active in preventing this. Titulescu's removal would ensure that Carol's personal involvement in government was increased.[29] At the same time, Carol resented the frequent interference of the French government in Romania's internal affairs. In 1935, for instance, the French government had forced the Romanians to turn down a German offer to help organise the Romanian armaments industry.[30] Carol may have regarded a shift in foreign policy towards Germany as a counterbalance to French influence within Romania which would also create the preconditions for establishing his own internal control over Romanian affairs by the removal of the powerful Titulescu.

Carol's personal attitude towards Germany was ambiguous. He clearly retained an admiration for the traditions of Imperial Germany. Carol's royal house of Hohenzollern-Sigmaringen was a cadet branch of the German imperial family. Carol had completed his military education in Potsdam prior to the First World War where he had become friendly with his cousin, Prince Friedrich of Hohenzollern-Sigmaringen. Thereafter, Prince Friedrich remained an important conduit between Carol and German leaders. According to Carol's most recent biographer, while in Germany Carol 'was impressed with the strength and efficiency of the German army and rapidly became a germanophile. He was also captivated by the Kaiser....'.[31] Carol's attitude towards National Socialism is less clear. According to his son King Michael, Carol 'had a hateful opinion of Hitler. For a king, Hitler could be nothing other than a dangerous parvenu'.[32] While Carol may have had no admiration for the racial and social revolutionary aspects of Nazism, he admired fascism's authoritarian and militaristic tendencies, which were embodied after 1938 in his own royal dictatorship. Carol certainly appreciated the ability of the Nazi regime to revive the German economy by economic planning, and he maintained his early admiration for the German army. Economic collaboration with Germany and help to build up the Romanian war industry were major contributants to Carol's wish to build closer links with the Reich from the mid-1930s. The pro-French Nicolae Titulescu's position as foreign minister made such large-scale collaboration with the Reich impossible.

The onset of the Great Depression in 1929 had revealed the economic weaknesses underlying the French security system in Eastern Europe. Despite France's role as a creditor and investor in Romania, she was able to do little to help her ally overcome the Depression. In particular, since France was agriculturally self-sufficient and employed a system of imperial preference, the French government could do little to absorb the agricultural produce of its East European allies. The fall in the price of grain had left the agrarian countries of Eastern Europe with produce largely unsaleable on the world market. The situation was compounded by the flooding of the European market by cheap grain from the Americas and Australia.[33] As late as 1936 a proposed economic agreement between France and Romania failed as a result of France's inability to absorb

Romania's agricultural surpluses.[34] In addition, France was unable to supply Romania with sufficient war materials to meet the requirements of Romania's rearmament programme, which began in 1935.[35]

The agrarian structure of the Romanian economy made it difficult for Romania to establish large-scale trading links with her neighbours. The Danubian countries were all primarily agrarian and, therefore, had no need of Romanian agricultural produce. Even the more industrialised Czechoslovakia was unable to absorb Romanian surpluses. In 1936 only 21% of Romania's trade was with the Danubian countries.[36]

Under these circumstances, the traditional trading links with Germany, which had been central before the First World War, acquired increasing importance. Indeed, despite the importance of the western countries as investors in Romania after the First World War, in the 1920s Germany absorbed more of Romania's exports than France and Britain combined.[37] Trade between the two countries was, however, adversely effected by the Depression. In the early 1930s, the Romanian minister to Berlin, Nicolae Petrescu-Comnen, fought hard to encourage the Germans to increase trade with Romania, arguing that economic exchange would lead to increasing German political influence in Romania.[38] The Germans insisted on linking economic concessions to political goodwill. German leaders made it clear that they regarded Titulescu as having sided with the Reich's enemies.[39]

Despite this tactical response, the Germans were well aware of the importance of the economic link with Romania. As early as 1926, Foreign Minister Gustav Stresemann had recognised the importance of providing Romania and Yugoslavia with economic markets in Germany. In this way, it would be possible for Germany to create a breach in the French security system in Eastern Europe through the dislocation of the Little Entente.[40] This idea was taken up with renewed vigour by the German foreign ministry following the 1929 economic crash, when it became clear that neither France nor Britain was capable of providing the countries of Eastern Europe with major economic markets. A commercial agreement was signed with Romania in 1930 and a preference treaty in 1931. The German policy of autarky and agricultural protectionism made it difficult, however, for the foreign ministry to make substantial inroads into the economies of Eastern Europe. This remained the case in the first year of Nazi rule.[41]

Early in 1934, in a move away from autarky and agricultural protectionism, the Reich signed commercial treaties with both Hungary and Yugoslavia. The treaties guaranteed the agricultural produce of both countries a market in Germany at fixed prices.[42] Since Romanian foreign policy was still at that time in the hands of Nicolae Titulescu, German leaders aimed to break Little Entente unity by concentrating on drawing Yugoslavia into the German economic sphere.[43] By 1936, the Germans had succeeded in replacing the western powers as Yugoslavia's main trading partner.[44] This was to have substantial implications for Yugoslavia's foreign policy-direction in the mid and late 1930s and helped undermine the unity of the Little Entente.[45]

Although Romania was of relatively little economic interest to the Germans in 1933, there was a distinct change in attitude following the inauguration of Schacht's New Plan in September 1934. The New Plan was a response to the economic self-sufficiency pursued by states as a consequence of the Depression. This had resulted in Germany's exclusion from numerous foreign markets and consequent inability to earn foreign exchange to pay for imports of raw materials. The New Plan introduced controls over foreign trade and exchange to ensure the import of raw materials and foodstuffs. The concept of multilateral trade was thereby jettisoned in favour of clearing agreements or barter exchange with economies which were considered complementary to that of the Reich. In other words, the Reich was to trade with countries which produced raw materials and foodstuffs, rather than with other highly industrialised countries. Hence, the agricultural countries of South-East Europe took on a new significance for the Reich.

The concept of trade between complementary economies was also popular within economic circles in Romania. The advantage of the New Plan for the Romanians was that they were given a guaranteed market for their agricultural produce and raw materials at prices above world market levels. This provided considerable incentive for continued and deepening economic links with Germany. In addition, Romanian food stuffs and raw materials were exchanged for German industrial goods, which the Romanians were otherwise unable to buy due to lack of foreign exchange. Economic negotiations between Germany and Romania began in the autumn of 1934 and culminated in the signing of a commercial treaty in March 1935. This provided the Romanians with a secure market in Germany for their produce.[46] By 1937, Germany was already receiving 19% of Romania's exports and providing 29% of her imports.[47]

The aim of the traditionalist Reich foreign ministry in pursuing increased trade with South-East Europe remained that of creating a breach in Little Entente unity. By destroying the French security system in Eastern Europe, revision of Germany's borders would become possible.[48] In contrast, Germany's new Nazi leaders aimed both at driving a wedge into the French system in Eastern Europe and to prepare for a possible war. South-East Europe could not only supply the Reich with raw materials necessary for rearmament, but the area could also provide food supplies by an overland route which could not be cut off easily at time of war by blockade.[49] Romania was Europe's second largest supplier of oil, and her supplies were thus of particular importance to the Reich in her preparations for war. This factor accounts for Germany's renewed interest in the Romanian economy after 1934.[50]

The contrasting methods of the traditionalist Reich foreign ministry and Nazi leaders and organisations towards Romania may be illustrated by reference to Alfred Rosenberg's Aussenpolitisches Amt der NSDAP. The foreign ministry believed that political links between Germany and Romania would evolve out of economic collaboration. The foreign ministry did not, therefore, attempt to establish links with right-wing or pro-German politicians within Romania, preferring instead to maintain links with King Carol and his 'German-friendly' supporter Gheorghe Brătianu.[51] Rosenberg, on the other hand, sought to create a pro-German political coalition in Romania.[52] His office established contacts with sympathetic politicians such as Alexandru Vaida-Voevod, Constantin Argetoianu, Octavian Goga and A. C. Cuza, as well as with King Carol. Although Rosenberg failed to create a broadly-based pro-German coalition in Romania, he succeeded in uniting Octavian Goga's National Agrarian Party and A. C. Cuza's League of National Christian Defence as the National Christian Party in July 1935.[53] Officials from Rosenberg's office helped the new party in establishing their antisemitic and nationalistic programme. The National Christians soon developed fascist trappings, including a uniformed party militia.

As well as establishing links with potential allies amongst the Romanian establishment, a novel aspect of Rosenberg's policy towards Romania, and one used subsequently by other Nazi leaders, was the offer to guarantee Romania against Hungarian revisionism in return for Romanian goodwill and friendship towards the Reich. From 1933 onwards, Rosenberg sought to convince the Romanian minister to Berlin, Comnen, that support for Hungarian revisionism was no longer a factor in German foreign policy.[54] In 1935 Rosenberg offered King Carol a German–Romanian treaty of friendship, to include German recognition of Romania's borders, together with a large-scale commercial treaty. The plan fell through on account of Foreign Minister Titulescu's threat to resign if such a treaty were signed.[55]

Similar assurances regarding Hungarian revisionism were also given to Romanian officials by Hermann Göring. Although Göring had no official foreign-policy appointment, his closeness to Hitler ensured his involvement in many foreign-policy ventures. He built up considerable contacts in Austria, Poland and the Balkan countries.[56] In the autumn of 1934, Göring was sent by Hitler to Belgrade as the Reich's official representative at the funeral of King Alexander I of Yugoslavia. There Göring informed King Carol that the Reich was not disposed to back Hungarian revisionism against Romania. Göring's aim was both to help destroy the unity of the Little Entente and to shore up Germany's economic position in Romania. His declaration coincided with the opening of economic negotiations with the Romanians in the autumn of 1934. Göring's anti-revisionist declarations, however, were strongly denied by the foreign minister, von Neurath.[57] Similar declarations made by Göring over subsequent years were also denied by the foreign ministry, which remained more openly sympathetic to the cause of Hungarian revisionism. These conflicting attitudes led to considerable confusion in the Romanian camp.

Like Göring, the German Führer also showed a greater flexibility towards revisionism than the German foreign ministry. Hitler was quite prepared to temporarily jettison ideology in exchange for long-term goals. Hitler made a number of statements to Romanian officials throughout the 1930s to the effect that, in return for Romanian goodwill, Germany would not support Hungarian revisionist claims against Romania.[58] In order to strengthen Germany's political and economic influence in Yugoslavia and Romania, destroy Little Entente unity and isolate Czechoslovakia, Hitler was prepared to allow relations with Hungary to cool. The Yugoslavs, as well as the Romanians, were given assurances by Göring and Hitler regarding their frontier with Hungary. From 1936 onwards, Hitler encouraged the Hungarians to direct their revisionist claims against Czechoslovakia alone, in order that the Reich could maintain good relations with Yugoslavia and Romania.[59]

The inauguration of the Four Year Plan in 1936 increased the economic importance of Romania for the Reich. The plan was designed to make Germany ready for war within four years. Emphasis was placed on the creation of synthetic raw materials, with the import of food and raw materials as a temporary measure. The strength of the Reich's rearmament drive, however, and the inability to produce synthetic materials in sufficient quantities, resulted in a necessary increase of imports of raw materials and food stuffs. South-East Europe's mineral resources and, in particular Romanian oil, were of critical and growing importance to Germany. In 1940 Germany required Romania to supply three million tons of oil out of a total requirement of some ten to twelve million tons.⁶⁰ As Commissioner of the Four Year Plan, Göring was keen to promote economic links between Romania and Germany. From 1936 onwards he frequently gave verbal assurances that, in exchange for Romania's neutrality in foreign policy and economic collaboration, Germany would not back Hungarian revisionism against Romania. Such declarations continued, however, to be negated by the foreign ministry. This made it highly difficult for the Romanian government to ascertain the exact nature of German policy towards Romania.⁶¹

Over the years, a number of German historians of the 'structuralist' school have argued that Nazi foreign policy was many-stranded and unclear in its aims. The structuralists have argued, in particular, that the pressure of competing and frequently antagonistic German state and Nazi Party foreign-policy organisations forced the regime into often contradictory foreign-policy positions.⁶² German policy towards Romania in this period would appear to bear out this argument. The willingness of Nazi leaders to show flexibility in the issue of revisionism in order to bring Romania into the German orbit was at variance with the foreign ministry's more long-term approach of establishing political links through economic collaboration. In addition, the links existing between Nazi organisations such as the SS or the Auslandsorganisation der NSDAP, which dealt with Nazi members outside the Reich, and Romanian political groupings such as the Legionary movement (or Iron Guard) in the 1930s, served to muddy the picture still further. The infiltration by party organisations, such as the SS, into the foreign ministry structures further complicated the foreign-policy making process.⁶³

The confusion of foreign-policy organisations has resulted in numerous gaps in our knowledge of German foreign-policy making. Perhaps because of his accumulation of administrative offices within the Third Reich, Göring's role in foreign-policy making has received relatively little serious attention by historians.⁶⁴ Yet his role in defining German policy towards Romania throughout the 1930s was clearly considerable. His frequent declarations regarding a German guarantee against Hungarian revisionism in exchange for Romanian foreign-policy neutrality towards Germany were taken seriously, if warily, by Romanian officials. Göring's declarations were thus instrumental in the shaping of Romania's policy of neutrality and goodwill towards the Reich which began after the dismissal of Titulescu on 29 August 1936.

The direct role of Germany in the downfall of Titulescu in the summer of 1936 remains unclear. Certainly, a number of the pro-German politicians with whom Rosenberg's Aussenpolitisches Amt had contact were instrumental in campaigning for his dismissal. 'Titulescu files' were drawn up in Bucharest and Berlin from 1933 and included material allegedly justifying his dismissal. The German file was apparently brought from Germany to King Carol by Octavian Goga in the summer of 1936, following Goga's trip to Germany in which he met most of the Reich leadership.[65] Whatever the extent of German complicity in Titulescu's downfall, his position in the Romanian government was untenable by the summer of 1936. His pro-Soviet policies became more distasteful to Romanian politicians in July 1936 when the outbreak of the Spanish Civil War renewed fears of Soviet interference in European affairs.

On 17 July 1936, Octavian Goga wrote a letter to King Carol calling for the dismissal of Titulescu. Although Goga's strongly pro-German inclinations were at variance with those of the majority of Romanian politicians, his reasons for calling for Titulescu's dismissal were widely shared. Goga criticised Titulescu for estranging Romania from her traditional allies, such as Poland, and from Germany and Italy, while seeking to bring Romania into an alliance 'with our old enemy Russia'. With Italy and Germany becoming ever more powerful in Central Europe, Goga expressed his fear that Romania risked becoming isolated between Russia and a German–Italian bloc which might support Hungarian revisionism. On the other hand, argued Goga, if Romania cultivated foreign-policy neutrality towards Germany, the Reich would be disposed to guarantee Romania's territorial integrity.[66]

In the cabinet reshuffle of 29 August 1936 Titulescu was replaced as foreign minister by Victor Antonescu. The period following Titulescu's dismissal saw a distinct, if subtle, change in Romanian policy towards Germany. Romanian foreign policy continued to be based, as it had been since the First World War, on ensuring Romania's territorial integrity. This was believed to be best protected during the Titulescu era by remaining within an essentially anti-German collective security system. From 29 August 1936 onwards, the Romanian foreign ministry, under King Carol's personal direction, believed the Romanian borders would be best safeguarded by pursuing a course of unofficial neutrality between, and friendship towards, all the Great Powers. In respect of the western powers, this policy necessitated the gradual consolidation of relations with Great Britain, in order to compensate for the weakness of France. It was the link with Germany, however, which had been the weakest of Romania's Great Power relationships since the end of the First World War. It was thus the consolidation of good relations with Germany that required special attention within this new policy of neutrality between the powers. The Romanian government pursued the Reich's goodwill from 1936 onwards and in so doing actively sought not only economic advantages but also potential protection against Soviet and Hungarian territorial claims. This resulted in Germany gradually reassuming the important position she had held for Romania before the First World War.[67]

Notes

1 Such is the view of Romanian inter-war history adopted by the 'dinosaurs' of the communist era. See, for example, the numerous works by Eliza Campus, including *Mica Înțelegere*, Bucharest, 1968 and *Din politica externă a României, 1913–1947*, Bucharest, 1980, esp. pp. 452–556. This view is sustained by another prolific historian from the communist era, Viorica Moisuc. In her *Diplomația României și problema apărării suveranității și independenței naționale în perioada martie 1938–mai 1940*, Bucharest, 1971, Moisuc blames the West for its 'appeasement' of Germany in 1938, even while Romania remained true to her allies. These ideas have been propagated by other historians of the communist era, who give little hint of any attempts by the Romanian government to reach accommodation with Germany: see, for instance, Ioan Talpeș, *Diplomație și apărare. Coordonate ale politicii externe românești 1933–1939*, Bucharest, 1988, and Mircea Mușat and Ion Ardeleanu, *România după Marea Unire*, Vol. 2, Part II-a, Bucharest, 1988, esp. pp. 1402–1532.
2 Thus, we see Mircea Mușat, a historian of the communist era, writing his *1940. Drama României Mari*, Bucharest, 1992, on behalf of the extreme right-wing party, România Mare. Mușat argues that in 1940 the Romanians were the innocent victims of the 'appeasing' West and of the brutal, cynical Axis powers. Viorica Moisuc has again argued, with even greater ferocity than before 1989, that Romania in the inter-war era was the victim of western 'appeasement' of Germany. Indeed, the West is held more culpable than the Reich itself for Romania's fate: Viorica Moisuc, *Premisele izolării politice a României, 1919–1940*, Bucharest, 1991, esp. pp. 331–72.
3 Andreas Hillgruber, *Hitler, König Carol und Marschall Antonescu. Die deutsch-rumänischen Beziehungen, 1938–1944*, Wiesbaden, 1965.
4 Dov B. Lungu, *Romania and the Great Powers, 1933–1940*, Durham and London, 1989.
5 For social and economic problems in inter-war Romania, see Henry L. Roberts, *Rumania: Political Problems of an Agrarian State*, New Haven, 1951, esp. pp. 89–206.
6 Gheorghe Tătărescu, *Patru ani de guvernare, noiembrie 1933–noiembrie 1937*, no place of publication, no date, p. 23.
7 For a general overview of Romania's inter-war foreign policy, see Frederic C. Nanu, *Politica externă a României, 1918–1933*, Iași, 1993 and Keith Hitchins, *Rumania 1866–1947*, Oxford, 1994, pp. 426–50.
8 Hitchins, *Rumania 1866–1947*, pp. 136–54; for the economic importance of Germany for Romania, see György Ránki, *Economy and Foreign Policy: The Struggle of the Great Powers for Hegemony in the Danube Valley, 1919–1939*, Boulder and New York, 1983, pp. 4–5.
9 Hans Tonch, *Wirtschaft und Politik auf dem Balkan. Untersuchung zu den deutsch-rumänischen Beziehungen in der Weimarer Republic unter besonderer Berücksichtigung der Weltwirtschaftkrise*, Frankfurt, 1984, pp. 157–8.

Introduction 15

10 For a general overview of Titulescu's foreign policy, see Ion M. Oprea, *Nicolae Titulescu's Diplomatic Activity*, translated by Andrei Bantaș, Bucharest, 1968.
11 For Titulescu's policy towards the Soviet Union, see Nicolae Titulescu, *Politica externă a României (1937)*, (eds) George G. Potra, Constantin I. Turcu and Ion M. Oprea, Bucharest, 1994, pp. 100–39 (104).
12 Lungu, *Romania and the Great Powers*, p. 60.
13 Ibid, pp. 80–1.
14 On the fall of Titulescu, see I. Chiper and Fl. Constantiniu, 'Din nou despre cauzele înlăturării din guvern a lui Nicolae Titulescu (29 august 1936)', *Revista română de studii internaționale*, 2, nr 6, (1969), pp. 37–53. See also, Oprea, *Nicolae Titulescu's Diplomatic Activity*, pp. 155–70.
15 For Romanian anti-bolshevism, see Lungu, op. cit., pp. 53, 60.
16 I. Chiper and Fl. Constantiniu, op. cit., pp. 40–2.
17 As early as 1928, the Romanian minister to Berlin, Nicolae Petrescu-Comnen, had asked German representatives if, in the event of a Soviet threat to Romania, Germany would act as a friendly go-between: Tonch, *Wirtschaft und Politik auf dem Balkan*, p. 83.
18 Ibid, pp. 135–40.
19 I. Chiper and Fl. Constantiniu, 'Din nou despre cauzele înlăturării din guvern a lui Nicolae Titulescu', pp. 37–8.
20 Nicole Jordan, *The Popular Front and Central Europe: The Dilemmas of French Impotence, 1918–1940*, Cambridge, 1992, p. 128.
21 I. Chiper and Fl. Constantiniu, op. cit., p. 44.
22 Ibid, p. 44; in June 1936 at a League of Nations session, Titulescu enquired of Léon Blum: '... if on 7 March you failed to defend yourself, how are you going to defend us against an aggressor?' Cited in Oprea, *Nicolae Titulescu's Diplomatic Activity*, p. 139.
23 Alvina Lazea, 'Probleme ale cooperării militare româno-franceze în anul 1936', *Studii revistă de istorie*, 22, nr 1, (1969), pp. 105–27 (106–7).
24 Lungu, *Romania and the Great Powers*, pp. 71–2.
25 Ibid, p. 12.
26 Oprea, *Nicolae Titulescu's Diplomatic Activity*, pp. 129–36.
27 (ed.) Sherman David Spector, 'Relapse into Bondage 1918–1947: The Political Memoirs of Alexandre Cretzianu, Free Romania's Last World Diplomatist': Chapter 1: 'The Fall of Titulescu', *Southeastern Europe*, 11, nr 2, (1984), pp. 237–50 (237–41).
28 I. Chiper and Fl. Constantiniu, 'Din nou despre cauzele înlăturării din guvern a lui Nicolae Titulescu', pp. 39–40.
29 Ibid, pp. 38–40; Oprea, op. cit., pp. 166–7.
30 Jordan, *The Popular Front and Central Europe*, pp. 125–7.
31 Paul D. Quinlan, *The Playboy King: Carol II of Romania*, London, 1995, p. 25.
32 Mircea Ciobanu, *Convorbiri cu Mihai I al României*, Bucharest, 1991, p. 122.
33 For the effect of the Depression on Romania, see Roberts, *Rumania: Political Problems of an Agrarian State*, pp. 170–87.
34 Jordan, *The Popular Front and Central Europe*, p. 128.
35 For an account of the decline of French economic influence in Eastern Europe and the problem of armament supplies, see David E. Kaiser, *Economic Diplomacy and the Origins of the Second World War: Germany, Britain, France and Eastern Europe, 1930–1939*, Princeton, 1980, pp. 197–217.

16 Introduction

36 Jordan, op. cit., p. 135.
37 Barry Crosby Fox, 'German Relations with Romania, 1933–1944', unpublished PhD thesis, Dept of History, Western Reserve University, September 1964, p. 15.
38 See, for instance, Comnen's discussion with State Secretary von Bülow in June 1933: MAE, 71/Germania, Vol. 74, pp. 17–20, Royal Legation of Romania in Berlin to the Foreign Minister, Letter nr 1835, 9 June 1933, signed Comnen.
39 Gerhard L. Weinberg, *The Foreign Policy of Hitler's Germany: Diplomatic Revolution in Europe, 1933–1936*, Chicago, 1970, pp. 118–19, 233.
40 Tonch, *Wirtschaft und Politik auf dem Balkan*, pp. 62–70.
41 Kaiser, *Economic Diplomacy and the Origins of the Second World War*, pp. 14–56.
42 For the Hungarian and Yugoslav treaties of 1934, see William S. Grenzebach, *Germany's Informal Empire in East-Central Europe: German Economic Policy Toward Yugoslavia and Romania, 1933–1939*, Stuttgart, 1988, pp. 33–46.
43 (eds) Wilhelm Deist, Manfred Messerschmidt, Hans-Erich Volkmann, Wolfram Wette, *Das Deutsche Reich und der Zweite Weltkrieg*, Vol. 1, Stuttgart, 1979, p. 634. See also, Hans-Jürgen Schröder, 'Der Aufbau der deutschen Hegemonialstellung in Südosteuropa 1933–1936', in (ed.) Manfred Funke, *Hitler, Deutschland und die Mächte. Materialen zur Aussenpolitik des Dritten Reiches*, Düsseldorf, 1976, pp. 757–73, esp. 758–60; Wilhelm Treue, 'Das Dritte Reich und die Westmächte auf dem Balkan, *Vierteljahreshefte für Zeitgeschichte*, 1, (1953), pp. 45–64; J. Kozeński, 'South-Eastern Europe in Nazi Expansionist Plans', *Polish Western Affairs*, 21, nr 1, (1980), pp. 47–58.
44 Hans-Jürgen Schröder, 'Deutsche Südosteuropapolitik 1929–1936. Zur Kontinuität deutscher Aussenpolitik in der Weltwirtschaftskrise', *Geschichte und Gesellschaft*, 2, nr 1 (1976), pp. 5–32: by 1938 the German share of trade with all the Balkan countries, including Hungary and Greece, was between 40 and 50% (ibid, p. 5).
45 For a detailed account of the German–Yugoslav economic relationship, see Hans-Jürgen Schröder, 'Südosteuropa als "Informal Empire" Deutschlands 1933–1939. Das Beispiel Jugoslawien', *Jahrbücher für Geschichte Osteuropas*, 23, (1975), pp. 70–96.
46 For the New Plan, see Antonin Basch, *The Danube Basin and the German Economic Sphere*, London, 1944, pp. 170–84; R. J. Overy, *The Nazi Economic Recovery 1932–1938*, London, 1982, p. 30, and Grenzebach, *Germany's Informal Empire in East-Central Europe*, pp. 235–37 and ibid, pp. 69–79 for the 1935 Romanian–German economic treaty.
47 Roberts, *Rumania: Political Problems of an Agrarian State*, p. 214.
48 See a memorandum to this effect, dated 13 March 1933, by the State Secretary at the Foreign Ministry, von Bülow, in (ed.) Wolfgang Michalka, *Das Dritte Reich. Dokumente zur Innen- und Aussenpolitik*, Munich, 1985, pp. 216–23.
49 Basch, *The Danube Basin and the German Economic Sphere*, p. 171; for the mineral resources of South-East Europe, see Norman Rich, *Hitler's War Aims: Ideology, The Nazi State and the Course of Expansion*, London, 1973, p. 182.
50 Martin Broszat, 'Deutschland-Ungarn-Rumänien. Entwicklung und Grundfaktoren nationalsozialistischer Hegemonial und Bundnispolitik, 1938–1941', *Historische Zeitschrift*, 206, (1968), pp. 45–96 (50).

Introduction 17

51 Hillgruber, *Hitler, König Carol und Marschall Antonescu*, p. 11.
52 For Rosenberg's policy towards Romania and his links with Carol and the Romanian right-wing, see Seppo Kuusisto, *Alfred Rosenberg in der nationalsozialistischen Aussenpolitik, 1933–1939*, Helsinki, 1984, pp. 204–43 and Radu Lecca, *Eu i-am salvat pe evreii din România*, Bucharest, 1994, pp. 80–135.
53 *Trial of the Major War Criminals Before the International Military Tribunal*, Vol. 25, Nuremberg, 1947, pp. 34–47, Document 007-PS, 'Short Report on the Activities of the Office of Foreign Affairs of the NSDAP from 1933 to 1943', signed Rosenberg, see esp. pp. 43–7.
54 Kuusisto, op. cit., pp. 223–5, 230.
55 Lecca, op. cit., pp. 113–18.
56 R. J. Overy, *Goering: The 'Iron Man'*, London, 1984, pp. 32–4.
57 Stefan Martens, *Hermann Göring 'Erster Paladin des Führers' und 'Zweiter Mann im Reich'*, Paderborn, 1985, pp. 40–6; see also Hans Mommsen, 'Reflections on the Position of Hitler and Göring in the Third Reich', in (eds) Thomas Childers and Jane Caplan, *Reevaluating the Third Reich*, New York, 1993, pp. 86–97.
58 As, for instance, in his discussion with Gheorghe Brătianu in November 1936. See Chapter 1 below for a discussion of this.
59 Broszat, 'Deutschland-Ungarn-Rumänien', pp. 45–56.
60 Maurice Pearton, 'British Policy towards Romania 1939–41', in (ed.) Rebecca Haynes, *Occasional Papers in Romanian Studies*, nr 2, London, 1998, pp. 59–92 (76).
61 Göring's declarations will be discussed in future chapters. For the Four Year Plan, see Norman Rich, *Hitler's War Aims: Ideology, The Nazi State and the Course of Expansion*, London, 1973, pp. 180–5 and Grenzebach, *Germany's Informal Empire in East-Central Europe*, pp. 96–130.
62 See, for instance, Hans Mommsen, 'National Socialism: Continuity and Change', in (ed.) Walter Laqueur, *Fascism: A Reader's Guide*, London, 1976, pp. 179–210; Martin Broszat, 'Soziale Motivation und Führer-bindung des Nationalsozialismus', *Vierteljahreshefte für Zeitgeschichte*, 18, nr 4, (1970), pp. 392–409. For the administrative confusion of the Third Reich as a whole, see Norman Rich, *Hitler's War Aims*, pp. 12–37. Hillgruber's *Hitler, König Carol und Marschall Antonescu* belongs to the older 'intentionalist' school, which believed in the primacy of Hitler in foreign-policy decision making.
63 For a full account of State and Nazi Party foreign-policy organisations and their workings, see, Hans-Adolf Jacobsen, *Nationalsozialistische Aussenpolitik 1933–1938*, Frankfurt, 1968, esp. pp. 16–319. The effect of confused German foreign-policy making on the outcome of the January 1941 Iron Guard rebellion in Romania has been discussed by Rebecca Haynes, in 'German Historians and the Romanian National Legionary State 1940–1941', *Slavonic and East European Review*, 71, nr 4 (October 1993), pp. 676–83.
64 An exception to much of the sensationalist literature is Stefan Martens, *Hermann Göring 'Erster Paladin des Führers' und 'Zweiter Mann im Reich'*, Paderborn, 1985. See also Alfred Kube, *Pour le merité und Hakenkreuz. Hermann Göring im Dritten Reich*, Munich, 1986, esp. pp. 91–103 for Göring's visit to Belgrade in 1934 and subsequent clashes with the foreign ministry.
65 I. Chiper and Fl. Constantiniu, 'Din nou despre cauzele înlăturării din guvern a lui Nicolae Titulescu', pp. 48–50.

66 Arh. Stat., Casa Regală, Dosar nr 7/1936, p. 9, the so-called 'Vittel Letter' from Octavian Goga to King Carol II, 14 July 1936.
67 As early as the summer of 1936, Romanian army generals stated that if France were to become diplomatically isolated, and the states of Central Europe were forced to choose between Germany and the Soviet Union, they would choose Germany: Jordan, *The Popular Front and Central Europe*, pp. 188–9.

1
Victor Antonescu and Romania's Foreign Policy Readjustment, September 1936 to December 1937

With the dismissal of Titulescu in the cabinet reshuffle of 29 August 1936, King Carol finally secured his authority over the direction of Romania's foreign policy. Although the new foreign minister, Victor Antonescu, had been minister in Paris from 1922–5, he had little of Titulescu's international influence and prestige. In contrast to Titulescu, Antonescu and all subsequent foreign ministers were ultimately dependent upon King Carol in the execution of foreign policy. The king's appointment of the francophile Antonescu suggested that the orientation of the country's diplomacy would remain pro-French, as it had been under Titulescu. Indeed, scrutiny of Victor Antonescu's public declarations during his time as foreign minister from 1936 to late 1937 certainly seem to confirm that Romania's foreign policy remained securely based on her traditional alliances.[1]

Yet Antonescu's public speeches conceal the change in foreign policy which took place during his ministry. The breakdown of the French-backed collective security system and the re-emergence of Germany as an assertive Great Power by the mid-1930s necessitated a realignment of Romanian foreign policy. Although there was no formal change of alliances, the Antonescu ministry inaugurated a shift towards a position of informal neutrality between the Great Powers and a corresponding diminution of Romania's foreign-policy obligations.[2] The relationship with Germany, comparatively neglected under Titulescu, now required careful cultivation. While Romania's traditional alliances, and her links with the West were to be maintained, Carol and the foreign ministry also sought to establish closer relations with the Reich. In pursuing a policy of informal neutrality between the powers and developing stronger links with Germany, the Romanians were influenced by the policies of their Polish and Yugoslav allies who were already accommodating themselves to the growth of German power.[3]

Both the Romanian government and the German foreign ministry were agreed that political relations between their two countries should develop gradually out of economic cooperation.[4] During his conversation with the German minister in Bucharest, Dr Wilhelm Fabricius, on 7 December 1936, Victor Antonescu indicated King Carol's wish to 'draw nearer to Germany by every available means, within the framework of the existing treaties'. Antonescu added that closer links with Germany were to be pursued systematically, beginning with the further development of economic relations.[5]

Even during Titulescu's final year as foreign minister, the Romanian economy had begun to shift into dependency on that of the Reich, undermining Titulescu's pro-French line in foreign policy.[6] Increasingly, it was Germany alone which assured the Romanian government a market for Romanian agricultural produce and raw materials. In exchange, Romania received German machinery with which the Romanian government sought to expand the country's small industrial sector. The March 1935 economic accord with Germany obliged the Reich to import almost 30 million marks worth of agricultural produce, plus seven million marks worth of raw materials, in exchange for German goods.[7]

Purchase of German armaments became an increasingly important aspect of Romanian–German economic exchange following the fall of Titulescu. The Romanians were particularly disillusioned by the fact that they did not receive priority treatment in the receipt of armaments from their traditional suppliers: France, Britain or even Czechoslovakia, Romania's main source of armaments. Germany thus emerged as an alternative source of supplies. Under the 24 September 1936 protocols all oil exports to Germany from Romania, which exceeded the 25% limit agreed under the March 1935 treaty, could be paid for by the delivery of German armaments. Renewed requests for arms were made by Minister President Gheorghe Tătărescu later in the year.[8]

Economic relations formed an important part of the discussion which took place on 4 December 1936 between the Romanian minister to Berlin, Nicolae Petrescu-Comnen, and Field Marshal Göring. During this meeting, Göring offered to incorporate Romania into the Four Year Plan so as to provide Romanian produce with a guaranteed market in the Reich.[9] As Commissioner for the Four Year Plan from late 1936, Reich Air Minister and Commander-in-Chief of the Luftwaffe, Göring was an important contact for the Romanians. The 4 December discussion was only one of many meetings which took place between German and Romanian diplomats, economic experts and industrialists in the wake of Titulescu's fall from power.

In October 1936, the Romanian government rejected the Czechoslovak government's 'Danube plan' to create greater economic links between the Danubian countries. As Antonescu explained to Minister Fabricius, the government was against any economic settlement in the Danube Basin which would exclude Germany. The aim of the government, insisted Antonescu, was specifically to expand economic relations with the Reich.[10]

The increasing economic importance of Germany for Romania during the Antonescu ministry culminated in the economic agreement signed on 9 December 1937. As a result of this, the volume of trade between the two countries increased by one-third. Helmut Wohlthat, who headed the German economic delegation, reported back to Berlin that there was opposition among some members of the Romanian National Bank to the growing ascendancy of Germany in the Romanian economy. Wohlthat concluded, nevertheless, that the fact the economic agreement was signed during the visit to Bucharest of French Foreign Minister Delbos was 'proof of the growth of German influence which has taken place in the years since the conclusion of the commercial treaty of 1935'.[11]

During Wohlthat's audience with the king and leading politicians on 14 December 1937, Minister President Gheorghe Tătărescu outlined the Romanian government's economic plans. Based on what Tătărescu referred to as the 'economic community of interests' between Germany and Romania, these plans included proposals for German support to help develop the Romanian economy through the introduction of new technology to agriculture, exploitation of raw materials, exploration of new oil fields, expansion of the armaments industry and the development of the Romanian infrastructure. These proposals were to provide the blueprint for the economic treaty concluded between Romania and Germany in March 1939 and included provisions for legislation to increase the role of foreign capital in the Romanian economy.[12]

The idea that the agricultural economy of Romania and the Reich's industrial economy were complementary was by now becoming so widespread in Romania that even staunchly pro-western politicians, such as Ion Mihalache, a leader of the National Peasant Party, were agreed on the necessity for ever closer economic links with Germany. During the 15 December 1936 foreign-policy debate in parliament, in which he otherwise strongly advocated the maintenance of the French alliance, Mihalache observed that the economic link with Germany was of vital importance. Mihalache believed that 'the structure of the two countries makes possible a richer exchange than with any other country'.[13]

The Romanian government's attempts at improved relations with Germany were not limited to the economic sphere. The foreign ministry also sought to win German goodwill by refusing to extend any of Romania's foreign-policy obligations in order to prevent Romania coming into conflict with the Reich. By so doing, the Romanian foreign ministry was gradually steering Romania into a diplomatic position of informal neutrality between the Great Powers, in which closer ties with the Reich could develop.

Hardly had Titulescu left office than the new foreign minister was assuring German representatives that his government was no longer prepared to continue his predecessor's policy. On 6 September, Victor Antonescu confirmed to Fabricius that Titulescu's links with the Soviet Union were one of the main reasons for his fall from power. Antonescu continued 'that no alliance would be concluded with Soviet Russia...' and added that Romania wished to avoid being active in European affairs, owing to the danger that she would become the 'theatre of war between Germany and Russia'.[14] As a German foreign-ministry circular pointed out a few weeks after the cabinet reshuffle, 'In Titulescu's fall, we can see the possibility of a relaxation of Romania's foreign policy and certainly a weakening of the Soviet-friendly course.'[15]

The new direction in Romanian foreign policy was further encouraged by declarations made by Nazi Party leaders that the Reich had no interest in supporting Hungarian revisionist claims on Transylvania. Common anti-bolshevism and the question of Hungarian revisionism were important components of Gheorghe Brătianu's discussion with Hitler in November 1936. The politician and historian Brătianu was already known in Berlin as a staunch opponent of Titulescu's pro-Soviet line in foreign policy and as 'deutschfreundlich'.[16] As early as 1934, Brătianu had expounded in print his fears of Soviet expansion into the Balkans and advocated that Romania should improve her relations with Germany through increasing economic exchange.[17] While it is true that Brătianu, as leader of the splinter party, the Young Liberals, held no official foreign-policy position, he was in close contact with King Carol. Following his trip to Berlin in November, he reported his findings to Carol. The king subsequently used him as an unofficial 'ambassador' to Berlin on several occasions. Brătianu's foreign-policy ideas profoundly influenced Carol's policies during the 1930s. Brătianu himself was particuarly influenced by the foreign policies pursued by Poland, Yugoslavia and especially Belgium.[18]

During his discussion with Hitler on 16 November 1936, Brătianu confirmed that Romania was no longer seeking an alliance with the Soviet Union and that Romania was not to be incorporated into the Franco-Soviet pact of May 1935.[19] Indeed, Brătianu explained that Romania regarded herself as a bulwark against the spread of communism. Brătianu indicated that Romania, together with Poland and Yugoslavia, intended to pursue a 'form of neutrality' similar to that declared by Belgium on 14 October.[20] Brătianu added that the Romanian government wished to build up solid economic relations with Germany 'so as to be able to achieve good political relations'. In conclusion, however, he expressed concern that Axis support for Hungarian revisionist claims on Romania would prevent the Romanian government tying itself closer to the Reich.

Hitler sought to allay Brătianu's fears by advising him to read Alfred Rosenberg's article, 'Unterdrückte Völker und Revisionismus' in the *Völkischer Beobachter* of 15 November 1936. In this article, Rosenberg had pointed out Germany's lack of concern for Hungarian revisionism. Hitler confirmed this stance during his discussion with Brătianu and stressed that Germany had 'an interest in seeing an independent and strengthened Romania and Yugoslavia, which are barriers against bolshevism'. He concluded that if 'Romania becomes an outpost of European order, no nation will be more interested in her preservation than Germany'.[21]

While the Romanians were giving the Germans indications of their change of policy towards the Soviet Union and their 'neutral' attitude towards the Reich, they did not omit to stress that the alliance with France was still the core of Romania's treaty system. The king and his ministers hoped that relations between the western powers and Germany would improve. This would then create a stable foundation for lasting Romanian–German friendship without forcing Romania to favour one power bloc against the other. During his discussions with Fabricius on 7 October 1936, Carol informed the German minister that 'I am no friend of bolshevism and my wish is to place the policy of my country on closer and friendlier links with Germany. But... Romanian policy is the policy of the treaties with France, Poland and the Little Entente... If Germany succeeds in having better relations with France ... it would be possible for me to come out more openly.'[22]

The growing desire of the Romanian government to remain effectively neutral between the Great Powers was given expression during the meeting of the Permanent Council of the Little Entente at Bratislava in September 1936. Controversy surrounded the so-called 'Krofta project', proposed by the Czechoslovak government, to transform the Little Entente alliances, which were directed solely against the threat of Hungarian revisionism, into a mutual assistance pact against any aggressor. This would oblige Romania and Yugoslavia to come to Czechoslovakia's aid in the event of a German attack upon her. The Czechoslovak government proposed that following the signing of a Little Entente mutual assistance pact, France should conclude a treaty of alliance with the Little Entente with pledges of mutual assistance against any aggressor. Such plans would have effectively brought Romania and Yugoslavia into the Czechoslovak-Franco-Soviet security system.[23]

Romanian historians invariably blame the Yugoslav government for the failure to enlarge the scope of the Little Entente.[24] It is clear, however, that Romanian diplomats shared the Yugoslav fear of entering into an alliance system which could provoke German displeasure or lead to war with Germany. On 11 September 1936, Foreign Minister Antonescu met with his Yugoslav counterpart, Stoiadinović, who affirmed that he was against any accord which was aimed against Germany, Yugoslavia's most important trading partner. Antonescu, happy to comply with Stoiadinović's objections, replied that 'we can discuss the proposals and raise certain objections'. The two ministers agreed that 'they would not give a categoric refusal, but with friendly words would show that we ask respite to study the question.....'.[25]

Consequently, at the Bratislava meeting of the Little Entente, it was decided that the Czechoslovak mutual assistance project would be postponed. Confirmation of the importance which links with the Great Powers now played in the affairs of individual Little Entente states was expressed in the final communiqué of the conference. While the three member states were 'determined to increase their security by a still closer and more effective union of their forces than before', at the same time, 'each state will continue to foster lively and intimate contacts with the states with whom such contacts exist'.[26] This was in direct contradiction to the Czechoslovak government's proposal to add a clause to the planned mutual assistance pact to ensure that the Little Entente countries could only conclude agreements with neighbouring Great Powers if all three Entente members were in agreement.[27] Polish government circles, commenting on the Bratislava conference, noted that the final communiqué left Czechoslovakia free to develop her relations with the Soviet Union, while Romania, 'does not wish to restrain her relations with Poland or Germany'.[28]

The Little Entente's increasing division between Czechoslovakia, backed by her French ally, on the one hand and Romania and Yugoslavia on the other became apparent again a few months later. In early 1937, the French government put forward its proposals for a Franco-Little Entente pact which presupposed the prior conclusion of the Little Entente mutual assistance pact. The French foreign office hoped thereby to oblige Romania and Yugoslavia to come to the aid of Czechoslovakia in the event of a German attack. Victor Antonescu made no bones of the issue, informing French Foreign Minister Delbos that he saw no reason why his country should compromise itself towards Germany for the sake of Czechoslovakia. Instead of the proposed pact with the Little Entente as a whole, Antonescu suggested that France should sign three separate treaties with each of the Little Entente countries. Delbos refused, since such treaties would not oblige Romania or Yugoslavia to fight for Czechoslovakia.[29]

The proposed Franco-Little Entente mutual assistance pact was debated during the meeting of the Permanent Council of the Little Entente held at Belgrade from 1–2 April 1937. Minister Comnen in Berlin had already alerted his government during the preceding weeks to the importance with which German leaders regarded the potential adherence of Romania and Yugoslavia to a Franco-Little Entente mutual assistance pact. Such a pact, as the Germans pointed out to Comnen, would bring Romania and Yugoslavia into the Soviet collective security system and thereby make them potential enemies of the Reich.[30]

The declaration issued at the end of the Little Entente meeting mentioned Yugoslavia's 'psychological difficulties' as the reason for the postponement of the Franco-Little Entente pact.[31] It was clear, however, that the proposed pact was no more desirable for the Romanians than for the Yugoslavs. Antonescu admitted to Fabricius on 6 April that the pact had been laid to rest 'because it would interfere with the more favourable development of links with Germany and Italy', of which the German link was deemed the most important. The Yugoslav, Greek and Italian ministers in Bucharest were able to confirm to Fabricius that Romania's desire for good relations with Germany had indeed been the reason for Romania's reluctance to accept the pact.[32] As King Carol recorded in his diary, 'regarding the French and Czech attempts to deepen relations between the Little Entente and the Gallic Great Power... we have no interest in enlarging the number of our possible enemies (alias Germany).'[33]

The Romanian government objected to the proposed Franco-Little Entente pact not only because Romania's defence of Czechoslovakia could lead her into war with Germany. The proposed pact also brought up the issue of the Soviet Union's right of passage through Romania to help Czechoslovakia in the event of a German attack. Not only was this unacceptable to Romania herself, but it was also abhorrent to her Polish ally. The Polish government placed pressure on the Romanian government throughout the winter of 1936-37 to forbid the Soviets right of passage in any future conflict.[34] Romania's fear of the Soviet Union was also apparent during negotiations that winter for a Franco-Romanian mutual air aid pact. According to this proposed pact, Romanian airbases would be fitted out for French or allied, i.e. Soviet, use. As a result, King Carol refused to conclude the pact and in January 1937 he dismissed Air Minister Caranfil for giving his verbal assent to the deployment of French and allied air forces in Romania.[35]

The negotiations for the extension of alliances between the Little Entente and France thus revealed the growing disunity of the Little Entente. On the one hand, Czechoslovakia was incorporated into the Franco-Soviet security system and feared Germany's potential territorial claims upon her. On the other hand, Romania and Yugoslavia were more inclined to view Germany favourably both as a counterweight to the Soviet Union and on economic grounds. Although all three Little Entente countries remained united against Hungarian revisionism, the need to curry favour in Berlin had by 1936 become an important factor in Romanian and Yugoslav decision-making. Poland, Romania and Yugoslavia now increasingly took on the appearance of 'an anti-Soviet phalanx against the Moscow-Prague-Paris security system'.[36]

Writing in February 1937, a French foreign office official noted that Romanian foreign policy consisted of 'fear mixed with admiration for Germany, fear mixed with hatred of Russia'.[37] The attitude suggested by the French note was apparent during the foreign-policy debates in the Romanian parliament and press in the autumn of 1936. During these debates, Romanian politicians generally expressed warm feelings for the traditional alliances with France, the Little Entente and Poland.[38] Nevertheless, politicians increasingly questioned the extent to which Romania could rely on her French ally in the wake of what many Romanians regarded as France's apparent shift towards bolshevism in both domestic and foreign policy. The failure of both France and the League of Nations to respond adequately to Hitler's remilitarisation of the Rhineland in March 1936 also called into question the efficacy of the collective security system more generally. In addition, the re-emergence of Germany and the Soviet Union as Great Powers made it essential to reassess Romania's relationship with these countries. The foreign-policy debates reflected the growing desire within the Romanian establishment for informal neutrality between the Great Powers, and for the cultivation of improved relations with Germany. Many politicians also believed that any policies towards the Soviet Union which could jeopardise relations with Germany should be avoided. During these debates, few Romanian politicians seriously considered jettisoning Romania's traditional allies in favour of a wholesale alliance with Germany. Nevertheless, even the most ardent pro-westerners were aware of the need for accommodation with Germany.

The most important foreign-policy debates in parliament took place on 14 and 15 December 1936. Romania's relationship with Germany was the main concern during the debates.[39] On 14 December, Foreign Minister Victor Antonescu affirmed the importance of Romania's traditional alliances. He also put forward the government view that, 'there are no differences which divide us from Germany. Accordingly, we can regard with pleasure the further development of our relations with Germany.' The advocates of neutrality were led by Gheorghe Brătianu. In his speech, Brătianu affirmed his opposition to any extension of Romania's collective security obligations which could curtail her independence of action in foreign policy. He expressed the fears of many politicians when he stressed the dangers of encouraging the participation of the Soviet Union in European affairs. Brătianu went on to argue that German support for revisionism was no longer a threat to Romania, putting forward as evidence the Alfred Rosenberg article in the 15 November edition of the *Völkischer Beobachter*. On the basis of the Rosenberg article, Brătianu 'declared himself categorically in favour of an improvement of relations with Germany'.

Strong opposition to Brătianu's 'neutralist' view point came from Ion Mihalache, one of the leaders of the opposition National Peasant Party. On 15 December, Mihalache emphasised the importance of the French alliance in maintaining Romania's territorial integrity. Nevertheless, since Romania had no direct point of conflict with Germany, even Mihalache believed it prudent to sign a non-aggression pact with Germany based on recognition of Romania's borders. He concluded with the significant remark that in the event of war, Romania 'will naturally come into the camp of that country which best assures her frontiers'.[40] This implied that even the pro-western National Peasant Party would not rule out a future alliance with the Reich if maintenance of Romania's territorial integrity required it.

During these foreign-policy debates the number of politicians advocating a full-scale alliance with the Reich remained a small, albeit shrill, minority. Foremost amongst these was Octavian Goga, president of the antisemitic National Christian Party, who, together with his political ally, A. C. Cuza, had long-standing links in Germany. In September 1936, the National Christian Party had already declared its wish for a treaty with Germany based on recognition of Romania's borders.[41] On 20 November, Goga stated in a newspaper article that he regarded the National Christian Party and the Nazi Party as partners in the joint fight against the Jewish and bolshevik dangers to Europe.[42]

During a speech in parliament on 27 November, Goga pointed out the importance of the Rosenberg article in *Völkischer Beobachter* of 15 November, as a vindication of his argument for a treaty with Germany. Goga quoted Nicolae Filipescu, a leader of the pre-war Conservative Party, who had declared in 1916 that 'we go to war with hatred towards the Hungarians, with indifference towards Austria and with regret towards Germany'. Nevertheless, although Goga stressed his distrust of the socialist French government and rejected the Franco-Soviet treaty system, he did not seek to jettison the French alliance in order to create closer links with the Reich. Rather, he advocated freedom of action for the Romanian government in her foreign relations. Thus, like the more moderate Gheorghe Brătianu, Goga believed that Romania's foreign policy should not be dictated by her allies. Goga consequently endorsed the formula, already laid down at the Bratislava Little Entente conference in September, that each Little Entente country should have freedom of action in its relations with other countries.[43] Meanwhile, during the 14 December foreign-policy debate, A. C. Cuza, Goga's more immoderate political ally, recommended full-scale German–Romanian cooperation against bolshevism and Romania's immediate adhesion to the Anti-Comintern Pact.[44]

As a result of these foreign-policy debates, the German minister in Bucharest, Fabricius, reported to Berlin that 'a great change has taken place over the last few months in Romanian foreign policy which aims at closer links with Germany'. While King Carol, the ultimate foreign-policy decision-maker, had made it clear that Romania's alliances were to remain intact, many politicians were now supporting a measure of independence for Romania in her relations with her allies. Such a shift in foreign policy would leave the road open for the strengthening of links with Germany. Of importance in this regard, as Fabricius rightly observed, was the stress which even the pro-French National Peasant Party leader Mihalache now placed on good relations with the Reich.[45]

As a consequence of this renewed interest in strengthening links with Germany, the Romanian foreign ministry displayed considerable interest during late 1936 in the comments made by Nazi Party leaders regarding German policy towards Romania. Of crucial importance in this respect, was the conversation between the Romanian minister to Berlin,

Comnen, and Göring which took place on 4 December 1936. Göring reaffirmed Hitler's declarations made to Gheorghe Brătianu on 16 November in which the Führer had distanced Germany from the cause of Hungarian revisionism. In generous mood, Göring offered a German guarantee of Romania's territorial integrity and help to develop the Romanian army and economy. In return, the Romanian government was to agree not to enter any political 'combination' directed against Germany or to extend Little Entente obligations beyond mutual assistance against Hungarian aggression. Göring also asked that the Romanian government should prevent Soviet right of passage through Romania. If Romania abided by such a policy, Göring promised that Germany would ensure that Hungarian and Bulgarian revisionist claims would not be unleashed against her. He added that Germany had made no pledges towards Hungary to help her realise her revisionist claims. If Romania refused the olive branch, however, Germany would forge closer links with Hungary and Bulgaria.[46]

Comnen made no immediate reply to the offer, other than confirming that Romania would oppose demands made by the Soviet Union, or any other country, for right of passage across Romania. Comnen pointed out, however, that the German foreign ministry had minimised the anti-revisionist declarations that Göring had made to the Romanians in the past. Göring retorted that the foreign ministry pursued a traditional revisionist policy but that he had the authorisation of the Führer himself to make this declaration in Romania's favour. Göring reassured Comnen that Germany had no objections to the Polish–Romanian alliance which acted as a dam against Soviet expansion, or to Romania's alliance with France, provided it was not turned against the Reich. Germany, Göring concluded, required only that Romania enter no 'combination' against her.[47]

Göring's requests conformed to the Romanian government's growing desire for a position of unofficial neutrality between the Great Powers and for a contraction of Romanian foreign-policy obligations. This had already been given expression by the failure of the proposals to expand the Little Entente alliances. Nevertheless, there was confusion in the Romanian camp regarding the discrepancy between the remarks made by Nazi Party leaders and the comments coming from the German foreign ministry. Following his conversation with Hitler on 16 November 1936, in which the Führer had declared his lack of commitment to Hungarian revisionism, Gheorghe Brătianu had discussed the matter with German Foreign Minister von Neurath. While observing that Hungary should come to a peaceful understanding with her neighbours, von Neurath declared

Germany to be sympathetic to Hungary as a fellow-sufferer of the Versailles system.[48] On 25 November 1936, Comnen took up this question of the German attitude towards Hungarian revisionism with Alfred Rosenberg, head of the Aussenpolitisches Amt der NSDAP. Comnen pointed out that during the funeral of King Alexander of Yugoslavia in Belgrade in October 1934, Göring had made a declaration to Carol to the effect that Germany had no interest in backing Hungarian revisionism. Göring's declaration had, however, subsequently been played down by the German foreign ministry. Rosenberg reassured Comnen that Germany did not support Hungarian revisionist claims, citing as evidence his 15 November article in *Völkischer Beobachter*, which had the Führer's backing.[49]

Foreign Minister Antonescu considered Göring's overtures to be sufficiently important to ask Comnen for confirmation of his 4 December discussion with the Field Marshal.[50] Comnen confirmed that Göring's declaration had been made on Hitler's authorisation. Göring now awaited a reply from the Romanian government to his offer. As Comnen pointed out to Antonescu, the ambiguous attitude of the German foreign ministry made a Romanian response difficult. On the other hand, Comnen argued, it could be harmful to Romanian interests if Romania refused the help promised by the Nazi Party leadership.[51]

Despite Comnen's numerous post-war writings in which he distanced himself and his country from any suspicion of complicity with Germany, at the time Comnen clearly believed the declarations made by German party leaders to be of vital importance for Romania's future.[52] In a report dated 14 December 1936, Comnen summarised what he regarded as the current German attitude towards Romania. He believed Germany strove for economic and political influence in the Danube basin and that Nazi Party leaders were therefore willing to jettison political formulas which were no longer regarded as in German interests, in particular support for Hungarian revisionism which would alienate Romania and Yugoslavia. This German attitude, wrote Comnen, was vital for Romania's national interests since Göring was prepared to guarantee Romanian territorial integrity. Comnen observed in this connection that Germany appeared already to have provided Yugoslavia with a territorial guarantee, in the form of a secret treaty or 'gentlemen's agreement'.[53] The belief that Germany might already be guaranteeing Yugoslavia's borders, encouraged the Romanian government's inclination to coordinate her policies with those of her Yugoslav ally from late 1936 onwards.[54]

On 20 March 1937, Comnen finally gave his government's official reply to Göring's declarations of 4 December 1936. Comnen confirmed that the Romanian government would not abandon any of her alliances or League of Nations obligations. If Germany were to guarantee Romania's territorial integrity in a precise manner, however, Romania would give assurances not to conclude any alliance or agreement for troop transit with the Soviets. Comnen concluded that his government agreed not to take part in any 'combination' against Germany and to develop economic relations with her.[55]

Through this declaration, Comnen once again assured the Germans of Romania's foreign-policy neutrality towards the Reich and of Romania's interest in extending economic relations. More important, he made explicit the Romanian government's interest in a German guarantee of Romania's territorial integrity. It is therefore clear that the Romanian government did not 'refuse' Göring's offer of 4 December 1936, as Alexandru Cretzianu, a senior foreign ministry official, later claimed.[56] Although the Göring–Comnen talks did not constitute a formal agreement between the two countries, Göring's offer and Comnen's reply influenced subsequent Romanian foreign-policy decisions and were used as a justification in many of Romania's later requests towards Germany. Moreover, this was not to be the last discussion between Romanian and German officials regarding a territorial guarantee.

For its part, the Romanian foreign ministry continued to display a cautious interest in Göring's declarations and to maintain both diplomatic and unofficial contact with him. In the spring of 1937, Atta Constantinescu, Gheorghe Brătianu's political ally, met Göring and conveyed King Carol's thanks for the anti-revisionist declarations made by Hitler and Göring in late 1936. Göring replied that he and Hitler had 'accepted' all of Comnen's points put forward on 20 March in response to the offer of a guarantee. Göring confirmed that 'Hitler wished for an agreement with Romania at any price'.[57]

Thus, by the winter of 1936–37, relations between Romania and Germany, which had sunk so low in the last months of the Titulescu ministry, were improving. Unfortunately for the Romanians, just at this point a diplomatic 'incident' occurred which threatened to overturn the work so far of the Antonescu ministry.[58]

The Moța and Marin diplomatic incident was occasioned by the appearance of the German, Italian and Portuguese ministers at the funeral of Ion Moța and Vasile Marin on 13 February 1937. These two senior members of the Romanian Legionary movement, or Iron Guard, had died fighting on the nationalist side in the Spanish Civil War. The presence of the diplomats at the funeral suggested to many Romanian politicians that their respective governments were expressing political support for the Iron Guard.

Although the Romanian and German foreign ministries spent a month wrangling over the wording of the German explanation regarding the German minister's presence at the funeral, Carol and his government were anxious not to damage German–Romanian relations.[59] The formal ending of the dispute by the government's acceptance of Fabricius's communiqué of 8 March, in which he denied that his presence at the Guardist funeral implied any political support for the movement, was followed swiftly by a number of assurances to the Germans. On 12 March, Carol empowered Comnen to inform the Germans of his wish for closer economic relations.[60] The following day, Comnen assured Foreign Minister von Neurath that with regard to the proposed Franco-Little Entente pact, 'Romania is not disposed to take part, to use Göring's expression, in any "combination" directed against the Reich'.[61]

Despite the Romanian government's desire that the Moța and Marin affair should not disturb relations with Germany, King Carol regarded the possibility of German support for the Iron Guard as a serious matter. On 12 March, the day after the affair had been officially declared closed by Victor Antonescu in the Chamber of Deputies, Carol had a discussion with his German friend, Helmuth von Cramon. Carol indicated to von Cramon that if German money was indeed supporting the Iron Guard, it would be sufficient reason to 'break off relations with the Reich completely'.[62]

Both Carol and Minister President Tătărescu had not been above supporting the Guard against their mutual political opponents earlier in the decade. By 1937, however, the level of popular support for the Guard was such as to be a potential threat to the monarchy itself. Fabricius had recorded that Carol had been greatly affected by the huge Guardist presence at the Moța and Marin funeral.[63] Although there was no concrete evidence of German support for the Guard at this time, Fabricius's presence at the funeral could not but play on Carol's fears.[64] As Fabricius himself recorded on the day of the funeral, 'the honour done by Germany to the heroes of the Iron Guard who fell in Spain has evoked a lasting mood of solidarity...the German wreaths were everywhere pointed out and were borne at the head of the funeral procession today.'[65]

Carol's anger at the manifestation of German support for the Iron Guard, however, was a measure not of his anti-German feeling but of his insistence on being the controlling and central element in Romanian politics. Carol was determined that German government and party agencies should deal directly with him and not with his political opponents. It was an attitude visible again one year later during the trial of

Corneliu Zelea Codreanu, the leader of the Iron Guard, who stood accused of having political links with Germany. Carol's fears of German support for the Iron Guard were compounded by the movement's unswervingly pro-Axis foreign-policy position. This became particularly apparent in the foreign-policy discussions which preceded the general election held in late 1937.

Despite his electoral pact with the pro-western Iuliu Maniu, leader of the National Peasant Party, Codreanu made no bones of his pro-Axis inclinations. In response to Maniu's defence of the League of Nations and Romania's alliances, Codreanu declared, 'I am against the Little Entente. I am against the Balkan Entente and I have no attachment to the League of Nations in which I do not believe. I am for a Romanian foreign policy with Rome and Berlin. I am with the states of national revolution against bolshevism... Within forty-eight hours of a Legionary movement victory, Romania will have an alliance with Rome and with Berlin....'.[66]

Guardist foreign policy was given ideological underpinning by Mihail Polihroniade, the movement's foreign-policy ideologue. Polihroniade described bolshevism as 'hell on earth... a mockery against God' and rejected any alliance with the Soviets since it would automatically imply an alliance against Germany. Not only had Romania no quarrels with Germany, argued Polihroniade, but Germany had given proof that she was not committed to supporting Hungarian revisionism through the Rosenberg article of 15 November 1936. It was in Germany that Polihroniade indeed saw 'the only power capable of counter-balancing the Russian colossus in Central Europe'. He dismissed the oft-mentioned threat of Hungarian revisionism as a distraction from the Soviet danger.[67]

Polihroniade went on to reject the claim that Greater Romania existed on the basis of the Paris peace treaties which had followed the First World War. He believed, rather, that the treaties merely confirmed the Romanians' ethnic and historic rights. In a world of constantly shifting national interests, Polihroniade also rejected the idea that Europe was permanently divided into 'revisionist' and 'anti-revisionist' blocs. He consequently argued that there was no reason why Romania should remain bound to her traditional allies, if it was no longer in her interests to do so.[68]

The foreign-policy debate amongst Romanian politicians and intellectuals was deemed to be particularly necessary in 1937 as Romania's allies were increasingly adapting their foreign policies to accommodate the growth of Axis power in Eastern Europe. As a result, the Romanian government could no longer be sure of the help of certain allies in the event of aggression against Romania. Of particular importance was Yugoslavia's rapprochement in early 1937 with revisionist Bulgaria and Italy. The Yugoslav–Bulgarian Pact of Friendship signed in January 1937 violated Yugoslavia's Balkan Entente obligations to defend her allies, including Romania, from any Bulgarian attack. Under the Yugoslav–Italian Convention of March 1937, Italy agreed not to support Hungarian revisionism against Yugoslavia.[69] The Convention thus indirectly ensured that any Italian backing for Hungarian revision would be directed against Czechoslovakia and Romania, rather than Yugoslavia.

The Romanian foreign ministry and the majority of politicians reacted to Romania's increasing isolation by continuing to favour a freeze on any enlargement of the country's foreign-policy commitments. The Romanians hoped thereby to consolidate their position of informal neutrality between the Great Powers.[70] Even amongst staunchly pro-French politicians a belief in a contraction of Romanian foreign-policy obligations was visible.[71]

Gheorghe Brătianu remained foremost amongst the exponents of unofficial neutrality for Romania between the Great Powers. Developing this theme in a series of newspaper articles and interviews in 1937, Brătianu described two tendencies within Romanian foreign policy. According to the first, which he described as 'the international policy system in Romania', Romanian obligations could be extended within the collective security framework. This might be achieved, for example, by the extension of Franco-Little Entente links with the Soviet Union. The second tendency was for 'a Romanian policy in the international system', whereby collective security measures should only be entered into if they were in the specific interest of Romania. To this end, Brătianu advocated that a bloc of states, independent of the current ideological pressures of bolshevism or National Socialism, should be built up in Eastern Europe.[72] Brătianu believed close ties with Germany to be possible within this system, arguing that the Rosenberg article of 15 November 1936, and Hitler's subsequent declarations to him, reflected a growing German sympathy towards Romania. Romanian–German friendship would thus be conditional upon what Brătianu believed to be German acceptance of Romania's current borders.[73] Grigore Gafencu's attempts to create a bloc of neutral states in South-East Europe in late 1939 were based upon these ideas developed in 1936 and 1937.

Reporting to the German foreign ministry in October 1937, Fabricius stated that 'Romania's line was absolutely clear: no more alliances… Even with Germany she wants no alliance, but rather an increasingly close friendship.' Victor Antonescu had confirmed to Fabricius in early

October that 'Romania was increasingly determined to go along with Germany', and that he believed 'that France and England also desire a rapprochement with Germany'.[74] The Romanian government clearly hoped that Romania's closer ties with Germany would develop within the framework of improved relations between Germany and the western powers. This would then justify Romania's gradual diplomatic shift into a position of unofficial neutrality between the Great Powers which had been taking place during 1937.

Moreover, it was clear during the run-up to the election held in December 1937 that any enlargement of Romania's obligations towards her traditional allies had become politically unacceptable to the electorate. On 7 December Foreign Minister Antonescu informed Fabricius that the question of a Franco-Little Entente alliance was finally laid to rest since it 'would be a slap in the face to public opinion, prior to the elections'.[75]

King Carol himself had reason to welcome an opportunity to free himself from the traditional French connection through a policy of unofficial neutrality between the powers and closer relations with Germany. On 31 October 1937, Carol's cousin, Prince Friedrich of Hohenzollern-Sigmaringen, stated to Fabricius that Carol was displeased with the French for two reasons. First, France's wish that Romania should rearm only with the help of France and Czechoslovakia, and not Germany, angered Carol since neither France nor Czechoslovakia was fulfilling Romanian armament requirements. Secondly, the French minister in Romania was pressurising Carol to bring the National Peasant Party to power. King Carol, who had long been at loggerheads with the National Peasant leader, Iuliu Maniu, was keen to avoid creating a National Peasant government.[76] Apparently, pressure on Carol from France and Czechoslovakia had been very strong. Even prior to the elections, 'the French military attaché in Paris had made known the National Peasant Party list of ministers, put together in Paris and Prague'.[77]

Unfortunately for Carol, the National Liberal Party, through whom he hoped to govern, failed to win the necessary 40% of the vote in the December elections with which they could form a new government. Neither the National Peasants, who had polled 21% of the vote, nor the Iron Guard with 16%, were acceptable to Carol. The king, therefore, decided to form a government under Octavian Goga and A. C. Cuza whose National Christian Party had polled only 9% of the vote. Carol foresaw this government as a prelude to his long-held plan for a royal dictatorship. In his diary he recorded that he believed a Goga–Cuza government would 'not be of long duration', and that he would then be 'free to take stronger measures', free of party interests.[78] That 'stronger measures' might also include some changes in foreign-policy orientation is suggested in the 'German-friendly' politician Constantin Argetoianu's diary. Referring to Carol's plans to reinforce royal authority, Argetoianu, one of the leading advocates of a royal dictatorship, stated that this included a plan 'to aim foreign policy on to the path of realities but maintaining, nevertheless, for the moment our present alliances'.[79] The appointment of Goga as minister president accorded well with a foreign policy which, as Argetoianu implied, aimed at maintaining the traditional alliances while seeking close relations with the Axis powers (Argetoianu's 'path of realities'). Goga was both pro-monarchy, which corresponded to Carol's future plans on the domestic front, and also pro-German. The latter was particularly important as Germany's economic importance to Romania increased. At the same time, since Goga believed that Romania should retain her traditional alliances, he would accept pro-westerners in his cabinet.[80] As we will see in the next chapter, however, the king's policy was to render fruitless Goga's long-held wish for a treaty with Germany.

Notes

1 For a complete volume of speeches by Victor Antonescu protesting that Romania's foreign policy remained unchanged after the fall of Titulescu, see Biblioteca Naţională, Fond St Georges, Packet nr 34, Doc. nr 5–3, Volume entitled 'Victor Antonescu. Declarations, Discussions, Interviews, Minister of Foreign Affairs, 1 September 1936–31 December 1937'.
2 In a posthumous publication, former Foreign Minister Titulescu described the foreign policy of the Antonescu ministry as 'a tendency towards isolation, [and] the neutrality of Romania': Nicolae Titulescu, *Politica externă a României (1937)*, (eds), George G. Potra, Constantin I. Turcu and Ion M. Oprea, Bucharest, 1994, p. 56.
3 (ed.) Sherman David Spector, 'Relapse into Bondage 1918–1947: The Political Memoirs of Alexandre Cretzianu, Free Romania's Last World Diplomatist.' Chapter 2. 'Titulescu's Policy Without Titulescu', *Southeastern Europe*, 12, nr 1, (1985), pp. 103–24 (104).
4 Andreas Hillgruber, *Hitler, König Carol und Marschall Antonescu. Die deutschrumänischen Beziehungen 1938–1944*, Wiesbaden, 1965, p. 11. In 1940 Gheorghe Tătărescu wrote that the economic conventions signed with the Reich from 1936 onwards 'were the decisive steps towards collaboration between Germany and Romania': 'Evacuarea Basarabiei şi a Bucovina de nord', in Gheorghe Tătărescu, *Mărturii pentru istoriei*, (ed.) Sanda Tătărescu-Negropontes, Bucharest, 1996, pp. 225–42 (232).

5 DGFP, C, 6, Doc. nr 83, Minister in Romania to the Foreign Ministry, Bucharest, 9 December 1936. Wilhelm Fabricius had been counsellor at the German embassy in Turkey from 1932 to 1936. He was minister in Romania from April 1936 to January 1941.
6 Anthony Tihamer Komjathy, *The Crises of France's East Central European Diplomacy 1933–1938*, Boulder, CO, 1976, p. 144.
7 William S. Grenzebach, *Germany's Informal Empire in East-Central Europe: German Economic Policy Toward Yugoslavia and Romania, 1933–1939*, Stuttgart, 1988, pp. 69–72.
8 PA, Politische Abteilung IV: Po 2, Vol. 1, 5.1936–7.1937, German Legation in Bucharest to the Foreign Ministry, Tgb. nr 2840/36, 17 November 1936, signed Fabricius. Tătărescu was minister president from January 1934 to December 1937 and secretary general of the National Liberal Party. For the 24 September protocols, see Grenzebach, op. cit., pp. 92–4.
9 MAE, 71/Germania, Vol. 75, pp. 174–7, Legation in Berlin for transmission to HM the King, the President of the Council and the Ministers of Industry and Commerce, Tel. nr 3697, 4 December 1936, signed Comnen. Comnen was minister to Berlin from 1928 to 1931 and again from 1933 to 1938.
10 DGFP, D, 5, Doc. nr 145, Memorandum by the Minister in Romania, Berlin, 7 October 1937.
11 DGFP, D, 5, Doc. nr 154, Ministerialdirektor Wohlthat to Minister President General Göring, Berlin, 13 December 1937. Helmut Wohlthat was an official of the German Ministry of Economics from 1934. He was also appointed by Göring to collaborate with him on the Four Year Plan from 1938.
12 DGFP, D, 5, Doc. nr 155, Ministerialdirektor Wohlthat to Minister President General Göring, Berlin, 14 December 1937.
13 Arh. St., Casa Regală, Dosar nr 44/1936, pp. 3–27, Foreign Policy Declarations made by Ion Mihalache to the Parliamentary Commisson on 15 December 1936.
14 DGFP, C, 5, Doc. nr 528, Minister in Romania to the Foreign Ministry, Bucharest, 6 September 1936.
15 PA, Politische Abteilung IV: Po 2, Vol. 1, 5.1936–7.1937, AA Pol IV 2837 II Berlin to various German Embassies and Legations, 25 September 1936, signed Weizsäcker.
16 PA, Politische Abteilung IV: Po 2, Vol. 1, 5.1936–7.1937, Berlin, Note to Pol IV 3830, 23 October 1936, unsigned.
17 Gheorghe I. Brătianu, *Problemele politicii noastre externe*, Bucharest, 1934, pp. 53, 63, 72–6. In 1934 Brătianu had met Alfred Rosenberg and Göring in Germany. He informed them of his fears of the Soviet Union and that he wished to consolidate Bessarabia's incorporation into the Romanian state with German help: Radu Lecca, *Eu i-am salvat pe evreii din România*, Bucharest, 1994, p. 105.
18 Dov B. Lungu, *Romania and the Great Powers, 1933–1940*, Durham and London, 1989, pp. 90–1; Nicole Jordan, *The Popular Front and Central Europe: The Dilemmas of French Impotence, 1918–1940*, Cambridge, 1992, p. 204.
19 For Brătianu's discussion with Hitler see, DGFP, C, 6, Doc. nr 38, The State Secretary and Head of the Presidential Chancellery to the Foreign Minister, 16 November 1936; MAE, 71/Germania, Vol. 75, pp. 157–60, Gh. Brătianu,

Note on the discussion with the Führer, Berlin, 16 November 1936 at the Reich Chancellery.
20 In October 1936 the Belgian government had declared that article 16 of the League of Nations covenant could not be applied without Belgian consent. Under article 16, a League of Nations member was obliged to allow right of passage through its territory to armed forces of any League member operating to protect another League member which was the victim of aggression. Article 16 had serious implications for Romania, as the Soviet Union could use it to insist on right of passage through Romania in order to help Czechoslovakia in the event of a German attack: (ed.) Sherman David Spector, 'Relapse into Bondage 1918–1947: The Political Memoirs of Alexandre Cretzianu, Free Romania's Last World Diplomatist': Chapter 2, 'Titulescu's Policy without Titulescu', *Southeastern Europe*, 12, nr 1, (1985), pp. 103–24 (122–4).
21 DGFP, C, 6, Doc. nr 38, The State Secretary and Head of the Presidential Chancellery to the Foreign Minister, 16 November 1936.
22 PA, Politische Abteilung IV: Po 2, Vol. 1, 5.1936–7.1937, German Legation in Bucharest to the Foreign Ministry, Tgb. nr 2487/36, Political Report, 7 October 1936, signed Fabricius.
23 C. A. Macartney and A. W. Palmer, *Independent Eastern Europe*, London, 1962, pp. 354–6.
24 See, for example, Mircea Mușat and Ion Ardeleanu, *România după Marea Unire*, Vol. 2, Part II-a, Bucharest, 1988, p. 1414.
25 MAE, Mica Înțelegere, Vol. 15, pp. 58–60, Discussion held on 11 September 1936 between Minister Victor Antonescu and Under-Secretary of State, Victor Badulescu, with President Stoiadinović regarding the questions to be discussed at the Conference of the Little Entente in Bratislava.
26 MAE, Mica Înțelegere, Vol. 15, unnumbered, Procès-Verbal de la session ordinaire du Conseil Permanent de la Petite Entente tenue à Bratislava les 13 et 14 Septembre 1936.
27 Nicole Jordan, *The Popular Front and Central Europe*, p. 201.
28 MAE, Mica Înțelegere, Vol. 15, pp. 312–16, Letter from the Romanian Consul at Lvov to Constantin Viscoianu, Minister Plenipotentiary at Warsaw, 21 September 1936.
29 Jordan, op. cit., pp. 243–5.
30 MAE, 71/Germania, Vol. 75, pp. 259–62, Legation in Berlin to the Foreign Ministry, Tel. nr 3746, 13 March 1937, signed Comnen; ibid, pp. 276–7, Legation in Berlin to the Foreign Ministry, Tel. nr 3760, 31 March 1937, signed Comnen.
31 MAE, 71/1920–1944, Dosare Speciale, Vol. 272, pp. 136–7, Procès-Verbal de la session ordinaire du Conseil Permanent de la Petite Entente tenue à Beograd, le 1er et 2 Avril 1937.
32 PA, Politische Abteilung IV: Po 2, Vol. 1, 5.1936–7.1937, German Legation in Bucharest to the Foreign Ministry, Tgb. nr 899/37, 6 April 1937, signed Fabricius.
33 Arh. St., Însemnări Zilnice, Carol II, roll 21, Vol. 2, 17 May 1937, pp. 87–8. The Franco-Little Entente pact was once again put on the agenda by the Czechoslovaks during the Little Entente conference at Sinaia in August 1937. The question was again postponed. The Romanian government also failed to follow up a Czechoslovak proposal for a mutual assistance pact between their

two countries put forward following the Belgrade meeting: MAE, Mica Înțelegere, Vol. 52, pp. 315–88 (363–71), M. Mitilineu, 'Romanian Relations with the Former Little Entente (1918–1938)', November 1942.
34 Jordan, *The Popular Front and Central Europe*, pp. 246, 273.
35 Ibid, pp. 245–6.
36 Günther Reichert, *Das Scheitern der Kleine Entente, 1933–1938*, Munich, 1971, p. 123.
37 Quoted in ibid, p. 250.
38 See, for example, the foreign-policy debate held on 3 December 1936: PA, Politische Abteilung IV: Po 2, Vol. 1, 5.1936–7.1937, German Legation in Bucharest to the Foreign Ministry, Tgb. nr 3079/36, 3 December 1936, signed Fabricius.
39 For what follows on the 14 December debate see, PA, Politische Abteilung IV: Po 2, Vol. 1, 5.1936–7.1937, German Legation in Bucharest to the Foreign Ministry, Tgb nr 3168/36, 14 December 1936, signed Fabricius.
40 Arh. St., Casa Regală, Dosar nr 44/1936, pp. 3–27, Foreign Policy Declarations made by Ion Mihalache to the Parliamentary Commission on 15 December 1936.
41 Bundesarchiv, Berlin, NS 43/60, Letter from the Aussenpolitisches Amt der NSDAP to Führer's Adjutant, Wiedemann, 4 September 1936, signed Schickedanz.
42 Mihai Fătu, *Cu pumnii strînși. Octavian Goga în viața politică a României (1918–1938)*, Bucharest, 1993, pp. 163–5.
43 MAE, 71/România, Vol. 357/1, p. 130, *Universul*, 29 November 1936: Chamber of Deputies, 27 November 1936, 'Necesitatea raporturilor cu Germania'.
44 PA, Politische Abteilung IV: Po 2, Vol. 1, 5.1936–7.1937, German Legation in Bucharest to the Foreign Ministry, Tgb nr 3168/36, 14 December 1936, signed Fabricius.
45 Ibid.
46 MAE, 71/Germania, Vol. 75, pp. 178–83, Legation in Berlin, Only for HM the King, the President of the Council, the Foreign Minister and the Under-Secretary of State, Tel. nr 3698, 4 December 1936, signed Comnen.
47 Ibid.
48 DGFP, C, 6, Doc. nr 36, Memorandum by the Foreign Minister, Berlin, 16 November 1936.
49 MAE, 71/Germania, Vol. 75, pp. 168–71, Legation in Berlin to the Foreign Ministry, Tel. nr 3692, 25 November 1936, signed Comnen.
50 MAE, 71/Germania, Vol. 75, p. 188, Victor Antonescu to Comnen, Tel. nr 68407, 9 December 1936, signed Antonescu.
51 MAE, 71/Germania, Vol. 75, pp. 195–8, Legation in Berlin, Personal for Victor Antonescu, Tel. nr 6300, 11 December 1936, signed Comnen.
52 See, for example, N. P. Comnène, *I Responsabili*, Verona, 1949, esp. pp. 260–1. In his *Anarchie, dictature ou organisation internationale?*, Geneva, 1946, pp. 169–75, Comnen discusses the fall of Carol's regime in 1940, the installation of the pro-German General Antonescu regime and the malign influence of Germany in Romania. (General Antonescu is described as a 'Gauleiter' for the Germans.) Yet in September 1940, Comnen offered his services to General Antonescu on the basis of his experience as minister to Berlin and foreign minister to help build up relations with Germany: Arh. St., P. C. M., Dosar nr

473/1940, pp. 4–9, Letter from N. P. Comnen at the Rome Embassy to General Antonescu, 10 September 1940. In addition to his attempts to strengthen economic relations with Germany, Comnen clearly placed considerable significance on the verbal guarantees given by German leaders. During his discussion with Fabricius on 9 December 1936, Victor Antonescu described Comnen as having a 'mania' for extracting such statements from German leaders: DGFP, C, 6, Doc. nr 83, Minister in Romania to the Foreign Ministry, Bucharest, 9 December 1936. Early in 1937, Fabricius reported that although the Romanians sought closer links with Germany, they did not intend to bind themselves to the Reich through a treaty, 'as Comnen so constantly urges them to do': DGFP, C, 6, Doc. nr 197, Minister in Romania to the Foreign Ministry, Bucharest, 11 February 1937.

53   MAE, 71/Germania, Vol. 75, pp. 199–209, Legation in Berlin to the Foreign Minister, Tel. nr 3941, 14 December 1936, signed Comnen.

54   For the Romanian foreign ministry's interest in the Reich guarantee of Yugoslavia, see DGFP, C, 6, Doc. nr 83, Minister in Romania to the Foreign Ministry, Bucharest, 9 December 1936. For the development of Yugoslavia's relations with Germany, especially under Stoiadinović, see J. B. Hoptner, *Yugoslavia in Crisis 1934–1941*, Columbia, 1962, pp. 46–166. For Romania's relations with Yugoslavia, see, Eugene Boia, *Romania's Diplomatic Relations with Yugoslavia in the Interwar Period, 1919–1941*, Boulder and New York, 1993, esp. pp. 202–84. Göring had apparently offered Yugoslavia a territorial guarantee against Hungary and Italy in June 1936: Hoptner, op. cit., pp. 46–7. In January 1938 Hitler offered Stoiadinović a guarantee of Yugoslavia's borders with Hungary: Boia, op. cit., p. 231. Romania's tendency to coordinate her policies with Yugoslavia was confirmed by Fabricius in his end-of-year report: PA, Deutsche Gesandschaft Bukarest, IA 5a, Vol. 1, 1935–39, German Legation in Bucharest to the Foreign Ministry, Tgb. nr 3288/36, Annual Political Report for 1936, 23 December 1936, signed Fabricius.

55   MAE, 71/Germania, Vol. 75, pp. 264–79, Absolutely Secret, Comnen to the Foreign Minister, Tel. nr 37056, 25 March 1937, signed Comnen.

56   Alexandru Cretzianu, *The Lost Opportunity*, London, 1957, p. 19. Cretzianu was secretary general at the foreign ministry between 1939 and 1941. In his memoirs, however, Cretzianu admitted that although Carol did not wish to jettison the collective security system, he could not reject Göring's offer of 4 December 1936. Carol, therefore, 'insisted that a formula be found which would leave us free for the future and would avoid the appearance that we wished to participate in any bloc directed against Germany'. See (ed.) Sherman David Spector, 'Relapse into Bondage 1918–1947: The Political Memoirs of Alexandre Cretzianu, Free Romania's Last World Diplomatist': Chapter 2, 'Titulescu's Policy without Titulescu', *Southeastern Europe*, 12, nr 1, (1985), pp. 103–24 (121).

57   MAE, 71/Germania, Vol. 75, pp. 298–300, Discussion between Göring and Atta Constantinescu; ibid, pp. 308–11, Letter from Royal Romanian Legation, Berlin, to Victor Antonescu, nr 1202, 19 April 1937, signed Comnen.

58   MAE, Dosare Speciale, Vol. 376/1, pp. 22–3, unnumbered telegram, Gheorghe Tătărescu to Victor Antonescu, 16 February 1937, signed Tătărescu.

59   MAE, Dosare Speciale, Vol. 376/1, pp. 55–6, Tătărescu to Minister Comnen, Tel. nr 9453, 17 February 1937, signed Tătărescu. For a detailed discussion of this diplomatic 'incident', see Rebecca Ann Haynes, 'Romanian Policy towards

Germany, September 1936–September 1940', unpublished PhD thesis, University of London, 1997, pp. 59–63. The incident may well have been inspired by domestic conflicts rather than by foreign-policy concerns. Fabricius later recorded that he had dined with members of the Romanian government on the evening following the funeral and there were no complaints regarding his presence at the funeral. Only on the following day did his attendance 'become an issue whereby the National Peasant Party hoped to bring down the Tătărescu regime': PA, Politische Abteilung IV: Po 5, Vol. 1, 5.36–8.37, German Legation, Bucharest, Tgb. nr 669/37, 11 March 1937, signed Fabricius.
60 Arh. St., Însemnări Zilnice, Constantin Argetoianu, Dosar nr 72, Vol. 1, 12 March 1937, p.169.
61 MAE, 71/Germania, Vol. 75, pp. 259–62, Legation in Berlin to the Foreign Ministry, Tel. nr 3746, 13 March 1937, signed Comen.
62 Arh. St., Însemnări Zilnice, Carol II, roll 21, Vol. 1, 12 March 1937, pp. 9–10. Von Cramon and Carol trained in the same regiment together in Potsdam before the First World War. In 1930 Carol had sent von Cramon as a special envoy to Hindenberg and Hitler subsequently used him as a special envoy to Romania.
63 PA, Politische Abteilung IV: Po 5, Vol. 1, 5.36–8.37, German Legation in Bucharest to the Foreign Ministry, Tgb. nr 669/37, 11 March 1937, signed Fabricius.
64 PA, Politische Abteilung IV: Po 2, Vol. 1, 5.1936–7.1937, German Legation in Bucharest to the Foreign Ministry, Tgb. nr 2487/36, Political Report, 7 October 1936, signed Fabricius.
65 DGFP, C, 6, Doc. nr 197, Minister in Romania to the Foreign Ministry, Bucharest, 11 February 1937.
66 Arh. St., Însemnări Zilnice, Constantin Argetoianu, Dosar nr 72, Vol. 3, 30 November 1937, pp. 325–6. Romanian elections were normally 'fixed' by the government. Elections had been called for 20 December 1937 as a result of the expiration of the four-year term of the parliament elected in December 1933. On 14 November 1937, Codreanu and Maniu, together with Gheorghe Brătianu's Young Liberals and Constantin Argetoianu's Agrarian Party, concluded a 'non-aggression pact' in order to prevent Carol and the National Liberal government from 'fixing' the elections to ensure the return of another Liberal government. For an overview of the domestic political situation in inter-war Romania, see Keith Hitchins, *Rumania, 1866–1947*, Oxford, 1994, pp. 377–426.
67 Mihail Polihroniade, 'Tineretul și politica externă', *Randuiala*, 3, Bucharest, 1937, p. 9. Polihroniade was also the editor of the Guardist newspaper, *Buna Vestire*.
68 Ibid, pp. 12, 20.
69 The German government had encouraged a rapprochement between Yugoslavia and Italy in order to disrupt the Little Entente and move Yugoslavia closer to the Axis: Gerhard L. Weinberg, *The Foreign Policy of Hitler's Germany: Starting World War II, 1937–1939*, Chicago, 1980, pp. 216–17.
70 For Romania's increasing isolation within the Little and Balkan Ententes, see Nicolae Titulescu, *Politica externă a României (1937)*, (eds) George G. Potra, Constantin I. Turcu and Ion M. Oprea, Bucharest, 1994, pp. 69–86. Titulescu's book was written as a condemnation of the foreign policy of the Tătărescu

government since Titulescu's fall from office. He condemned the government for allowing Romania's allies to pursue their own policies according to national interests, while leaving Romania's obligations towards her allies intact.
71 Even the pro-French historian Nicolae Iorga believed Romania should refuse any foreign-policy commitments which were not in her immediate interests: MAE, 71/România, Vol. 357/1, unpaginated, *Naţionalul*, 19 February 1937, 'Politica României este hotărîte numai de ea'.
72 MAE, 71/România, Vol. 4, p. 383, *Timpul*, 'Politica sistemelor internaţionale în România şi politica românească în sistemele internaţionale', and Georges I. Brătianu, *La politique extèrieure de la Roumanie*, Bucharest, 1937.
73 MAE, 71/România, Vol. 4, p. 271, *Curentul*, 'G. Brătianu despre politica României faţa de Germania. Care e rolul Micii Înţelegeri şi al alienţei cu Polonia?' See also, Mihai A. Antonescu, *Politica externă a României*, Bucharest, 1937, p. 25, in which he advocated the creation of a bloc of neutral states between the Baltic and Black Seas. Mihai Antonescu was foreign minister during the General Antonescu dictatorship.
74 DGFP, D, 5, Doc. nr 145, Memorandum by the Minister to Romania, Berlin, 7 October 1937.
75 DGFP, D, 1, Doc. nr 65, German Minister in Romania to the German Foreign Ministry, Bucharest, 7 December 1937.
76 PA, Politische Abteilung IV: Po 2, Vol. 2, 9.37–2.39, German Legation in Bucharest to the Foreign Minstry, Tgb. nr 3172/37, 31 October 1937, signed Fabricius. For further details of Maniu's fight against Carol's authoritarian tendencies, see Ioan Scurtu, *Istoria Partidului Naţional Ţărănesc*, Bucharest, 1994, pp. 265–82.
77 Bundesarchiv, Berlin, NS 10/89, Aktennotiz! Berlin, 30 November 1937, signed Schickedanz.
78 Arh. St., Însemnări Zilnice, Carol II, roll 21, Vol. 3, 2 November to 31 December 1937, pp. 226–8. For Carol's long-standing wish to set up an authoritarian regime, see Larry L. Watts, *Romanian Cassandra: Ion Antonescu and the Struggle for Reform, 1916–1941*, Boulder and New York, 1993, pp. 133–6.
79 Arh. St., Însemnări Zilnice, Constantin Argetoianu, Dosar nr 72, Vol. 3, 10 November 1937, pp. 246–7.
80 Paul A. Shapiro, 'Prelude to Dictatorship in Romania: The National Christian Party in Power, December 1937–February 1938', *Canadian–American Slavic Studies*, 8, nr 1, (Spring 1974), pp. 45–88 (66–9).

2
'Friendly with the Whole World': The Goga–Cuza Government and the Comnen Foreign Ministry, December 1937 to December 1938[1]

The short-lived Goga–Cuza government installed in late December 1937 did little to speed up the process of rapprochement with the Reich, despite Octavian Goga's desire for an alliance with Germany.[2] The cabinet was in fact divided between pro-westerners and those who sought strong links with the Axis powers. This division reflected King Carol's decision to steer a neutral course between the Great Powers. Within this policy of informal neutrality between the powers, Romania's traditional alliances and western links were to be maintained. At the same time, relations with the Reich were to be gradually strengthened. With the king ultimately in control of foreign policy, there was to be no room for an overt pro-German policy as originally advocated by Goga and as still called for by his political partner, A. C. Cuza.

The appointment of the anti-bolshevik, pro-German Octavian Goga at the head of the government represented an assurance for Germany of Romania's good intentions towards her and confirmed that Romania would not enter into closer relations with the Soviet Union. As the Romanian minister to Berlin, Comnen, informed Foreign Minister von Neurath, the new Romanian government 'represents an evolution in the normalisation of our relations with Germany' and was 'a complete guarantee regarding our relations with Russia'.[3]

At this stage, Goga was probably the best known Romanian in Germany. Hitler described the coming to power of the Goga government and its subsequent policies as the 'first happy event of the New Year'.[4] Goga was not the only pro-German in the new government. Although his outspokenly germanophile and antisemitic political ally, A. C. Cuza, was relegated to minister without portfolio, his son, Gheorghe Cuza, became minister of labour. Other pro-Germans in the cabinet included Ion Gigurtu, as minister of trade and industry, Eugen Savu, as financial minister and Irimescu, the air and sea minister.[5]

Some of the most important cabinet posts were, however, taken by pro-westerners. Thus, Armand Călinescu of the National Peasant Party, became minister of the interior.[6] General Ion Antonescu was appointed minister of national defence, with General Teodorescu as his undersecretary.[7]

Istrate Micescu, the new foreign minister, was a member of the National Christian Party. Although pro-German, Micescu had promised to follow Carol's commands and the advice of the former foreign minister, Victor Antonescu, in keeping with Carol's determination to keep ultimate control of foreign policy.[8] Nevertheless, the sharp ideological divisions which existed in this heterogeneous cabinet led to a number of highly contradictory foreign-policy announcements, even by Carol's otherwise loyal foreign minister.

On 31 December 1937, Micescu informed members of the diplomatic corps that the general aim of policy was to create lasting links with Italy and Germany as soon as possible.[9] Yet within a fortnight of this declaration, the 'German-friendly' Constantin Argetoianu was complaining in his diary of Micescu's pronouncements in favour of the League of Nations and of the alliance with Czechoslovakia.[10] Micescu's itinerary of foreign capitals in mid-January 1938 did not include the Axis capitals, but instead Geneva, home of the League of Nations, Belgrade and Prague. In the Czechoslovak capital, Micescu assured his hosts that Romania would respect her Little Entente obligations.[11]

Minister President Goga's foreign-policy declarations also reflected this ambivalence between pro-German statements and assurances of Romania's loyalty to her traditional allies. On 31 December 1937, Goga assured Fabricius of his wish for a treaty of friendship with Germany. On the following day, Goga stressed in a newspaper article his desire for a new commercial treaty with the Reich. At the same time, he stated his wish to maintain the traditional links with France and to strengthen ties with Britain.[12] In keeping with this position, Goga, on his elevation as minister president, sent telegrams of friendship both to Romania's traditional allies (Czechoslovakia, France, Poland and Yugoslavia) as well as to Italy and Germany.[13]

Goga's New Year telegram to Hitler constituted one of the government's few concrete attempts to foster the German connection during its brief term of office. In his telegram, Goga spoke of his 'unshakeable determination to maintain good and cordial relations with Germany....'. Goga, nevertheless, made it clear that his desire for close ties with Germany was dependent on the Reich's recognition of Romania's territorial integrity. He alluded to previous remarks made to him by the Führer in which the latter had apparently referred to the 'the natural relations between the two countries and of the vital rights of Romania, whose present boundaries are incontrovertibly justified by the principle of nationality'. As a result of Goga's direct reference to Romania's territorial integrity, the Reich chancellery deemed it inadvisable for the Führer to give a direct reply to the telegram which might thereby have alienated Hungary. Consequently, Fabricius was directed to simply convey Hitler's 'gratitude' for the declaration.[14]

Foreign-policy contradictions were to some extent inherent within the policy of neutrality between the powers which Carol wished to pursue. Goga clearly did not regard his foreign-policy statements as having been in contradiction to the king's aims. Speaking in defence of his cabinet's foreign policy five days after its dismissal, Goga explained that his aims had been to 'retain our existing alliances and pacts of friendship, and to seek to enlarge the circle of our sympathisers beyond our borders. In this regard I was in perfect concord with the declarations of His Majesty and never departed a millimetre from the line laid down.'[15] As Carol himself stated in an interview with a German newspaper on 6 February 1938, he was a supporter of Romania's traditional alliances. At the same time, he wanted Romania, like her Polish and Yugoslav allies, to extend her relationships 'in all directions'.[16]

Even without this inherently equivocal foreign-policy line, contradictory statements and aims were all the more likely in view of the fact that the government now included a vocal pro-German element for the first time since the First World War. Conflict soon emerged between the more pliable Goga, who was prepared to comply with royal wishes, and the more vocally pro-German A. C. Cuza. On 10 January, Cuza demanded that Romania should leave the League of Nations or else he and his son would leave the coalition.[17] Meanwhile, Cuza's interview with an Italian newspaper, in which he declared the League of Nations to be 'a society of Jews, constituted to dominate the nations', and that he regarded the League as 'dead but unburied', totally ruined the effect of Micescu's trip to Geneva. Carol was apparently furious with Cuza.[18]

At the same time as it pursued the policy of informal neutrality between the Great Powers, the Goga government inaugurated a radical antisemitic domestic policy. The government introduced legislation specifically aimed at curtailing what many Romanians at the time regarded as the disproportionate position of the country's small Jewish minority in the economy and higher education.[19] The result of these measures was to bring the economy to a standstill as Jews boycotted work and withdrew their money from the banks. The Jewish World Congress and the Federation of Jewish Societies of France petitioned the League of Nations to investigate the situation in Romania. The British and French governments subsequently put pressure on Romania to comply with the 1919 Minorities' Protection Treaty under which Romania was obliged to treat her citizens equally regardless of nationality.[20]

The Goga–Cuza government fell from power largely as a result of western displeasure at its antisemitic measures. Goga later informed Fabricius that two days before Carol dismissed him on 10 February, the French minister to Bucharest, Thierry, had informed him that if Romania did not honour the Minorities' Protection Treaty, France would consider herself absolved from any obligations to protect Romania and to provide the Romanian government with army credits.[21] Without any formal commitment from Germany to guarantee Romania's frontiers, Carol could not afford to alienate his western guarantors. At the same time, the extreme right-wing nature of the Goga–Cuza government had roused the wrath of the Soviet Union. Following the disappearance of Butenko, the Soviet chargé d'affaires, from Bucharest, the Soviets claimed he had been murdered by Romanian fascists. Although Butenko subsequently surfaced in Italy, denouncing the bolshevik system, the Soviets continued to demand the punishment of his 'murderers'.[22] With the government thus commanding no respect abroad and divided at home by armed clashes between Călinescu's ministry of the interior security forces, Cuza's paramilitary *Lancieri*, and the Iron Guard, Carol dismissed the Goga government.

The Reich had little cause to bemoan the downfall of Goga. As Ernst von Weizsäcker, director of the political department at the German foreign ministry, pointed out in a foreign-ministry circular, 'we found in [Goga], as an admirer of the present German form of government, a far-reaching understanding for the new Germany; beyond that the short duration of his government prevented a serious diplomatic exchange of views with him'.[23] Most importantly, in view of the Reich's economic interests in Romania, the chaos created by the regime's antisemitic legislation had impeded the flow of Romanian agricultural produce and petroleum to the Reich.[24] Consequently, the inauguration of King Carol's royal dictatorship in February 1938 was accepted calmly in Germany. The pro-western Călinescu and Antonescu retained their positions in the new government but, as Fabricius reported, the new cabinet included a 'number of people who are not against cooperation with Germany'. He therefore expected the government's policies to take their 'usual course', especially in economic matters.[25]

Reporting on the character of the royal dictatorship to the German foreign ministry, Weizsäcker noted its nationalistic, Christian and antisemitic character. The new regime abolished the 1923 constitution and deprived the parliament of power. Ministers were made solely responsible to the king, who had the power to issue decrees with the force of law. Weizsäcker observed that both Carol and Gheorghe Tătărescu, temporary acting foreign minister in the new government, had declared their wish for gradual rapprochement with Germany. Weizsäcker regarded article 91 of the new constitution to be an important step in this direction since it prevented the passage of foreign troops through Romania. He correctly surmised that this would put a stop to Soviet demands to pass through Romania to help Czechoslovakia in the event of a German attack.[26]

The elevation of the Romanian minister to Berlin, Nicolae Petrescu-Comnen, first as under-secretary of state at the foreign ministry on 10 February and then as foreign minister on 30 March 1938, was greeted warmly in Berlin.[27] On 6 April, in a declaration to the press, Comnen, although stressing the importance of Romania's traditional alliances, pointed out that his 'long mission in Berlin has given me the opportunity to understand our relations with Germany in great detail'. Comnen concluded that he sought to develop relations with the Reich, especially in the economic and cultural spheres.[28]

King Carol and Foreign Minister Comnen were, nevertheless, determined to maintain an essentially neutral course in foreign policy, while pursuing German friendship. This was especially important in view of the increase in German power resulting from the Anschluss of Austria on 13 March. The Romanians wished neither to antagonise the Germans, nor to find themselves entirely dominated by the enlarged Reich. The appointment of Comnen, who had long years of diplomatic experience during the Titulescu era, would also help Romania retain her links with the West and her traditional allies.[29] At the same time, Comnen's experience in Berlin would help to strengthen relations with Germany.[30]

Romanian historians invariably blame the West for 'appeasing' Hitler by refusing to take action to prevent the Anschluss.[31] Yet by 1938, the Romanian government had long regarded the Anschluss as a natural development. On 19 March, Carol informed Fabricius that he had regarded the Anschluss as inevitable for some while.[32] Furthermore, the Little Entente had long since decided to take no military action in the event of an Anschluss, regarding it as an affair for the Great Powers. In the summer of 1936, the Little Entente chiefs of staff decided that any military measures against Austria or Hungary in the event of a Habsburg restoration would only take place if both Germany and Italy remained strictly neutral. Military action in the event of a German Anschluss of Austria was not foreseen.[33]

The reaction of the Romanian foreign ministry to the Anschluss on 13 March 1938 was in keeping with this non-interventionist approach. Neither France nor Britain were willing to take military action against the German entry into Austria. Foreign Minister Comnen therefore issued a circular to all Romanian legations abroad to the effect that 'Romania has never considered the Anschluss as a local problem... but as a European problem which depends in the first place on the actions of the interested Great Powers'. Comnen continued that Czechoslovakia, Yugoslavia and Hungary now all shared common borders with the enlarged Reich, but had received assurances from Germany that their borders would not be violated. Consequently, the Romanian government did not consider it necessary to take any initiatives in the matter.[34]

Both the king and the foreign ministry were, nonetheless, well aware that the creation of a Greater German Reich reduced the value of the traditional alliance system.[35] In particular, the absorption of Austria gave the German Reich economic preponderance in the Danube basin. Germany's share of trade with South-East Europe increased on account of the addition of Austria's trade with the region, which included investments in the Romanian banking system.[36] In keeping with the policy of informal neutrality between the Great Powers, the Romanian government attempted to prevent the enlarged Germany from totally dominating the Romanian economy. During the Romanian–German economic negotiations in May and June 1938, Romanian representatives attempted to dissuade German negotiators from including Romania's economic conventions with the former Austrian state into Romania's clearing agreements with Germany. Such a move would have greatly increased petroleum exports to Germany. Although the Reich succeeded in including Romanian trade agreements with Austria in the clearing agreement signed on 21 June 1938, the Romanians were able to limit the amount of petroleum to be exported to Germany.[37]

The Romanian government also began a series of measures to try to increase trade with the western countries. During May and June 1938, Foreign Minister Comnen attempted to encourage Britain and France to cooperate with Romania in strengthening economic relations. On 18 June, former Minister President Gheorghe Tătărescu visited London with the aim of increasing commercial exchange with Britain. Tătărescu informed the British that the Romanian government was ready to do business with the Reich 'but did not want to give Germany a monopoly'.[38] Nevertheless, Germany's absorption of Austria's trading agreements with Romania had the inevitable result of increasing Romania's economic dependence on the Reich. The Greater Reich now absorbed some 27% of all Romanian exports.[39]

King Carol's decision to intensify the process of eliminating the Iron Guard as a political force was a further consequence of the Anschluss. Carol's decision was initiated and encouraged by Minister of the Interior Armand Călinescu, who regarded the Anschluss as part of a German step-by-step plan for political and economic domination of the Danube basin. Călinescu believed that Germany would use the Iron Guard as a tool to put pressure on the Romanian government to comply with German wishes. He therefore advocated the liquidation of the Guard and the arrest of Codreanu, the movement's leader.[40]

Despite Călinescu's personal opinions, however, Carol's decision to crush the Iron Guard should not be seen as part of an anti-German foreign-policy reaction on his part. As Weizsäcker pointed out in a German foreign-ministry circular, 'even though in Romania the movement which ideologically appears most closely to approach our own *Weltanschauung*, namely the Iron Guard, is being most vigorously fought, we, nevertheless, have no cause for unease... Carol will persist in his repeatedly expressed desire to come to a closer relationship with Germany.' Rather than part of an anti-German policy, Weizsäcker recognised Carol's clampdown on the Iron Guard as 'a signal of his desire for internal independence'.[41] Carol's strengthening of his domestic position was particularly important in view of the dangerous degree of public support for the Guard, manifested during the Moța and Marin funeral and the election of 1937. Simultaneously, however, Carol sought by crushing the supposedly German-backed Guard to ensure that all German contacts would be conducted through the monarchy alone, and thereby ensure his complete control over the country's foreign policy.

Romanian historians have traditionally regarded the Iron Guard as the most important element in a German backed 'fifth column', also consisting of members of the ethnic German minority in Romania and other right-wing groups. The aim of the 'fifth column' was to bring down the royal government and divert Romania from her loyally pro-western course. According to this view, from 1933 onwards 'Hitlerite

Germany found in the Iron Guard a docile and faithful partner'.[42] In this respect, historians have reflected the contemporary belief that the Guardists had full German support. In view of the Guard's pro-Axis foreign-policy orientation and their solidarity with Nazi antisemitic measures, this is perhaps hardly surprising.[43]

The most comprehensive account of the Iron Guard to date, however, offers little evidence that the movement was financed and coordinated by Germany.[44] The German foreign ministry, as we have seen, favoured a policy of gradual rapprochement with Carol, beginning on an economic basis. They consequently took little notice of the Iron Guard.[45] This attitude was to continue throughout the forthcoming Codreanu trial in May 1938. Links between Rosenberg's Aussenpolitisches Amt and the Iron Guard were also slender. Rosenberg did attempt to unify the Guard with Goga and Cuza's political parties at the time of the creation of the National Christian Party. The attempt failed due to the personality clash between Codreanu and his erstwhile political ally, A. C. Cuza.[46] In the winter of 1936–37 Rosenberg once again tried to establish links between the Guard and radical elements within the ethnic German minority in Romania. These attempts failed due to Codreanu's links with Iuliu Maniu and the National Peasant Party which culminated in Codreanu's electoral pact with Maniu in November 1937, with which Rosenberg had little sympathy.[47]

Of more ultimate significance were the loose links which existed by the mid-1930s between the Guard and Nazi Party organisations such as the SA, SS and Goebbels' propaganda ministry.[48] While there is no evidence of financial help from these agencies, Codreanu was known to have received money from a German agent, Schepky, and also apparently from Arthur Konradi, head of the Romanian-German Chamber of Commerce in Bucharest.[49] But while Codreanu lived the movement was never dependent on German finances. In fact, the Guard's main financial support came from the organisation 'Friends of the Legion'. Contributors had at various times included King Carol himself, as well as his brother Prince Nicolae.[50] It was only after the murder of Codreanu in November 1938 and the subsequent flight of substantial numbers of Guardists into exile in Germany that the movement became heavily influenced by the Nazis. It was at this point that links previously made with organisations such as the SS were to bear fruit.

In view of the tendency amongst historians to stress the Guard's links with Nazi Party organisations, it should also be pointed out that King Carol did not limit his contacts with the Reich to official diplomatic channels. He frequently used unofficial emissaries, such as Gheorghe

Brătianu, to treat with the German foreign ministry, Rosenberg's Aussenpolitisches Amt and German party leaders. He also established direct links between his own monarchical organisations and the Nazi Party. Collaboration between the Guard of the Country (*Straja Ţării*), the king's youth movement, and the Hitler Youth were begun in 1935. The commander of the movement, Sidorovici, was a good friend of the Hitler Youth leader, von Schirach.[51] This underlines the fact that Carol's crushing of the Iron Guard was not part of an anti-German foreign policy, but was intended to ensure that all contacts with Germany where conducted instead through the monarchy alone.

Codreanu was arrested on 16 April 1938 on the charge of insulting the royal minister, Nicolae Iorga.[52] On 19 April Codreanu received a six months sentence for damaging Iorga's honour. Allegations of German support for the Guard were a major factor in Codreanu's second trial, held between the 23 and 27 May 1938 before a military court in Bucharest. He was charged with having formed a paramilitary organisation 'for the overthrow of the existing social order', and of having for this purpose 'accepted foreign funds and entered into relations abroad'. Codreanu was further accused of writing to Hitler in 1935 stating that he wished to carry out a National Socialist revolution in Romania with German support. He had apparently also proposed a political and economic alliance with Germany.[53]

The German foreign ministry did not attempt to interfere in Codreanu's trial. Fabricius refused to intervene even when members of the Guard approached him to intercede for Codreanu.[54] In view of Germany's reserve towards Codreanu, Minister of the Interior Călinescu was able to reassure Fabricius that 'the Romanian government wished to avoid anything that might in any way involve Germany in these proceedings....'. Consequently, Germany was not even mentioned by name in the indictment issued against Codreanu.[55] On 27 May 1938, Codreanu was sentenced to ten years' hard labour although the prosecution failed to establish that he had communicated secretly with Hitler in 1935. Codreanu had denied writing the relevant letter and of having any contact with Germany.[56]

The Romanian government had good reason to act cautiously towards Germany even as the Iron Guard was being crushed. By the spring of 1938 the Sudeten crisis had already begun to threaten the peace of Europe. In Romanian historiography, Romania is portrayed as being loyal to its obligations to Czechoslovakia to the last. In the traditional account, both Romania and Czechoslovakia were let down only by the 'appeasement' policies of Britain and France.[57]

In reality, the 1938 Czechoslovak crisis was marked by a desperate attempt by Romania to evade her treaty obligations towards Czechoslovakia in order to avoid the possibility of finding herself at war with Germany. At the same time, the Romanian government made every effort to deny right of passage through Romania to the Red Army to aid its Czechoslovak ally. The Romanians feared that the entry of the Red Army into their country might bring Romania into the theatre of war between Germany and the Soviet Union and would be followed by the permanent Soviet occupation of Bessarabia.

Throughout the Sudeten crisis, the Romanian government's attempts to remain neutral towards Germany in any possible conflict were complicated by Romania's Little Entente obligations towards Czechoslovakia. While Romania was not obliged to help the Czechoslovaks against Germany, she was bound to give them military aid in the event of an attack by Hungary. The Romanian government feared that Hungary would take advantage of the current crisis to regain former Hungarian Slovakia, which had been granted to Czechoslovakia under the Treaty of Trianon. If the Hungarians were working in collusion with the Reich, a Romanian counterattack on Hungary would lead to war with Germany. As King Carol noted in his diary on 23 May 1938, so long as Hungary did not enter any conflict, 'we can conform to our policy of not entering automatically against Germany, and therefore in principle remain neutral'.[58] It was further possible, however, that a German strike against Czechoslovakia might be launched from Hungarian soil. In this case, the Romanian foreign ministry was unclear how it should react. On 2 September, after research into their Little Entente obligations, the Romanian foreign ministry confirmed that the Little Entente countries had no obligation to attack Hungary in a case when Hungary adopted a *passive* attitude towards the violation of her neutrality by German troops participating in an attack against another Little Entente member state.[59] The Romanian foreign ministry, however, remained uneasy regarding its position in the event of German use of Hungarian territory to launch an attack, especially in the event of Hungary also taking up a belligerent attitude towards Czechoslovakia. On 9 September, the Romanian minister to Berlin, Radu Djuvara, pointed out to Weizsäcker, now state secretary at the German foreign ministry, that the Romanian government was unclear whether German use of Hungarian territory for an attack on the Czechoslovaks would be a *casus foederis* for Romania. Djuvara requested on behalf of his government that Germany should desist from launching an attack from Hungarian territory and should not force Hungary to take up arms against Czechoslovakia.[60] Carol and his advisers, however, subsequently decided officially that Romania would not intervene even in the event of a Hungarian attack on Czechoslovakia.[61] On 27 September, the day following this decision, Fabricius reported to Berlin that the Romanians 'do not wish for war with Germany and would do their utmost to prevent one; they wish to remain neutral'.[62]

In the weeks before Munich, German leaders proved ready to rein in Hungarian actions in order to allow Romania and Yugoslavia to remain neutral in a possible war. A German foreign-ministry memorandum of 18 August recorded that Hungary was to be advised 'to await Czechoslovak provocation as a pretext for war in the event of a German–Czechoslovak conflict, and to prepare the way for the Romanians and Yugoslavs to evade their treaty obligations'.[63] On 28 September, Göring informed the Yugoslav representative in Berlin that if Hungary became militarily involved in Czechoslovakia 'it will take a form such that Romania and Yugoslavia's obligations will be inoperative'. Göring repeated his previous promises that the Reich would guarantee Romania and Yugoslavia against Hungarian revisionism provided they remained neutral towards Germany and avoided involvement with the Soviets.[64]

During 1936 and 1937 Romanian officials had given frequent assurances to German leaders to the effect that Romania would not allow the passage of Soviet troops across Romanian soil. During the Sudeten crisis, Romanian officials continued to give the Germans such assurances. The Romanians were doubtless encouraged in this policy by further promises of a territorial guarantee made by German party leaders. In late April 1938, Hitler spoke to Djuvara, the Romanian minister to Berlin, of the Reich's intention to respect national frontiers in South-East Europe. Hitler authorised Djuvara to inform the king and Foreign Minister Comnen that he was prepared to guarantee Romania's frontiers.[65] At the end of May 1938, Minister Djuvara informed Field Marshal Göring that Romania would not allow the Soviet Union right of passage across the country. Djuvara pointed out that the question of Soviet right of passage was also of concern to the Polish government, which would also not allow the Soviet army to pass through its territory.[66] In mid-September, as the Sudeten crisis reached its climax, the Soviet Union was still pressurising Romania to allow her the right of passage. In an effort to avoid Franco-Soviet endeavours to force Romania to declare her attitude in the event of a German–Czechoslovak conflict, Foreign Minister Comnen refused to take over chairmanship of the League of Nations assembly. At the same time, in an attempt to tread a neutral path between Germany and the West, Comnen had not issued an official denial that

Soviet troops were to pass through Romania so as not to weaken the position of Czechoslovakia, France and the Soviet Union in their negotiations with Germany.[67] Regardless of this, however, it was by now quite clear that the Romanians would not allow Soviet right of passage. On 9 September Djuvara had informed Weizsäcker on Foreign Minister Comnen's instructions that Romania was in agreement with Poland that it was in Romania's 'vital interest' that 'Russia should be prevented from interfering via Romanian territory'.[68] Later in the month, the Romanian minister to Rome informed Italian Foreign Minister Ciano, in the name of the Romanian government, that Romania had refused to bow to Soviet pressure to grant right of passage. As in Djuvara's earlier conversation with Weizsäcker, Romania's alliance with anti-Soviet Poland was brought out as justification for the Romanian decision. As the Romanian minister informed Ciano, '... the alliance with Poland would take precedence over any obligation to Prague'.[69] The Romanians were again encouraged by Hitler's declaration to Djuvara on 23 September that Germany set great store on the Polish–Romanian alliance as a barrier against the Soviet Union. Consequently, said Hitler, Germany would ensure that Romania's borders were respected in the event of any changes to the status of Czechoslovakia.[70]

The question of Soviet right of passage through Romania was complicated by Czechoslovakia's purchase of Soviet aircraft which had to be flown to Czechoslovakia through Romanian airspace. On 30 April, Foreign Minister Comnen pointed out to Fabricius that his government could not prevent the flight over Romania of Russian aircraft purchased by Czechoslovakia since this was in accordance with 'international usage'.[71] German officials monitored the flight through Romanian airspace of Soviet aircraft purchased by the Czechoslovaks which began in May. By September some three hundred planes had been delivered. The approval for these flights had apparently been given by the Romanian General Staff under a Czechoslovak threat of an embargo on further arms deliveries to Romania. The condition laid down by the Romanians was that the planes were to carry Czechoslovak markings, carry no arms and fly non-stop over Romanian territory.[72]

While the Czechoslovaks were buying aircraft from the Soviets, the Romanian government was keen to build up its own air industry with German help. This ambition provided another reason for the Romanians to wish to retain German favour during the Sudeten crisis. France's failure to supply anti-aircraft guns and planes ordered in 1937, led the Romanian government in August 1938 to authorise a further barter of petroleum and cereals in exchange for war materials from Germany.

The agreement marked a further stage in Romania's growing dependence for arms on Germany, rather than on Czechoslovakia and France.[73] In mid-September, Göring invited the Romanian air attaché to Berlin, Gudju, to inspect German air installations.[74] One week later, Göring communicated to Gudju, 'the Reich government's satisfaction with the attitude taken by Romania in regard to possible passage of Russian troops'.[75] Reconstruction of the Romania air industry with German help was to be a major feature of the economic accord between Romania and Germany signed in March 1939.

Romania's wish for neutrality towards the Reich was also evident in the pressure exerted on Czechoslovakia throughout 1938 to come to a solution to the Sudeten question compatible with German interests. Immediately after the Anschluss in March, Carol informed Fabricius that he had asked the British government to put pressure on the Czechoslovaks to grant concessions to the Sudeten Germans.[76] In early August, the Romanian minister to Prague, Radu Crutzescu, made it plain to Czechoslovak Foreign Minister Beneš that 'a Czech–German agreement would be received by us with unspoken relief'. Crutzescu suggested that the Czechoslovak government should turn 'anti-German public opinion [in Czechoslovakia] in a more conciliatory direction'.[77] A few days later, Foreign Minister Comnen reported to Fabricius that he had stressed to Beneš 'Romania's wish for a solution to the Sudeten question, satisfactory to Germany'.[78]

The reality of Romania's foreign-policy position in the autumn of 1938 was that a pro-Soviet Czechoslovakia was not of sufficient value to Romania to risk a war with Germany. As King Carol recorded in his diary on 1 September 1938, he had informed Comnen that Romania's foreign policy should be based on strong relations with Britain and France and on 'fidelity to our alliances'. Romania should not, however, allow her commitments to bring her into conflict with Germany, which Carol wished to avoid 'at any price'.[79]

Despite the Romanian government's conciliatory attitude towards Germany during the Sudeten crisis, the events leading up to the signing of the Munich agreement on 30 September were sufficient to shake the faith of Romanian politicians in the West's ability and desire to uphold the Paris peace settlement.[80] Paradoxically, however, Munich also reinforced the Romanian government's belief in the need to maintain informal neutrality, or what became known as 'equilibrium', between the Great Powers. Munich sounded the final death-knell of the collective security system in Eastern Europe. As Argetoianu observed, 'The tribunal of the Great Powers is re-established as in the time before the war.'[81] The Romanian government, at least temporarily, 'assumed that the Reich [had] entered into friendly relations with England and France' and that in future major European disputes would be arbitrated by the same four Munich powers.[82] Hence, King Carol and his government were determined to concentrate on building up strong bilateral relations between Romania and the Great Powers as well as with Romania's smaller allies and neighbours. Direct consultation between leaders of state was to be an important aspect of the recalibrated policy. In keeping with this policy, King Carol planned to visit France, Britain and Germany in the autumn of 1938. The king aimed to retain a free hand in foreign policy in order to remain neutral in any ideological or physical conflict between the Great Powers. Building up Romania's armed forces was also an important part of the policy of neutrality between the powers.[83] Within this policy of neutrality or 'equilibrium' between the Great Powers, however, the relationship with Germany was of ever-increasing weight.

The Munich settlement gave the Reich clear geo-political and economic hegemony in Central and South-East Europe. Through the effective absorption of all Czechoslovak trade and foreign investments, Munich transformed Germany into the dominant trading partner for all the countries of Central and South-East Europe. In Romania, Germany took over Czechoslovak investments in the textile, chemical and metallurgical industries, as well as in banking.[84] Moreover, the effective incorporation of the whole Czechoslovak economy into that of the Reich, transformed Germany overnight into Romania's main armaments supplier.[85]

Although King Carol still hoped to encourage the western powers to increase their investments in the Romanian economy, he also positively sought to exploit Germany's economic hegemony in the region by encouraging full-scale German cooperation in building up the Romanian economy. On 7 October 1938, Fabricius reported that Carol had instructed Constantinescu, the pro-western minister of economics, to place no further obstacles in the way of economic expansion with the Reich.[86] In early November, the king indicated to his German friend, von Cramon, that he wanted to collaborate with Germany to transform agrarian Romania into an industrialised country. Carol pointed out that he also wished to build up the Romanian armed forces and had empowered the Romanian air minister to carry out negotiations with Germany regardless of any coming offers from Britain and France.[87] It was thus clear that Germany was already regarded as of greater economic importance than the western countries, even before Carol's trip to Britain and France in mid-November 1938.[88]

Romanian historians have tended to blame Romania's increasing economic dependency on Germany as the direct result of Britain's lack of economic interest in Romania in late 1938.[89] Research carried out by western historians, however, suggests that by the spring of 1938 the British foreign office was already drawing up plans to shore up British economic interests in South-East Europe. While both the British foreign office and prime minister believed that German economic preponderance in the area was inevitable, they did not believe that Germany should be allowed an entirely free hand.[90] Even before Carol's trip to London from 15 to 18 November, the British foreign secretary, Lord Halifax, had agreed to the purchase of 200,000 tons of Romanian wheat. Halifax also agreed to increased petroleum purchases and British assistance for the creation of a Black Sea naval base. During his visit to London in November, Carol pressed Chamberlain for assistance to build the naval base, and to develop Danube trade. Chamberlain was apparently keen to send a commercial mission to Bucharest to discuss these possibilities.[91]

Romania's trading relations with Britain were, however, problematic. Britain, like France, employed a system of imperial preference, thus raising a barrier against many agricultural products which Romania would have liked to export to Britain. Furthermore, and perhaps more important, Britain was also reluctant to enter into long-term economic plans which could have helped Romania restructure her economy.[92] By contrast, Germany was by now Romania's premier trading partner and had long since been absorbing Romania's agricultural produce. Göring, as Commissioner of the Four Year Plan, had already expressed his interest in a long-term economic plan with Romania during a discussion with Constantin Argetoianu on 18 November.[93] During their meeting at Berchtesgaden on 24 November, Carol and Hitler both pointed out their desire for better commercial relations between their two countries. On 26 November, in his discussion with Göring, Carol placed particular emphasis on his wish to conclude a trade and clearing agreement with Germany, together with a five to ten-year economic plan. Carol also stressed that he wanted German help to build up the Romanian armaments industry.[94]

As well as the economic implications of the Munich agreement, German supremacy in the region made Romania and Hungary competitors for German arbitration on the question of territorial revision. The annexation of the Sudetenland by Germany in October 1938 had immediately raised the possibility of Hungarian annexation of Slovakia and Ruthenia, the eastern-most tip of Czechoslovakia (also known as the Carpatho-Ukraine) which bordered on to Romania. The Romanian government feared that an enlarged Hungary would then lay claim to Transylvania. More specifically, Ruthenia provided the Romanians with their only direct line of communication into central Czechoslovakia and, through it, the shortest route to Germany. The Romanian foreign ministry feared that if direct communication with Czechoslovakia was lost, arms supplies from Czechoslovakia or Germany would have to pass through potentially hostile Hungarian territory. Moreover, the loss of the direct route to the Reich would vitally affect Romania's economic relations with Germany.[95]

Following the Munich agreement, Romanian representatives pleaded with the Reich not to gratify Hungarian territorial claims. Foreign Minister Comnen utilised earlier declarations he had made to Reich leaders that Romania would not enter any alliance against Germany. By so doing, he sought to justify his request that Romanian security should not be endangered by the enlargement of Hungary. On 6 October 1938, Comnen informed the German foreign ministry that the Romanian government wished to retain the common frontier with Czechoslovakia. He went on to say that 'Germany solemnly declared to us that we could count on her help to retain our actual borders if we did not enter into a combination aimed against the Reich. Calculating it is in her interest, Romania has abstained from any act that could be considered hostile to the Reich. Now is the time for [Germany] to respect her engagements to us.'[96]

The particular importance of sustaining good relations with Germany was made clear by the Axis' decision to award southern Slovakia to Hungary under the terms of the Vienna Award of 2 November 1938. Although the future of Ruthenia was left unresolved, the fact that the Award was made without consulting the western powers revealed that the Axis powers were fast becoming the sole arbiters of the fate of Central and South-East Europe.[97]

During his meeting with Hitler on 24 November, Carol asked to know the German attitude towards Hungarian revisionism and the the fate of Ruthenia. Hitler replied that he had advised the Hungarians to moderate their territorial claims. He stressed that although the Reich was not directly interested in the Ruthenian issue, he was against Hungarian attempts to overturn the 2 November Vienna Award which had left Ruthenia within Czechoslovakia.[98]

Although the question of a German guarantee of Romania's territorial integrity did not come up during Carol's discussions in Germany, Göring did discuss the matter during his informal meetings with Gheorghe Brătianu and Constantin Argetoianu which took place in early November. Brătianu and Argetoianu's trips had been authorised by Carol with the express aim of ascertaining the degree of German support for Hungarian revisionism. During his discussions, Brătianu stressed to Göring Romania's wish 'to be vis-à-vis Germany as Yugoslavia is from the economic and political view, especially regarding Hungary'. Göring pointed out that Germany had ensured that Hungary would not unleash revisionist claims upon Yugoslavia and would do the same for Romania. Germany, Göring added, required a clear indication that Romania would retain foreign-policy neutrality towards the Reich.[99] In his conversation with Constantin Argetoianu on 18 November, Göring alluded to the possibility of a territorial guarantee against both Hungary and the Soviet Union in return for a Romanian assurance of foreign-policy neutrality and a long-term economic agreement.[100] This was the first time that Göring had hinted at a possible German guarantee for Romania against the Soviet Union.

Germany's new hegemony in Central and South-East Europe served to increase Romania's geographical isolation from the West and thereby increased the value of the Reich as a potential supporter against the Soviet Union. Moreover, the Sudeten crisis itself had brought to the fore the dangerous possibility of the Red Army's entry into Romanian territory and reacquisition of Bessarabia.[101]

On 29 September, the day preceding the signing of the Munich agreement, the Romanian Court Marshal Flondor informed Fabricius of the king's wish for closer relations with Germany. Carol was particularly anxious to know if Germany would render Romania assistance in the event of a Soviet attack. The following day, Fabricius met with one of Carol's most trusted personal attendants, Mocsonyi, chief master of the hunt, who again impressed upon Fabricius Carol's hopes that close relations with Germany would protect Romania against Hungarian and Soviet threats. King Carol had apparently declared that he 'would rather see the Germans as enemies in his country than the Russians as friends'.[102]

During Carol's discussions with Hitler and Ribbentrop in late November, the king once again gave his assurance that Romania 'would never permit the passage of Russian troops' through the country. Carol even denied to Ribbentrop 'that the Little Entente had ever been an ally of France...'.[103] While technically correct, Carol's comment revealed the extent to which Romania was becoming oriented towards Germany rather than France.

Unfortunately, relations between Romania and Germany were soured immediately upon Carol's return to Romania by the murder of the imprisoned Iron Guard leader, Codreanu, on the night of 29/30 November. During Carol's absence abroad, a number of Iron Guard bombings and antisemitic attacks had taken place, imperilling the stability of the royal regime. Consequently, while on his way back from Germany to Romania, Carol gave his consent to Armand Călinescu's plan to dispatch Codreanu.

The German government reacted furiously to the news of the murder. Hitler was particularly angered by an official communication from Bucharest which claimed that during his meeting with Carol, Hitler had said he was prepared to sacrifice Codreanu. A link had thereby been made between Carol's visit to Hitler and the murder.[104] Hitler ordered decorations handed out by Carol during his trip to Germany to be returned. A German decoration which was to have been presented to Crown Prince Michael was also withheld.[105] The German press responded with severe attacks on the Romanian government.[106] The latter, keen to build up the relationship with Germany, was dismayed at the response of both Hitler and the press.[107] It thus became tactically necessary for Carol and his ministers to increase the pace of accommodation with the Reich in order to restore Germany's goodwill towards Romania. It was to undertake this task that Carol appointed Grigore Gafencu as foreign minister in late December 1938.

Notes

1 MAE, 71/România, Vol. 5, p. 229, *Dreptatea*, 28 January 1938, 'Friendly with the Whole World' was the title of an article by Theodor Emandi, former Romanian minister to Prague, describing the foreign policy pursued by the Goga government. Emandi asked whether either the western powers or the Axis would preserve trust in Romania 'in our policy of equilibrium and friendship with the whole world'.
2 The government was created on 28 December 1937 and dissolved on 10 February 1938. The brevity of the government's time in office may account for the lack of primary documents relating to Romania's foreign policy during this period. Many of the secondary works used in this section are themselves based on newspaper articles of the period. The main secondary work is Paul A. Shapiro's, 'Prelude to Dictatorship in Romania: The National Christian Party in Power, December 1937–February 1938', *Canadian-American Slavic Studies*, 8, nr 1, (Spring 1974), pp. 45–88.
3 MAE, 71/Germania, Vol. 76, pp. 16–18, Legation in Berlin to the Foreign Ministry, Tel. nr 3800, 17 January 1938, signed Comnen.
4 MAE, 71/Germania, Vol. 76, pp. 21–7, Legation in Berlin to the Foreign Ministry, Tel. nr 3805, 21 January 1938, signed Brabetzianu.
5 Gigurtu had studied in Germany and, as general director of the Mica mineral company, had close economic ties with Germany. He was to lead the pro-Axis government from 4 July to 4 September 1940. Savu was a former director of the Romanian National Bank and was friendly with Fabricius. Irimescu was also known to be pro-German. For this information, see Shapiro, op. cit., p. 71.

6   Dov B. Lungu, *Romania and the Great Powers, 1933–1940*, Durham and London, 1989, p. 117.
7   Antonescu had been military attaché in Brussels, London and Paris between 1922 and 1926. Fabricius confirmed that both Antonescu and Teodorescu were pro-French: DGFP, D, 5, Doc. nr 169, Minister in Romania to the Foreign Ministry, Bucharest, 10 February 1938. Gheorghe Barbul, who became Antonescu's chief of cabinet during the war, confirms that the mixed cabinet was composed on foreign-policy grounds with Antonescu as a guarantee to the West that Romania would not fight against them and with Goga as the guarantee for Germany: Gheorghe Barbul, *Memorial Antonescu. Al treilea om al Axei*, Iași, 1992, p. 8.
8   Shapiro, 'Prelude to Dictatorship in Romania', p. 71.
9   PA, Politische Abteilung IV: Po 2, Vol. 2, 9.37–2.39, Note, Foreign Ministry Pol IV 138, Berlin, 3 January 1938, signed Heinburg.
10 Arh. St., Însemnări Zilnice, Constantin Argetoianu, Dosar nr 73, Vol. 1, 10 January 1938, p. 42.
11 Florea Nedelcu, 'Cu privire la politica externă a României în perioada guvernării Goga–Cuza', in (ed.) Viorica Moisuc, *Probleme de politică externă a României 1919–1939. Culegere de studii*, Bucharest, 1971, pp. 278–9.
12 Ibid.
13 Mihai Fătu, *Cu pumnii strînși. Octavian Goga în viața politică a României (1918–1938)*, Bucharest, 1993, p. 170–2.
14 DGFP, D, 5, Doc. nr 157, Memorandum by an Official of the Presidential Chancellery, Berlin, 1 January 1938, signed Kiewitz.
15 Arh. St., Casa Regală, Dosar nr 40/1938, pp. 4–9, Reasons for the fall of the National Christian Government. Explanation given by Octavian Goga, former President of the Council, at the meeting of the National Christian Party Council on 15 February 1938.
16 Arh. St., Casa Regală, Dosar nr 240/1938, Vol. 1, pp. 53–5, Agenția Telegrafică Română, Orient Radio-Rador, 7 February 1938, King Carol's interview with Prince Anton Rohan for the *Berliner Tageblatt* of 6 February 1938.
17 Arh. St., Casa Regală, Dosar nr 31/1938, p. 53, report by *Haint* of Warsaw, 13 January 1938.
18 Arh. St., Însemnări Zilnice, Constantin Argetoianu, Dosar nr 73, Vol. 1, 21 January 1938, p. 69.
19 For details of these antisemitic measures, see (ed.) Arnold J. Toynbee, *Survey of International Affairs 1937*, Vol. 1, Oxford, 1938, p. 429.
20 DGFP, D, 5, Doc. nr 179, Circular of the Foreign Ministry, Berlin, 9 March 1938, signed Weizsäcker.
21 PA, Politische Abteilung IV: Po 5, Vol. 3, 2.38–8.38, German Legation in Bucharest to the Foreign Ministry, Tgb. nr 442/38, 12 February 1938, signed Fabricius.
22 (ed.) Sherman David Spector, 'Relapse into Bondage 1918–1947. The Political Memoirs of Alexandre Cretzianu, Free Romania's Last World Diplomatist': Chapter 4, 'The Royal Dictatorship', *Southeastern Europe*, 15, Parts 1–2, (1988), pp. 99–113 (102–4).
23 DGFP, D, 5, Doc. nr 179, Circular of the Foreign Ministry, Berlin, 9 March 1938, signed Weizsäcker.

24 William S. Grenzebach, *Germany's Informal Empire in East-Central Europe: German Economic Policy Toward Yugoslavia and Romania, 1933–1939*, Stuttgart, 1988, p. 189.
25 Amongst those listed by Fabricius as 'German-friendly' were Marshal Averescu, Vaida-Voevod, Cancicov and Argetoianu: PA, Politische Abteilung IV: Po 5, Vol. 3, 2.38–8.38, German Legation in Bucharest to the Foreign Ministry, Tgb. nr 434/38II, 13 February 1938, signed Fabricius.
26 DGFP, D, 5, Doc. nr 179, Circular of the Foreign Ministry, Berlin, 9 March 1938, signed Weizsäcker.
27 Arh. St., M. P. N, Agenţii, Dosar nr 30, pp. 3–4, Romanian Legation in Berlin to the Foreign Ministry, Tel. nr 124, 1 March 1938, signed Press Attaché Ilcuş; ibid, pp. 14–15, Romanian Legation in Berlin to the Foreign Ministry, unnumbered telegram, 7 March 1938, signed Press Attaché Ilcuş.
28 Arh. St., M. P. N., Presa Internă, Dosar nr 382, pp. 93–5, Declarations made to the press by N. P. Comnen, Foreign Minister, 6 April 1938.
29 Comnen was apparently still an adherent of collective security: Lungu, *Romania and the Great Powers*, p. 146.
30 Gerhard L. Weinberg, *The Foreign Policy of Hitler's Germany: Starting World War II, 1937–1939*, Chicago, 1980, p. 235.
31 See, for instance, J. Benditer, 'Anschlussul şi unele consecinţe ale lui asupra politicii externe a României', *Studii şi cercetari ştiinţifice istorie*, filiala Iaşi, 7, fasc. 2, (1959), pp. 135–56.
32 PA, Politische Abteilung IV: Po 5, Vol. 3, 2.38–8.38, German Legation in Bucharest to the Foreign Ministry, Tgb. nr 876/38, 19 March 1938, signed Fabricius. Foreign Minister Titulescu had also informed the Germans during his time in office that he regarded the Anschluss as inevitable: Günter Reichert, *Das Scheitern der Kleine Entente, 1933–1938*, Munich, 1971, pp. 82–3.
33 MAE, Dosare Speciale, Austria A1, Vol. 272, 22 December 1937, p. 93, 'Secret. The Attitude of the Little Entente Regarding the Question of a possible Anschluss', signed Timiraş.
34 MAE, 71/România, Vol. 415 bis, p. 7, Tel. nr 15645 for Circulation to all Legations, 16 March 1938, signed Comnen.
35 MAE, Dosare Speciale, Austria A1, Vol. 272, pp. 216–31, Memo, Evolution of the Anschluss Question from 11 July 1936 to its Realization, 18 March 1938, signed Timiraş.
36 Antonin Basch, *The Danube Basin and the German Economic Sphere*, London, 1944, pp. 201–3.
37 Viorica Moisuc, *Diplomaţia României şi problema apărării suveranităţii şi independenţei naţionale în perioada martie 1938-mai 1940*, Bucharest, 1971, pp. 36–44.
38 PRO, FO 371/R5760/223/37, Letter from Sir Frederick Leith-Ross to Mr Harvey, 21 June 1938.
39 Henry L. Roberts, *Rumania: Political Problems of an Agrarian State*, Harvard, 1951, p. 215.
40 Armand Călinescu, *Însemnări politice 1916–1939*, (ed.) Al. Gh. Savu, Bucharest, 1990, 13 March 1938, pp. 383–4.
41 DGFP, D, 5, Doc. nr 179, Circular of the Foreign Ministry, Berlin, 9 March 1938, signed Weizsäcker.
42 Mihai Fătu and Ion Spălăţelu, *Garda de Fier. Organisaţie teroristă de tip fascist*, Bucharest, 1980, p. 102. See also, for example, Florea Nedelcu, 'Date noi

privind legăturile Gărzii de Fier cu Nazismul', *Revista de istorie*, 32, nr 7, (1979), pp. 1351–4; Petre Ilie, 'Relațiile dintre Garda de Fier și Germania nazista', in *Împotriva fascismului. Sesiunea științifică privind analiza critică și demascarea fascismului în România*, București, 4–5 martie 1971, Bucharest, 1971, pp. 83–95.

43   Armin Heinen, *Die Legion 'Erzengel Michael' in Rumänien. Soziale Bewegung und politische Organisation*, Munich, 1986, p. 340. For the Guard's reaction to German antisemitic measures, see ibid, pp. 244, 251.

44   Ibid, pp. 322–41. Heinen's findings are also corroborated by Francisco Veiga, *Istoria Gărzii de Fier 1919–1941. Mistica ultranaționalismului*, Bucharest, 1993, pp. 251–5.

45   Ibid, p. 254; Heinen, op. cit., p. 245.

46   *Trial of the Major War Criminals before the International Military Tribunal*, Vol. 25, pp. 34–47, Document 007-PS. 'Short report on the activities of the office of Foreign Affairs of the NSDAP from 1933 to 1943', signed Rosenberg.

47   Seppo Kuusisto, *Alfred Rosenberg in der nationalsozialistischen Aussenpolitik, 1933–1939*, Helsinki, 1984, pp. 236–8.

48   Radu Lecca, *Eu i-am salvat pe evreii din România*, Bucharest, 1994, p. 95.

49   MAE, România R6, Dosare Special, Vol. 487, p. 15, From the Romanian Legation in Switzerland, Bern, to Foreign Minister Comnen, Tel. nr 933, 21 May 1938, unsigned; Lecca, op. cit., p. 109. Konradi was also commercial attaché at the German Legation and Landesgruppenleiter of the NSDAP in Romania.

50   Heinen, *Die Legion 'Erzengel Michael' in Rumänien*, p. 341.

51   MAE, 71/Germania, Vol. 80, p. 32, *Universul*, 5 August 1940, 'Declarations made by Sidorovici to the press regarding the opening of the "International Exhibition" in Vienna'.

52   This was the result of Codreanu's letter to Nicolae Iorga accusing him of 'intellectual dishonesty' for calling for Iron Guard shops to be closed, having himself recommended to Codreanu that he take measures to compete with Jewish traders: Prince Michel Sturdza, *The Suicide of Europe: The Memoirs of Prince Michel Sturdza, Former Foreign Minister of Romania*, Boston, 1968, pp. 113–15.

53   DGFP, D, 5, Doc. nr 203, Minister in Romania to the Foreign Ministry, Bucharest, 17 May 1938.

54   Ibid.

55   Ibid.

56   For the full transcript of Codreanu's trial, see (eds) Kurt W. Treptow and Gheorghe Buzatu, *Corneliu Zelea Codreanu în fața istoriei*, Vol. 1, 'Procesul' lui Corneliu Zelea Codreanu (Mai, 1938), Iași, 1994.

57   The secondary literature to this effect is vast. Foreign Minister Comnen began this defensive interpretation shortly after the war. See, N. P. Comnène, *Preludi del grande dramma (Ricordi e documenti di un diplomatico)*, Rome, 1947, esp. pp. 3–201. For later works, see, for example, J. Benditer, 'Atitudinea guvernului român fața de Cehoslovacia în lunile premergătoare München-ului (mai–septembrie 1938)', *Studii revistă de istorie*, 9, nr 5, 1956, pp. 7–20; Eliza Campus, *Mica Înțelegere*, Bucharest, 1968, esp. pp. 290–317; Viorica Moisuc, *Premisele izolării politice a României*, 1919–1940, Bucharest, 1991, pp. 341–51.

58 Arh. St., Însemnări Zilnice, Carol II, roll 21, unnumbered volume, 23 May 1938, p. 240.
59 MAE, Dosare Speciale, Cehoslovacia C7.b., Vol. 308, pp. 31–3, Unsigned Note in Connection with the Possible Passage of German troops through Hungary for an Attack on Czechoslovakia, 2 September 1938.
60 DGFP, D, 2, Doc. nr 447, Minute by the State Secretary for the Foreign Minister, Nuremberg, 9 September 1938.
61 Lungu, *Romania and the Great Powers*, pp. 132–4.
62 DGFP, D, 2, Doc. nr 650, German Minister in Romania to the Foreign Ministry, Bucharest, 27 September 1938.
63 DGFP, D, 2, Doc. nr 367, Unsigned Foreign Ministry Memo, Berlin, 18 August 1938.
64 Comnène, *Preludi del Grande Dramma*, p. 138.
65 MAE, 71/Germania, Vol. 76, pp. 56–8, Legation in Berlin to the Foreign Ministry, Tel. nr 3888, 22 April 1938, signed Djuvara.
66 MAE, 71/1920–1944, Dosare Speciale, Cehoslovacia C7, Vol. 301, pp. 133–4, From the Legation in Berlin to the Foreign Ministry, Tel. nr 32428, 30 May 1938, signed Djuvara.
67 DGFP, D, 2, Doc. nr 462, German Consul General at Geneva to the Foreign Ministry, Geneva, 12 September 1938.
68 DGFP, D, 2, Doc nr 447, Minute by the State Secretary for the Foreign Minister, Nuremberg, 9 September 1938.
69 DGFP, D, 2, Doc. nr 609, Unsigned Foreign Ministry Minute for the Foreign Minister, Berlin, 26 September 1938.
70 MAE, Dosare Speciale, Cehoslovacia C7.b., Vol. 303, p. 264, Legation in Berlin to the Foreign Ministry, Tel. nr 38208, 23 September 1938, signed Djuvara.
71 DGFP, D, 2, Doc. nr 142, German Minister in Romania to the Foreign Ministry, Bucharest, 30 April 1938.
72 DGFP, D, 2, Doc. nr 236, German Minister in Romania to German Foreign Minister, Bucharest, 3 June 1938; ibid, Doc. nr 300, Memorandum by the Air Attaché of the German Embassy in Poland (Gerstenberg), Warsaw, 19 July 1938; ibid, Doc. nr 445, German Chargé D'Affaires in Romania to the German Foreign Minister, Bucharest, 9 September 1938, signed Stelzer.
73 Lungu, *Romania and the Great Powers*, p. 125; the agreement was signed in September, see Gheorghe Zaharia and Ion Calafeteanu, 'The International Situation and Romania's Foreign Policy between 1938 and 1940', *Revue roumaine d'histoire*, 18, 1, (1979), pp. 84–90 (85).
74 MAE, 71/Germania, Vol. 76, pp. 96–7, Legation in Berlin to the Foreign Ministry, Tel. nr 3897, 15 September 1938, signed Djuvara.
75 MAE, Mica Înțelegere, Vol. 52, pp. 315–88, (375), M. Mitilineu, 'Romanian Relations with the States of the former Little Entente (1918–1938)', November 1942.
76 PA, Politische Abteilung IV: Po 2, Vol. 2, 9.37–2.39, German Legation in Bucharest to the Foreign Ministry, Tgb nr 1148/38, 9 April 1938, signed Fabricius.
77 MAE, 71/1920–1944, Dosare Speciale, Cehoslovacia C7, Vol. 302, pp. 143–5, Report nr 2130/C from the Legation in Prague to Minister Comnen, 12 August 1938, signed Radu Crutzescu.

78 DGFP, D, 2, Doc. nr 361, German Minister in Romania to the German Foreign Minister, Bucharest, 15 August 1938.
79 Arh. St., Însemnări Zilnice, Carol II, roll 21, Vol. 6, 1 September 1938, p. 408.
80 See, for example, Argetoianu's comments on the agreement: Arh. St., Constantin Argetoianu, Însemnări Zilnice, Dosar nr 73, Vol. 3, 22 September 1938, p. 12.
81 Arh. St., Însemnări Zilnice, Constantin Argetoianu, Dosar nr 73, Vol 3, 1 October 1938, p. 33.
82 DGFP, D, 5, Doc. nr 228, Minister in Romania to the Foreign Ministry, Bucharest, 30 September 1938.
83 For Carol's policy of 'equilibrium' between the Great Powers, see, N. N. Petrașcu, *Evoluția politică a României în ultimii douăzeci de ani (1918–1938)*, Bucharest, 1939, esp. pp. 129–36.
84 Basch, *The Danube Basin and the German Economic Sphere*, pp. 204–5.
85 Mark Axworthy, *Third Axis, Fourth Ally: Romanian Armed Forces in the European War, 1941–1945*, London, 1995, p. 38.
86 DGFP, D, 5, Doc nr 231, Minister in Romania to the Ministry of Foreign Affairs, Bucharest, 7 October 1938.
87 Bundesarchiv, Berlin, R43 II/1486a, Letter from von Cramon to Hitler, Göring and Ribbentrop, 10 November 1938.
88 PA, Politische Abteilung IV: Po 2, Vol. 2, 9.37–2.39, German Legation in Bucharest to the Foreign Ministry, Tel. nr 251, 21 November 1938, signed Fabricius.
89 See, for instance A. Niri, *Istoricul unui tratat înrobitor. (Tratatul economic româno–german din martie 1939)*, Bucharest, 1965, pp. 135–8.
90 David Britton Funderburk, *Politica Marii Britanii fața de România, 1938–1940. Studiu asupra strategiei economice și politice*, Bucharest, 1983, pp. 61–92; Simon Newman, *March 1939: The British Guarantee to Poland*, Oxford, 1976, pp. 33–5.
91 Newman, op. cit., pp. 44–9. See also, PRO, FO 371/R9213/3/37, Viscount Halifax to Sir M. Palairet (Bucharest), Tel. nr 367, 17 November 1938.
92 Newman, op. cit., p. 108. A foreign office memo pointed out some of the numerous problems in Britain's trading relations with Romania, including the disparity between the world price of wheat and Romania's higher prices and bad credit record: PRO, FO 371/R9239/223/37, Memorandum signed Mr Ingram, 14 November 1938.
93 Arh. St., Însemnări Zilnice, Constantin Argetoianu, Dosar nr 73, Vol. 3, 22 November 1938, p. 195, Note taken with regard to my Meeting with Marshal Göring at Berlin on 18 November 1938.
94 DGFP, D, 5, Doc. nr 254, Memorandum by the Foreign Minister. Conversation of the Führer with the King of Romania in the presence of the Reich Foreign Minister, Berchtesgaden, 24 November 1938; ibid, Doc. nr 257, Berlin, 30 November 1938, Minute on the Conversation between the Field Marshal and King Carol of Romania on Saturday, 26 November 1938.
95 MAE, Mica Înțelegere, Vol. 29, pp. 130–42, Conference held on 18 October [1938], taking place at Galați, on the yacht *Luceafarul*, between HM King Carol II of Romania, Col. Beck, Foreign Minister of Poland and Comnen, Foreign Minister of Romania.

96 MAE, 71/Germania, Vol. 76, pp. 112–13, Foreign Minister Comnen to the Legation in Berlin, Tel. nr 59924, 6 October 1938, signed Comnen. See also Comnen's request to the Germans on 26 October: Arh. St., Casa Regală, Dosar nr 165/1938, Vol. 2, p. 107, To the Legation in Berlin from Comnen, unnumbered telegram, 26 October 1938, signed Comnen.

97 On this issue, see Anthony Komjathy, 'The First Vienna Award (November 2, 1938)', *Austrian History Yearbook*, 15–16, (1979–80), pp. 131–56.

98 DGFP, D, 5, Doc. nr 254, Memorandum by the Foreign Minister. Conversation of the Führer with the King of Romania in the presence of the Reich Foreign Minister, Berchtesgaden, 24 November 1938. Ribbentrop added to his notes of this conversation that beforehand Hitler had said he would leave open the Ruthenia question. Ribbentrop noted that 'The basic idea of our policy towards Hungary and Romania at present should be to keep both these irons in the fire and shape matters in the German interest according to the way the situation develops'.

99 MAE, 71/Germania. Vol. 76, pp. 175–87, Note on a Conversation between Marshal Göring and Atta Constantinescu and Gheorghe Brătianu in Berlin on 6 November 1938.

100 Arh. St., Însemnări Zilnice, Constantin Argetoianu, Dosar nr 73, Vol. 3, 22 November 1938, p. 195, Note taken with regard to my meeting with Marshal Göring at Berlin on 18 November 1938.

101 In 1937 the Soviet press had begun to make renewed claims on Bessarabia and the first border incidents for many years took place on the Dniester frontier: Lungu, *Romania and the Great Powers*, p. 102.

102 DGFP, D, 5, Doc. nr 227, Minister in Romania to the Foreign Ministry, Bucharest, 29 September 1938; ibid, Doc. nr 228, Minister in Romania to the Foreign Ministry, Bucharest, 30 September 1938; PA, Politische Abteilung IV: Po 2, Vol. 2, 9.37–2.39, German Legation, Bucharest, to the Foreign Ministry, Tgb nr 3380/38, 30 September 1938, signed Fabricius.

103 DGFP, D, 5, Doc. nr 254, Memorandum by the Foreign Minister. Conversation of the Führer with the King of Romania in the presence of the Reich Foreign Minister, Berchtesgaden, 24 November 1938.

104 MAE, 71/Germania, Vol. 76 bis, pp. 29–30, Legation in Berlin to the Foreign Ministry, Tel. nr 39029, 17 January 1939, signed Brabetzianu.

105 Ulrich von Hassell, *Vom Andern Deutschland. Aus den Nachgelassenen Tagebücher 1938–1944*, Zürich, 1947, p. 41.

106 MAE, 71/Germania, Vol. 76, p.173, *Berliner Börsenzeitung*, 4 December 1938.

107 DGFP, D, 5, Doc. nr 260, Legation in Romania to the Foreign Ministry, Bucharest, 4 December 1938, signed Klugkist.

3
Grigore Gafencu: The Persistence of 'Equilibrium' between the Great Powers, December 1938 to March 1939

The first three months of Grigore Gafencu's foreign ministry, which culminated in the signing of the Romanian–German economic accord in March 1939, present a problem for the historian. The foreign policy conducted during this period can be read in a variety of ways. On the one hand, there is evidence of increased willingness on the part of the Romanian government to tie itself to Germany. On the other hand, evidence suggests that the Romanian government's overall foreign-policy strategy remained that of retaining neutrality, or 'equilibrium' as Gafencu called it, between the Great Powers.

Romanian historians, in discussing this period, have stressed German pressure on Romania as determining the direction of Romanian foreign policy. According to such accounts, this German pressure increased in severity following the murder by Carol's government of the supposedly German-backed Codreanu in November 1938. This pressure was exerted through a so-called 'fifth column' consisting of Iron Guardists, members of the ethnic German minority, and an assortment of Romanian fascists and right-wingers. The belief that Romania was forced to sign the March 1939 economic accord in the face of German pressure is supported by those historians who regard Germany as a direct military threat to Romania in March 1939. Romanian historians have thus argued that the economic treaty of 23 March was signed by Romania in order to conciliate Germany and to forestall the German military threat. The treaty itself resulted in the subordination of the Romanian economy to German interests, leading inevitably to

Romania's entry into the war on the Axis side. According to this view, economic conciliation of Germany was made unavoidable as a result of western political and economic indifference to the fate of South-East Europe.[1]

The period from the appointment of Gafencu as foreign minister to the signing of the German–Romanian economic accord in March 1939 did indeed see an increased willingness by the Romanian government to draw closer to the Reich. While pursuing a policy of equilibrium between the Great Powers, Romania's relationship with Germany was acquiring ever greater significance. As a result of the international events of 1938, in particular the Anschluss and the Munich agreement, Germany had secured for herself geo-political hegemony in Central and South-East Europe. This not only increased the Reich's economic importance for Romania, but also indicated Romania's need to compete with revisionist Hungary for German goodwill. Hence many of Gafencu's policies towards the Reich had already been planned in the months before he came to office. His policies of concessions towards the German minority in Romania, securing Germany's entry into the European Danube Commission and increased economic collaboration with Germany had all been foreseen in 1938 by Gafencu's predecessor as foreign minister, Nicolae Petrescu-Comnen. To these longer-standing factors which affected Gafencu's policy towards Germany, however, was added the immediate need to placate the Germans, who were still angered by the circumstances attending Codreanu's murder.[2] Gafencu's immediate task was to speed up the implementation of the planned concessions in an effort to conciliate Germany. It was this forced pace of relations with Germany between December 1938 and March 1939 which temporarily upset the policy of equilibrium between the powers.

Gafencu's pursuit of a German guarantee of Romania's territorial integrity in exchange for Romanian economic concessions was a central aspect of Gafencu's policy towards Germany. It was, moreover, the issue of a German guarantee which formed the background to the diplomatic incident known as the 'Tilea affair' of March 1939. The 'Tilea affair' indicated that Gafencu's policy towards Germany had opened up divisions within the Romanian government, with some individuals favouring stronger relations with the western powers rather than Germany. At the same time as he sought a guarantee from Germany, Gafencu was increasingly disposed to regard the Reich as a potential mediator in Romania's quarrels with Hungary. The foreign ministry's growing tendency to coordinate its foreign policy with that of the Reich can be seen in the events surrounding the settling of the Ruthenian issue in late

March 1939. Despite growing collaboration with the Reich, however, the period of December 1938 to March 1939 ended with Gafencu successfully retaining equilibrium between the Great Powers.

*

On 21 December 1938, Carol replaced Comnen as foreign minster with Grigore Gafencu who was to retain this post until June 1940.[3] Already during the course of 1938, Gafencu had moved away from his original belief in collective security, in favour of the theory that Romania should seek to maintain 'equilibrium' between the Great Powers. In October 1938, the British legation in Bucharest reported that the newspaper edited by Gafencu, *Timpul*, was showing 'a certain tendency towards trimming [its] sails in the direction of Germany, the *leit-motif* being that whilst it is desirable for Romania to maintain her friendships with her old allies and friends, this does not necessarily preclude her forming new ones'.[4] This policy of 'equilibrium' was expressed in Gafencu's inaugural speech as foreign minister given on Radio Bucharest on 29 December 1938. Romania, Gafencu declared, watched with interest any efforts at rapprochement between the Great Powers of the West and Central Europe. The king's trip to London, Paris and Berlin in November 1938 was proof of Carol's desire for closer relationships with all the powers which had collaborated together at the Munich conference. 'The equilibrium and peace of the continent', said Gafencu, 'depends in great measure on the spirit of understanding and feeling of solidarity of these states.' At the same time, it is clear that the relationship with the Reich was becoming of ever greater weight within Romania's Great Power relationships. As a result of the Munich agreement, argued Gafencu, Germany now had a 'new significance' for Romania.[5]

In keeping with this policy of equilibrium between the Great Powers, King Carol and Gafencu introduced new personnel into Romania's diplomatic missions in Germany, Britain and France. Former Minister President Gheorghe Tătărescu was appointed ambassador to Paris on 9 December 1938. On 1 February 1939, Viorel Tilea, who had extensive contacts in Britain, took up his post as minister to London. Early in 1939 Radu Crutzescu was appointed minister to Berlin on the recommendation of the 'German-friendly' Gheorghe Brătianu, who had himself declined the post, preferring instead to offer his services as an informal bridge between Romania and the Reich.[6]

Foreign Minister Gafencu's first task was to show the Germans that, notwithstanding Codreanu's murder, there had been no intention of damaging German interests in Romania. During a visit by German foreign minister Ribbentrop to Warsaw in January 1939, the Romanian minister to Warsaw hastened to assure him that Romania strove for reconciliation with Germany, in particular through strengthened economic relations. Although Ribbentrop confirmed that he welcomed economic collaboration with Romania, the Romanian minister reported to Gafencu that, 'on the political plane, the attitude of the German foreign minister is in the final analysis fairly reserved'. Ribbentrop's 'reserve' towards Romania was confirmed by Fabricius, who pointed out to Gafencu that German belief in the Romanian regime had been shaken by the events of late November. The Reich now awaited 'economic solutions and the clearing of the atmosphere of distrust'.[7]

To the frosty tone of German leaders was added the fear of a potential German or Hungarian attack on Romania. A study produced by the High Command of the Army in January 1939 expressed fears that Germany might try to use her new geo-political hegemony to launch an attack on Romania in order to dominate the whole course of the Danube river.[8] Gafencu also feared that Hungary might exploit German resentment towards Romania to further her own revisionist claims against Romania. This possibility seemed all the stronger with Hungary's entry into the Anti-Comintern Pact in January 1939.[9]

As a result of these fears, Romanian military and political leaders decided on a policy of conciliation of Germany.[10] In his meeting with a number of government ministers on 23 January 1939, Gafencu put forward two hypotheses with regard to German policy towards Romania. In the worse case, Gafencu conjectured that Germany might attack Romania, under the pretext of her current anger following Codreanu's murder, in order to secure domination of the Danube basin. Gafencu's more favourable hypothesis was that the Reich sought a gesture of goodwill from Romania.[11] In early 1939 Gafencu, therefore, recommended a number of measures designed to conciliate Germany. Three measures were highlighted: concessions to the German minority in Romania, the admittance of Germany into the European Danube Commission (EDC), and economic concessions. Although all these measures had been foreseen in 1938, Gafencu's policy had a novel element. Gafencu hoped to link Romania's economic concessions to receipt of a German guarantee of Romania's territorial integrity.

German leaders had often hinted that the German attitude towards a country was influenced by how well that country treated its German minority. This had been most recently pointed out by Göring to Carol during their meeting on 26 November 1938.[12]

In 1930 the number of Germans in Romania numbered some 760,000. The communities were divided between the Banat, Transylvania, Sathmar (Maramureş,) the Bukovina and Bessarabia, with a small number in the Regat.[13] In 1921 these German groups were united in one organisation, the Verband der Deutschen in Rumänien. In 1935 the Verband had been taken over by Fritz Fabritius and renamed the Volksgemeinschaft der Deutschen in Rumänien. Fabritius had been in contact with Hitler since 1920, and now proceeded to run the Volksgemeinschaft on National Socialist lines. Fabritius claimed autonomy for the German minority in Romania and the freedom to cultivate links with Nazi Germany.[14] On 6 February 1938, Octavian Goga, in one of the few pro-German actions of his government, recognised the Volksgemeinschaft as the exclusive official organ of the minority in Romania.[15]

Nevertheless, all was by no means well in relations between minority and government. Since the creation of Greater Romania, the government had been pursuing policies to 'romanianise' the country's economy and institutions in which the ethnic minorities were often more highly represented than ethnic Romanians. Although the Germans were a relatively favoured minority and retained a high degree of cultural freedom, they frequently suffered as a result of Romanian anti-minority legislation.[16]

The growing conflict between Germany and Czechoslovakia over the treatment of the Sudeten German minority in the summer of 1938 made the Romanian government aware of the need to treat its minorities with care. A discontented German or Hungarian minority could become a destabilising factor in Romania's relations with Germany and Hungary. Under a council of ministers' decree of 1 August 1938, the right to use place names in minority languages was assured. The minority statute of 4 August 1938 additionally guaranteed the use of a national-minority language in parishes where that nationality represented a majority of inhabitants.[17]

Following the Munich agreement in September 1938, the Romanians were given more indications of the importance which the Germans attached to the good treatment of the German minority in Romania. In October 1938, German newspapers reported with concern that Romanian policies to 'romanianise' industry were often at the expense of ethnic Germans. In addition, the right to education in the mother tongue was not always honoured.[18] At the same time, a number of direct contacts took place between Romanian representatives and German officials dealing with minority issues. Between 6 and 10 October 1938, Hans Hedrich, an ethnic German member of the Romanian senate, visited Berlin and met foreign ministry officials and representatives of the Volksdeutsche Mittelstelle (VoMi), the official Reich organisation dealing with the German minorities. On his return to Romania, Hedrich informed the Romanian government that the Reich regarded future political relations with Romania as developing out of self-determination for the German minority. In mid-October a Crown Council was called because it was believed that Hedrich's news was 'of the greatest importance for the possibilities of Romanian foreign policy'.[19] On 14 October, Pătraş, an official of the Romanian royal household, met Malletke, adviser on eastern questions at Rosenberg's Aussenpolitisches Amt in Berlin. Malletke assured Pătraş that both he and Rosenberg had agreed to offer Romania a frontier guarantee in return for greater rights for Romania's ethnic minorities.[20]

It seems likely that it was as a result of these discussions that Carol promised Göring during their meeting in November 1938 that he intended to re-examine Romania's minority policy. Within the existing legal framework, Carol wished 'to give the German minority groups who were good Romanian citizens the same rights and living conditions as the Romanians'.[21]

It was, however, only following Codreanu's murder and the appointment of Gafencu to the foreign ministry that the government began to make substantial concessions to the German minority. On 6 January 1939 a foreign ministry note confirmed the government's decision to bring the Volksgemeinschaft into the newly-established government party, the National Renaissance Front (FRN), and to accord them certain rights there.[22]

The accord for the entry of the ethnic Germans into the FRN was signed on 10 January 1939. German sections of urban and rural communes were to be represented in the high national council and the directorate of the FRN. German professional organisations were also incorporated into the FRN and the Germans were allowed to establish their own organisations for cultural, economic and social work. Gafencu declared the accord to be proof of 'the decision of the Romanian government to remove all difficulties which stand in the way of the resumption of relations of trust and friendship between Germany and us'.[23]

The next conciliatory measure to which Gafencu turned in early 1939 was the entry of Germany into the European Danube Commission (EDC). As with the decision to grant concessions to the German minority, the initial provisions leading up to Germany's entry into the EDC had already been made in 1938.

The EDC had been created as part of the 1856 Treaty of Paris which ended the Crimean War. Prussia had been instrumental in the creation of the EDC and Germany, as Prussia's legal successor, had been a member until the First World War. The EDC had technical and administrative powers, which included policing and judicial competence, over the Lower and Maritime Danube. During the inter-war period, member countries included Britain, France, Italy and Romania.[24] In May 1938 delegates at the Little Entente conference held at Sinaia decided that since, in the wake of the Anschluss, Germany now dominated the course of the Upper Danube, she should be granted admission to the EDC. Nevertheless, due to the wide prerogatives of the EDC, the Little Entente ruled that German entry should be preceded by modifications to the EDC's role in order to prevent any encroachments by the commission on Romanian sovereignty. On 18 August 1938, an accord was signed by Britain, France and Romania which outlined the powers of the EDC within the framework of Romania's sovereign rights.[25] The path was now open for German entry and on 2 March 1939, Britain, France, Germany, Italy and Romania signed an accord ratifying the Reich's entry into the EDC.[26] Among the benefits which Germany now enjoyed as a member of the EDC was free access to the Black Sea.[27]

Unfortunately for Gafencu, these moves to incorporate the ethnic Germans into the FRN and to bring Germany into the EDC failed to placate Hitler and the German press: both were still angered by the murder of Codreanu.[28] The Romanian government now decided on a policy of conciliation towards Germany based on economic collaboration and concessions. This policy of economic collaboration with Germany, conceived by King Carol following the Munich agreement, was speeded up by Gafencu in early 1939. The study produced by the High Command of the Army in January 1939 recommended the economic conciliation of Germany so as to forestall a potential German military threat to Romania. Nonetheless, the authors of the study were aware of the benefits to be gained by economic collaboration with Germany, 'which on the one hand would satisfy German requirements and on the other hand would bring about a blossoming of our state'.[29]

A similar conclusion was reached by Gafencu on 23 January 1939 in the course of discussions with royal ministers on how best to deal with the tense relations between Romania and Germany. The foreign minister recommended economic concessions to Germany. In exchange for German help in the exploration of new reserves, for example, Romania would offer to export more petroleum to Germany.[30]

Both Romanian and western historians have tended to regard the terms for economic collaboration between Germany and Romania which were discussed in February and March 1939 as having been laid down by Germany. According to their view, the economic terms were an attempt to subordinate the Romanian economy to Germany.[31] Documentary evidence shows, however, that it was the Romanian government which drafted the initial terms of economic collaboration upon which Hermann Wohlthat, Göring's chief economic negotiator, then based his proposals. As early as December 1937, in fact, the then minister president, Gheorghe Tătărescu, had discussed Romanian-drafted economic plans with Wohlthat which bore striking resemblance to those of the 1939 economic accord.[32] By early February 1939, an outline programme had been prepared under King Carol's supervision by Gafencu, Economics Minister Bujoiu, Armaments Minister Slavescu and Finance Minister Constantinescu.[33] The Romanian negotiators were apparently aware that their programme would give Germany predominance in the Romanian economy and they considered this to be in the country's interest. Indeed, it had been decided that 'Germany generally shall regain the position of economic predominance in Romania which she had before 1914'.[34] Based on Romanian proposals, Wohlthat drew up a plan for negotiation based on founding organisations to adapt Romanian production to German requirements, particularly in agriculture. Wohlthat's plan included arrangements for Romanian mineral resources and forests to be exploited jointly by the two countries and for Romania to be helped to expand her industry while respecting German export interests. The Reich was to help develop Romania's communications infrastructure. The Romanian armaments industry and airforce were also to be developed along German lines.[35]

The building up of the Romanian war industry with German help was especially important to King Carol in view of Bulgarian, Hungarian and Soviet territorial claims against Romania. Carol had discussed collaboration with Germany to this end with Göring in November 1938. In late January 1939, during air attaché Gerstenberg's trip to Bucharest, Carol had informed him of his decision to buy German military aircraft.[36] A week later, the Romanian air minister informed Gerstenberg of his government's decision to develop the Romanian airforce with German technical assistance. The Romanian government had decided that a deal worth from 13 to 15 million Reichsmarks should be incorporated into the proposed economic treaty.[37]

Indeed, it was the Germans, rather than the Romanians who were wary of these grandiose economic plans. On 16 February, Dr Clodius, deputy director of the economic policy department at the foreign ministry, wrote to Wohlthat in Bucharest. Clodius pointed out that as a result of the 10 December 1938 agreement, Germany already accounted for around 50% of Romania's foreign trade. A special programme would not greatly increase this and Clodius feared that 'some of the items contemplated for this agreement...will be more a question of fine words than of actual accomplishments'. The Reich foreign ministry thus initially advised the economic negotiators that a reserved attitude should be taken towards general economic coordination between Germany and Romania.[38] Nevertheless, the Reich foreign ministry gave its approval to the Romanian proposals following another conversation between Wohlthat and the Romanian negotiators which confirmed 'the unanimous stand of the Romanian government in favour of orienting the Romanian economy towards Germany'. As a result, the German foreign ministry authorised that the negotiations be conducted such that 'without political commitments, the greatest possible economic advantages are drawn from the present situation'. Proposals for directing the Romanian economy towards Germany were to be given favourable consideration, provided the Romanians made concessions on raw materials and petroleum. The Romanian government, so the German foreign ministry believed, should also show willingness to adapt agriculture and industrial production to fit German requirements.[39]

Gafencu was now determined to conclude an agreement for economic collaboration with Germany and was able to influence the course of economic negotiations with the Germans in Romania's favour by hinting at possible collaboration with the Reich's economic competitors.[40] Gafencu informed Wohlthat in late February of his intention to visit Berlin before any visits to London and Paris. He claimed that he had rejected economic feelers from the western governments in order to 'give expression to the earnest desire of the Romanian government to reach an understanding with Germany first of all'.[41] The Germans were fully aware of the economic negotiations being conducted with France between January and March, which resulted in the treaty of 31 March. Far more seriously, on 12 February a British business group led by Lord Semphill arrived in Bucharest and was received by Carol and his ministers. British proposals were based on those Carol had discussed during his November 1938 visit to London. Although the proposals were not as extensive as those being discussed between Germany and Romania, they included plans for the exploitation of forests, help to build up the Romanian armaments industry, and construction of a Danube–Black Sea canal. These plans greatly worried the Germans and added to the haste and pressure of the Wohlthat mission.[42] The Wohlthat negotiations thus began to take on the aspect of a 'trial of strength' between Britain and Germany in Romania. This 'trial' between the Great Powers was intensified as a result of the German invasion of Czechoslovakia on 15 March and the subsequent diplomatic incident known as the 'Tilea affair'.

The 'Tilea affair' has excited considerable interest amongst historians. The debate is concerned with the veracity of the claim made to the British foreign office by the Romanian minister to London, Viorel Tilea, that the Germans had issued Romania with an 'ultimatum' during the economic negotiations in March 1939. Despite all the ink which has flowed on the 'Tilea affair' and the German 'ultimatum', there has been little attempt to link Tilea's statements to the question of a German territorial guarantee for Romania.[43] Yet the 'Tilea affair' is only fully explicable against the background of Gafencu's attempts to win a guarantee of Romania's territorial integrity from the Germans. As well as its importance to the development of Romanian–British relations in 1939, the 'Tilea affair' tells us much about Romania's relations with Germany and suggests that the forced pace of Gafencu's conciliation of Germany was not favoured by all members of the Romanian political and economic leadership.

Tilea's declarations in London took place in the context of the increasing international tensions resulting from the Reich's invasion of Czechoslovakia on 15 March. On the same day, Hungary annexed Ruthenia, which bordered Romania. The Romanians, fearing a possible Hungarian attack on Transylvania, strengthened their frontier with Hungary. Border tension was to continue for several weeks. With the invasion of Czechoslovakia, the military balance of power in Central and South-East Europe had shifted overwhelmingly in favour of Germany and of her Hungarian ally. King Carol's reaction was that 'having in view the unexpected expansion of Germany, we must hasten the commercial negotiations with her and conclude them as quickly as possible'.[44] In keeping with Carol's overall foreign-policy objective of maintaining equilibrium between the Great Powers, he also decided 'to send the western powers an S.O.S.'.[45] Despite the policy of greater economic collaboration with Germany, Carol sought to ensure that western influence would not be entirely lost in the area. In this way, Romania would be able to maintain room for manoeuvre as an independent actor between the Great Powers.

In compliance with Carol's views, on 16 March Gafencu issued orders to Tilea, the Romanian minister to London, and Gheorghe Tătărescu, ambassador to Paris, to draw the attention of the British and French foreign offices to the dangers of having 'only one arbiter left in Europe who decides upon the security, the independence and the peace of nations'.[46] On 16 March, and before he had received Gafencu's orders, Tilea spoke to Sir Orme Sargent, assistant under-secretary at the foreign office. He informed Sargent that 'his government, from secret and other sources, had good reason to believe that within the next few months the German government would reduce Hungary to vassalage and then proceed to disintegrate Romania'.[47] At 6 am on 17 March, Tilea received an anonymous phone call. The caller spoke of harsh economic and political demands made by Germany on Romania. After taking this call, Tilea received his instructions from Gafencu, issued the previous day. On the afternoon of 17 March, Tilea spoke to Lord Halifax, the foreign secretary. He requested a British arms credit for Romania and went on that he feared that 'it was by no means to be excluded that the German government would make an almost immediate thrust upon Romania'. Tilea claimed that Germany had demanded a monopoly of Romania's exports and that Romanian industry be restricted in the interests of German exports. In return, Germany would be prepared to give Romania a territorial guarantee. Tilea added that 'this seemed to the Romanian government something very much like an ultimatum'. He asked to what extent Romania could count on British support and whether Britain and France would be prepared to support a regional anti-German bloc consisting of Romania, Poland, Yugoslavia, Greece and Turkey.[48] By the 18 March, *The Daily Telegraph* had turned Tilea's implied ultimatum into a clear-cut case of a German 'economic ultimatum' in which Romanian industry was to be shut down and all Romanian agricultural produce exported to Germany in return for a territorial guarantee.[49]

When news of the 'economic ultimatum' reached Romania, Gafencu immediately denied its existence. Gafencu was clearly greatly alarmed that such a claim would ruin the course of negotiations with Germany. On 19 March he ordered all Romanian foreign ministry missions abroad to deny that any such 'ultimatum' had been given. Romanian diplomats were to stress that negotiations between Germany and Romania were proceeding normally.[50] Given Gafencu's anger towards Tilea, it is clear that Tilea had overstepped the instructions he had received from Gafencu on the morning of 17 March. In a telegram to Gafencu on 18 March, Tilea stated that the news he had given to the foreign office in London had produced an 'extraordinary effect'. British parliamentarians and businessmen had told him that if Romania resisted any military attack, Britain would enter any ensuing war on Romania's side and would guarantee the Polish–Romanian–Yugoslav borders.⁵¹ Gafencu responded immediately to Tilea's telegram on 18 March, informing his minister that 'the false news which you have communicated to Lord Halifax and the whole foreign office with regard to Wohlthat's negotiations in Bucharest has indeed produced "an extraordinary effect"'. The 'effect', added Gafencu, was one both damaging to the economic negotiations with Germany and to the good name of Romanian diplomacy. Gafencu concluded that 'the general situation is sufficiently serious not to be disturbed even more through exaggerated fantasies... If we find ourselves one day truly in the face of a threat, no one will believe us when we ask for support....'. Having denied the ultimatum, Gafencu ordered Tilea to leave London for Bucharest.⁵² The Romanian government's denial of the ultimatum, however, was disbelieved in London. Gafencu was forced to accompany Sir Reginald Hoare, the British minister to Bucharest, to the king. Carol assured Hoare that while 'there was much in the German proposals that was unpalatable... no sort of exception could be taken to the manner in which they had been presented and pressed'.⁵³

Meanwhile, on 18 March, Sir Alexander Cadogan cross-examined Tilea on behalf of the British foreign office. Despite Gafencu's instructions to Tilea to deny the existence of the 'ultimatum', Tilea remained 'convinced of the truth of the ultimatum story'. Tilea added, however, that the ultimatum had been presented about ten days before the Czechoslovak crisis and had been turned down by the Romanian government. In a reference to possible conflicts regarding foreign and economic policy within Romania, Tilea said there were 'many crosscurrents' in Romania. Although he was convinced that the ultimatum had been presented and refused, 'what he now feared was that the refusal would not be maintained'.⁵⁴

Although there was no German 'ultimatum' as such, it seems highly likely that some form of political guarantee was offered by Germany. In return, Romania was expected to restrict its industrial growth in German interests. The Romanian ambassador to Paris, Gheorghe Tătărescu, confirmed to French officials that Tilea had been dealing with matters which were 'some weeks old'. Tătărescu went on to inform the US ambassador that Germany had demanded all Romanian grain and petroleum production for four years, together with the sole right to develop and exploit new oil fields. Romania had refused, and Tătărescu had added that 'the Germans had not pushed this demand and the negotiations now in progress were proceeding in a polite manner'.⁵⁵ Although Tătărescu made no mention of a political guarantee, Gafencu's linkage of economic concessions to Germany in exchange for a German guarantee of Romania's territorial integrity lay at the core of his policy towards the Reich in early 1939. By so doing, Gafencu intended to make concrete the many verbal promises of a guarantee which had been given by German leaders to Romanian officials over the preceding months and years. A guarantee of this type would have reduced the threat of Bulgarian, Hungarian and Soviet territorial claims against Romania and would serve to give Romania the protection of the major continental power, which, since the Munich agreement, had become the main arbiter of the fate of Central and South-East Europe.

Gafencu was encouraged in his policy by Göring's renewed declarations in the weeks preceding the opening of economic negotiations in February 1939. In late January, German air attaché Gerstenberg assured Gafencu on Göring's behalf that the promises of a German guarantee of Romania's territorial integrity, which had been made by German leaders to Carol and other Romanian politicians, still held.[56]

In February, the Romanian politician Gheorghe Brătianu once again visited Berlin to meet Göring at Carol's command. Göring assured Brătianu that the Reich had no interest in diminishing Romania territorially and added that 'if we see that you do not want to be our enemy, then, in Bismarck's words, we will not risk for Hungary the bones of a single Prussian grenadier...'.[57] Reporting his conversation to members of the Romanian legation in Berlin on the following day, Brătianu added that Hitler and Ribbentrop, as well as Göring, had confirmed that Romania would receive the same border guarantee against Hungarian revisionism which Yugoslavia had apparently received.[58]

Fuelled by these expectations, Gafencu had immediately attempted to link economic concessions to a guarantee following Wohlthat's arrival in Bucharest in early February to begin the negotiations. On 14 February, Gafencu tried to convince Wohlthat that peaceful economic collaboration with Germany over an extensive period required a clarification of political relations between the two countries. Gafencu requested that the numerous border assurances given to Romanian politicians by German leaders should now be formalised. Economic concessions by Romania were thus to be linked to Romanian territorial integrity.[59]

Gafencu again sought to extract a political guarantee from Wohlthat on 22 February by suggesting that an agreement between Germany and Romania could be based both upon an obligation not to take part in any political campaign aimed against the other, and upon an understanding to respect each other's alliances. Having failed thus far to extract a full political guarantee from Wohlthat, Gafencu conceded that he 'would be thankful for a simple but categoric recognition of borders' and confirmed that this policy had received the approval of King Carol and his government.[60]

The Reich foreign ministry's instructions to Wohlthat to conduct the economic negotiations such that 'without political commitments, the greatest possible economic advantages are drawn from the present situation' does not necessarily mean that no offer of a guarantee was made.[61] Such offers in the preceding months and years had, after all, come from Göring rather than from the foreign ministry. Wohlthat, who, during the negotiations with Romania, seems to have been acting both as Göring's economic negotiator and on behalf of the foreign ministry, may have received conflicting instructions. He may, nonetheless, have offered a guarantee on Göring's behalf in exchange for massive Romanian economic concessions.

Documentary evidence suggests that at some point following his return to Bucharest on 10 March, Wohlthat did offer to link economic concessions to a political guarantee or agreement. The guarantee was rejected by Romania, owing to the effect its acceptance would have had on western opinion in the wake of the international tension created by the German invasion of Czechoslovakia and British reactions to the 'Tilea affair'. On 23 March, following the eventual signing of the accord, Gafencu issued a circular to all Romanian foreign-ministry missions abroad in which he stated that the new economic accord was part of a long-term strategy that had been foreseen following the signing of the December 1938 economic agreement. Gafencu concluded that 'the Romanian government does not think it opportune in today's circumstances to bind to this economic accord a political accord so as not to give space for mistaken political interpretations'.[62]

Writing in his diary at Leipzig on 23 March, Constantin Argetoianu noted a political guarantee to be fundamental to the economic accord, and indeed as having been 'the point of departure for our negotiations'.[63] Argetoianu was therefore amazed to discover on his return to Bucharest that the economic accord had been signed without a political pledge on Germany's part. Although Fabricius had apparently given a verbal declaration that Germany would defend Romania's territorial integrity if attacked, the declaration had not been confirmed in the signed accord. Argetoianu discussed the question of a specific guarantee of Romania's frontiers with Armand Călinescu, the pro-western minister of the interior. Călinescu tried to convince Argetoianu 'of the uselessness of such a clause which would irrevocably divide us from France and England and from their help....'. Călinescu went on to argue that 'if Russia should attack us, the Germans will still come to our help even without a political treaty, especially if they have to defend the investments which they will make in our country'.[64]

Despite the Romanian government's protestations to the British, after Tilea's declarations in London, that discussions with Germany were proceeding normally, the economic negotiations were clearly conducted in a tense atmosphere. The German and Hungarian occupations of Czechoslovakia and Ruthenia led to rumours of an imminent invasion of Romania. Under these circumstances, a number of the Romanian negotiators became worried by certain economic concessions which they feared could affect Romanian sovereignty.[65]

Following Tilea's statements to the British foreign office, western pressure on Romania to prevent the signing of the accord led Wohlthat to change his drafts for the agreement. Since 'the conclusion of a secret treaty was no longer possible... [Wohlthat] changed the texts into that of a state treaty which could, if necessary, be published, and a secret protocol of signature incorporating the objects and reciprocal promises of the two governments, which were not suitable for publication'.[66] It is certainly possible that the secret treaty or secret protocol may have been intended to include a political guarantee or other political agreement.[67] This would certainly fit with Tilea's fears, expressed to the British on 18 March, that the Romanians had refused the ultimatum but 'what he now feared was that the refusal would not be maintained'.[68] By 20 March, the texts of the treaty which Wohlthat had already agreed with Economics Minister Bujoiu could not be signed because, 'Bujoiu could, in the tense political situation, no longer obtain the approval of the other ministers'.[69] At this point, Wohlthat began to exert what Constantin Argetoianu described in his diary as Wohlthat's 'sweet pressure'. On Wednesday 22 March, Wohlthat informed Gafencu that he would leave Romania on the evening of the 23rd and requested direct negotiations with him or the king. This was obviously an attempt to force the pace by threatening to break off the talks. Discussions then ensued between Bujoiu, Gafencu, Călinescu and Wohlthat. The accord was finally signed on Thursday 23 March; Wohlthat's task being made easier by the fact that Carol wanted a prompt conclusion of negotiations.[70]

After the signing of the accord, Gafencu complained to Fabricius of 'the enormous pressure which up to the last moment had been exerted on the government from abroad, in order to prevent the conclusion of the Wohlthat treaty'.[71] British pressure may well have contributed to the Romanian government's decision to reject a German guarantee, or any other form of political treaty, fearing thereby that Romania would appear as having fully entered the German camp. Such an appearance would have destroyed the Romanian government's attempt to balance itself between the Great Powers.

The fears of some of the Romanian economic negotiators in the last days of discussions, and Viorel Tilea's declarations to the British foreign office, suggests that the Romanian establishment was to some extent divided as to the wisdom of Gafencu's policy of stronger political and economic links with Germany. The relationship with Germany had, since Munich, become of increasing significance within Romania's Great-Power relationships. Nevertheless, in keeping with the policy of equilibrium, the king and the foreign ministry still sought to maintain strong links with Britain and France. The problem with such a policy was that individual actors within the Romanian establishment might favour stronger links with one or another Great Power. Minister Tilea himself clearly favoured stronger political and economic links with Britain rather than with Germany. He had long been known as an anglophile and had undertaken some of his education at the London School of Economics. He had been a member of the Romanian legation in London immediately after the First World War and was co-founder and acting-president of the Anglo-Romanian Society. He received the CBE in 1938 for furthering better relations between Britain and Romania. He was thus well known in both political and business circles in London.[72] At the time of the economic negotiations with Germany, Tilea was discussing with the British the formation of an Anglo-Romanian trading company on behalf of the Romanian industrialist Max Auşnit.[73]

Tilea was also concerned about the implications of Germany's occupation of Czechoslovakia for Romania's rearmament programme and clearly favoured rearmament with British rather than German support. In his talk with Sir Orme Sargent on 16 March, Tilea requested a British loan for ten million pounds to replace the Czechoslovak arms due to Romania which he feared would be lost owing to the German occupation of Czechoslovakia. He repeated these fears and the request for a loan to Halifax the following day. Tilea had apparently been seeking a British loan for arms for some time without success. The Czechoslovak crisis gave a new justification to his demands.[74] On 22 March Tilea was still in London, despite three attempts by Gafencu to force him to return to Bucharest. Tilea was convinced that under the present circumstances the British would finally grant Romania an arms credit.[75]

At the same time, Tilea believed the German military threat to Romania to be genuine. This would account for Tilea's attempts to interest the British in the formation of an anti-German 'bloc' in Eastern

Europe. The urgency of Tilea's requests to the British were compounded by his fears for his place of birth which was multi-ethnic Transylvania. He had already alerted Halifax on 14 March that 'the process by which Germany had induced Slovakia to declare its independence could be applied equally in other countries which had not got a homogeneous population'. He gave as examples a possible German-backed secession of Croatia from Yugoslavia and Transylvania from Romania. By 17 March, Tilea appears to have believed that Transylvania was on the verge of German occupation.[76] Such fears led to what Sir Reginald Hoare described as the 'impulsive naiveté' with which Tilea set about convincing the British of the situation in South-East Europe.[77]

Tilea's 'unilateral policy' in London and his refusal to comply with Gafencu's order to return to Bucharest, raises the question as to whether Gafencu was in full control of foreign policy in March 1939. Hard on the heels of Wohlthat's arrival in Bucharest on 8 February, Gafencu questioned him as to 'what political news I had for the king, as he needed the support of the king vis-à-vis the other ministers in order to push the treaty through the cabinet'. According to Wohlthat, a reshuffle of the Romanian cabinet was expected in the event of any failure to conclude a treaty with Germany: 'The ministers who would have been replaced because their pro-German policy, which had been sanctioned by the king, had proved unsuccessful, were, Gafencu, Bujoiu, the minister of economics and Slavescu, the minister for armaments.'[78] This suggests that had the economic treaty failed, Carol might have been forced to pursue a more openly pro-British line and to appoint pro-British ministers. Gafencu's complaint to Fabricius of rumours circulating in an attempt to overthrow him, illustrates that Gafencu was fighting a personal battle for political survival.[79]

Minister President Armand Călinescu also seems to have not been fully committed to Gafencu's policy. His comments to Constantin Argetoianu regarding the 'uselessness' of a German political guarantee which would divide Romania from the western powers, suggests that Călinescu may have been instrumental in ensuring the rejection of any German offer of a guarantee.[80] Sir Reginald Hoare, the British minister to Bucharest, writing just a few months after the 'Tilea affair', stated that he regarded the pro-western Călinescu, as 'temperamentally, more disposed to resist the Germans than Gafencu, being a man without fear'.[81] It was Călinescu, in fact, who had recommended Tilea to Carol as minister to London. The existence of a secret code through which Călinescu communicated with Tilea in London in special cases has led some commentators to conclude that Călinescu was Tilea's anonymous caller on the morning of 16 March.[82] The true identity of Tilea's caller is, however, more surprising.

During his cross-examination by Sir Alexander Cadogan on 18 March, Tilea informed him that the anonymous caller through whom he had received the information regarding the severe demands being made by the German economic negotiators had been 'a private source'. On further questioning, he declared his informant 'to be the general manager of a big Romanian industrialist, who had come especially to Paris to pass the news on to him'.[83] A letter written by Tilea in 1946 reveals the caller to have been Adrian Dumitrescu, general manager of the industrialist Nicolae Malaxa, who had been ordered by Malaxa to inform Tilea of the German economic demands.[84] King Carol's diary reveals that a meeting held on 20 March 1939 between the king, Călinescu, Bujoiu, Court Minister Urdăreanu and Malaxa to discuss the German proposals, had been instigated by Malaxa, who was worried by the provisions of the draft accord. On the day of the signing of the accord, 23 March, Carol recorded that Malaxa was angry about the treaty, fearing that it gave the Germans the right to interfere in the process of industrialisation in Romania.[85]

At first sight, Malaxa's involvement in trying to alert the British to the possible dangers of the economic accord seems unlikely. He had trained as an engineer in Germany and his vast industrial concerns had close links with German industry. Malaxa's enterprises dealt with metallurgy and armaments and included interests in Reşiţa, the largest metallurgical company in Romania, with its German connections.[86] Moreover, following the Nazi–Soviet Pact of August 1939, Malaxa was one of those who were to call upon King Carol to enter into decisive rapprochement with Germany.[87] The explanation of Malaxa's behaviour, however, can be found in the nature of government during the royal dictatorship.

Carol's unofficial 'camarilla' consisting of his cronies and favourites had been important ever since his ascent to the throne in 1930. During the early part of the decade, the camarilla had been used to undermine the mainstream political parties and to create an alternative focus for political life in the country. With the abolition of parliamentary government and the establishment of Carol's personal dictatorship in early 1938, the influence of the camarilla became even more central to the governing of the country. Bankers and industrialists, such as Argetoianu, Malaxa, Gigurtu and Bujoiu, as well as politicians, formed an important part of the camarilla and were often appointed to important official political positions. The economic interests of members of the camarilla could thereby influence government policy. Malaxa himself, although he had no political position, was close to the king and was allowed a free hand in those government ministries and services which affected the prosperity of his industrial affairs.[88] Indeed, Malaxa's metallurgical and armament concerns were amongst the few such companies in Romania at that time which were not under ultimate Anglo-French or Czechoslovak control.[89] It is more than likely that Malaxa, despite his links with German industry, feared that undue German influence in the Romanian economy would curtail the large degree of autonomy that he had built up in that sphere. Following Carol's fall from power in September 1940, Malaxa threw in his lot with the Iron Guard in order to prevent General Antonescu taking his industrial complexes under state control.[90] Given the important influence of individuals within the camarilla, it is not surprising that Gafencu was unable to prevent the acting out of unilateral policies during the complicated events of March 1939.

King Carol himself was committed to economic cooperation with Germany, despite his policy of maintaining strong links with all the Great Powers. Fearing, however, that internal divisions regarding the degree of economic coordination with the Reich were displeasing to the Germans, Carol put out informal feelers to confirm his government's desire for cooperation. On 3 March, Carol informed Fabricius that he would send Constantin Argetoianu to the Reich to assure the Germans of the Romanian government's 'true intentions'.[91] On 17 March, the very day on which Tilea awakened the British to the German 'ultimatum', Carol invited Göring to the anniversary celebration in May of King Carol I's birth. Court Minister Ernest Urdăreanu, who made the offer on Carol's behalf, informed Fabricius that Carol regarded Göring's acceptance 'as of great significance for future politics in South-East Europe and towards Soviet Russia'. His acceptance would give expression to 'Germany's leading economic position in the future economic formation of this area'.[92] The king himself was by this stage one of the most important industrialists in the country. By the time of his abdication in 1940, Carol had shares in forty companies and banks, including Malaxa and Reşiţa both of which had significant German links. Carol also had shares in German domestic companies, including AEG and Deutsche Bank.[93]

Despite Malaxa's fears, the signing of the accord did not signal the economic subjugation of Romania to Germany. Of immediate importance to the Romanians was the successful resolution of their problem with regard to weapons bought in Czechoslovakia. On 18 March, Gafencu had requested that fifty waggon-loads of arms, held up in Czechoslovakia as a result of the German invasion, should be released.[94] On 22 March, Carol decided that the delivery of these arms, and other shipments ordered from the Czechoslovaks before the German invasion, was the *sine qua non* of the 23 March accord.[95] On 23 March, the Germans agreed to release the fifty waggon-loads of armaments and to guarantee the delivery of all arms ordered in Czechoslovakia. By the following day, Fabricius was able to record that the speedy delivery of the war materials had made a great impression in Romania. The press were hailing it as the first valuable result of cooperation under the treaty. The German pledge that arms from Czechoslovakia would continue to be delivered was a strong incentive for Romania to sign the treaty.[96]

The economic accord failed to shackle the Romanian economy to that of Germany. Even a contemporary American observer was willing to concede the great benefits derived by South-East Europe from the economic link with Germany.[97] While the accord laid out guidelines for future cooperation between the Germany and Romania in agriculture, industry, exploitation of natural resources and building up the country's infrastructure, there was no question of a German monopoly on Romanian exports. Article one stated that 'the economic plan shall take into account on the one hand German import requirements and, on the other hand, development possibilities for Romanian production and Romanian domestic requirements as well as the necessity for Romania to maintain economic relations with other countries'.[98] The trade agreements with France on 31 March and with Britain on 11 May 1939 were clear proof that Germany did not have a monopoly on the Romanian economy.[99] Until the onset of the war against the Soviet Union in 1941, the Romanian government retained sufficient freedom of economic action to ensure that Germany did not derive all the benefits which the accord was designed to bring her.[100]

For its part, the Romanian government was most keen to implement certain clauses of the accord, particularly those relating to armaments. On 4 April 1939, Fabricius reported that the Romanian air ministry had ordered thirty fighter-aircraft and fifteen spare engines from the Reich. The ministry wished to appoint commissioners under the terms of the March treaty as soon as possible to handle a project worth forty million Reichsmarks. It was the German side, rather than the Romanians, which was tardy in executing this particular aspect of the treaty. In May, Carol expressed his concern to Fabricius that Germany was slow in delivering arms in accordance with the treaty. Carol repeated that he 'was resolved to carry through Romania's great rearmament programme in conjunction with Germany'.[101]

For Foreign Minister Gafencu, the signing of the accord represented a great success for his policy towards Germany thus far. It ensured his continuation as foreign minister and opened up the possibility for him to visit Berlin, where he still hoped to convince the Germans to guarantee Romania. In order to ensure that other foreign governments would not be perturbed by Romania's increasing collaboration with Germany, however, Gafencu issued a circular on 25 March. In this he stated that Romania's rising volume of trade with the Reich did not signify a fall of trade with other countries. He went on to claim that the 'deepening of Romanian–German economic relations will have no consequence other than to raise Romania's economic potential and the living standards of the population'.[102] In a speech to the high council of the National Renaissance Front on 27 March, Gafencu stated that 'the accord promotes our highest aim, the consolidation of our country. Through armaments, technology and agriculture we will strengthen our country. It is the opportunity to strengthen and defend our independence.'[103] Gafencu's conduct during the negotiations in February and March 1939, belie his claim, made after the Second World War, that the only purpose of the accord had been to thwart German plans to invade Poland and Romania.[104]

The signing of the accord was greeted warmly by those economists and industrialists with overt pro-German inclinations, particularly on the grounds of complementary economic interests. The economist Mihai Manoilescu justified the accord on the grounds that both Romania and the other agricultural countries of Eastern Europe were unable to compete with western agriculture. It therefore made sense, in his opinion, for Romania to exchange her agricultural produce for German industrial goods and to create an isolated, protected economic area away from the pressures of the world economy.[105]

The willingness to accept large-scale foreign intervention in the Romanian economy represented a substantial change from the nationalist ideas current in the 1920s. The ruling National Liberal governments, in particular, had then believed that Romania should establish her industrial base without foreign intervention.[106] As a result of the Depression, however, nationalism was no longer seen as incompatible with acceptance of foreign capital. As Ion Gigurtu informed the chamber of deputies in June 1939, 'The different economic conventions, of which the most important are those concluded with Germany because we have complementary economies, can be an invaluable help for the advancement of the country's economy. Nothing must impede their application, since they agree with our economic interests... True nationalism cannot be against foreign help because it is only through this that we can raise the standard of living of the Romanian population.'[107]

Even Armand Călinescu, who had been less inclined for conciliation of Germany than Gafencu, approved of strengthened economic links with the Reich. In a speech to the High Council of the National Renaissance Front on 27 March, he pointed out that the accord was highly beneficial to Romanian agriculture and industry. Romania would be able to sell her agricultural produce and receive arms and industrial equipment in exchange. Agriculture would be invigorated by the encouragement of new cultivations and outlets. He also pointed out that the accord did not give Germany a monopoly in the Romanian economy, so that Romania's freedom of action was assured.[108]

The period of Romanian–German economic negotiations in March 1939 was also complicated by the resolution of the Ruthenian issue. The Vienna Award of November 1938 had assigned southern Slovakia to Hungary while leaving Ruthenia within the rump Czechoslovak state. Hungary, however, continued to harbour claims to Ruthenia, which had previously been part of the Hungarian kingdom. During the events of March 1939, the Romanian foreign ministry sought to coordinate its attitude towards the issue with that of the Reich.

During his discussions with Hitler and Göring in November 1938, King Carol had insisted that Ruthenia should remain a part of Czechoslovakia. Carol did not wish Ruthenia to be annexed by Hungary, as this would have lengthened the Romanian–Hungarian border. This would in turn jeopardise the security of Transylvania. A Hungarian occupation of Ruthenia, Carol had argued, would also imperil Romania's direct line of communication with Czechoslovakia and, through that country, to Germany.[109]

By early 1939, however, the Romanian government was moving towards accommodation with German wishes on the issue but hoped that Germany would be prepared, if necessary, to mediate with Hungary in Romania's favour. On 19 January Gafencu assured the German legation that 'if somehow Germany should reach the conviction that the [Ruthenian] state is not viable and thinks that a new division of this state is needed, we will not oppose a new study of the problem, which takes account of our interests'.[110] In a meeting with Călinescu and Gafencu on 14 March, the day on which Ruthenia declared its day-long independence, Carol decided that Romania should participate in any territorial changes which occurred in Ruthenia. Romania, Carol believed, should request the incorporation of a number of ethnically Romanian villages into the Romanian state, together with the railway line which linked

Romania to Poland. Romania, Carol concluded, should also request that any new Romanian–Hungarian border should be kept as short as possible.[111] On 15 March, as German troops entered Prague and Hungary occupied Ruthenia, Gafencu alerted Fabricius to the fact that Romanian military units were now on the frontier facing Ruthenia. Romania, declared Gafencu, 'will not stand idly by if Romanian villages and railway lines in [Ruthenia] are occupied by Hungary'.[112] It was clear, however, that for all Gafencu's belligerent talk, Romania was unwilling to occupy the Romanian villages without German agreement. As Gafencu pointed out, the government did 'not wish to do anything without German consent'. Gafencu requested, nevertheless, that Romania's 'just claim to these territories would not be overlooked'.[113]

Romania now hoped that Germany would mediate between themselves and the Hungarians. On 18 March, however, Fabricius informed Gafencu that the Reich did not wish to mediate but would give 'advice' in Budapest. Gafencu put forward Romania's claim to the railway linking Romania to Poland and to four villages in Ruthenia with majority Romanian populations. Gafencu added, however, that if Hungary did not agree, Romania was willing to abandon her claims.[114]

The Romanian government's unwillingness to fight for such modest territorial gains at a time of high international tension was confirmed by a Crown Council meeting on 19 March. King Carol argued that for political and strategic reasons, the Romanian villages should be occupied by Romania. His argument was unanimously rejected by the Council.[115] On 31 March, Fabricius recorded that Hungary had demanded recognition of the Ruthenian frontier and the relinquishment of the Romanian claims. Romania agreed to comply with Hungarian wishes.[116]

The growing tendency to accommodate Romanian foreign-policy decisions to the Reich's wishes had also been noticeable with regard to the decisions of the Balkan Entente in early 1939. The Romanian government was encouraged in this by Yugoslav leaders. In early February 1939, Gafencu visited Belgrade. Prince Paul agreed that the Balkan Entente conference, to be held in Bucharest on 16 February, was to avoid 'any terms or declarations which could arouse fears or suspicions that this organisation is aimed against one or the other of the European axes'.[117] Despite this decision to reaffirm the maintenance of equilibrium between the power blocs, moves were made to ensure accommodation with the Axis during the Balkan Entente conference, in which it was decided to recognise the Franco regime in Spain. Gafencu informed Fabricius that the Balkan Entente had decided that under no circumstances should the Entente become an instrument directed against

Germany. 'Quite the contrary, the Balkan Entente must realise that Germany's *Drang nach Osten* was a natural phenomenon.' Gafencu added that the Balkan countries should meet this 'by working closely with Germany, especially in economics'.[118]

The period from Gafencu's elevation to the foreign ministry in December 1938 to late March 1939 was marked by Gafencu's policy of swift reconciliation with the Reich. This was a tactical response both to German anger at the murder of the pro-German Codreanu and to the growth of German power in Central and South-East Europe as a result of Munich. Nevertheless, despite the disproportionate weight of Germany within Romania's Great Power relationships and the growing willingness to coordinate various aspects of Romanian foreign-policy decisions with German wishes, the period closed with Gafencu successfully retaining equilibrium between the powers. Despite the embarrassment caused by the 'Tilea affair', the Romanian government's request to Britain and France that the affairs of the region should not be left solely to German arbitration, found a response. The 'Tilea affair' and Germany's invasion of Czechoslovakia led to renewed interest by Britain and France in the fate of Eastern Europe. By late March, negotiations were well under way between the British and Romanian governments. These negotiations were to lead to the 13 April Anglo-French guarantee of Romania. At the same time, Gafencu still hoped to secure a territorial guarantee from the Germans, in the belief that the British would be in agreement with this. Two guarantees would secure Romania's position of equilibrium between the Great Powers. The pursuit of these guarantees, and the attempt to maintain equilibrium between the West and the Reich formed the core of the Romanian government's policies during the international events of the late spring and summer of 1939.

Notes

1 See, for instance, Viorica Moisuc, 'Tratatul economic româno-german din 23 martie 1939 și semnificația sa', *Analele institutului de studii istorice și social-politice de pe lîngă C. C. al P.C.R.*, 13, nr 4, (1967), pp. 130–46; H. Brestoiu, 'România ținta a expansiuni hitleriste', *Magazin istoric*, 21, nr 10, (247), (October 1987), pp. 12–16. A. Niri was the first Romanian historian to regard the treaty as a diplomatic action by the Romanian government to try to win time. She claims that in his talks with Carol in November 1938, Hitler ordered Carol to bring Codreanu to power. As a result, Carol proposed his own form of collaboration based on adaptation of the Romanian economy to German needs. While there is no concrete evidence to support the claim that Hitler demanded Carol bring Codreanu to power, Niri is correct to point out that proposals to adapt the economy to German needs came from the

Romanian side. See, A. Niri, *Istoricul unui tratat înrobitor. (Tratatul economic româno-german din martie 1939)*, Bucharest, 1965.
2 In his post-war writings, Gafencu described his task on coming to office in December 1938 as being to 'placate Germany and consolidate ties with the West and the Balkans'. Gafencu was not a member of the openly germanophile camp to which Goga and Codreanu belonged. In his book, however, Gafencu makes himself rather more pro-western and anti-German than the measures carried out during his term of office suggest. See, Grigore Gafencu, *The Last Days of Europe: A Diplomatic Journey in 1939*, translated by Fletcher-Allen, London, 1947, p. 25.
3 Gafencu was a member of the National Peasant Party and had been minister of communications and minister for industry and commerce in the early 1930s. His diplomatic experience consisted of a mere five months as undersecretary of state at the foreign ministry in 1932. He was also an old friend of the king. According to Lungu, Carol removed Comnen because he was 'unpopular in Berlin on account of his inability to free himself completely from the philosophy of collective security': Dov B. Lungu, *Romania and the Great Powers, 1933–1940*, Durham and London, 1989, p. 146.
4 PRO, FO 371/R8304/441/37, from Sir M. Palairet (Bucharest), Tel. nr 71, 13 October 1938.
5 MAE, 71/România, Vol. 5, pp. 500–5, Gafencu's Radio Presentation at Radio Bucharest, 29 December 1938; MAE, 71/România, Vol. 6, p. 4, *Universul*, 31 December 1938.
6 Livia Dandara, *România în viltoarea anului 1939*, Bucharest, 1985, pp. 95–6; DGFP, D, 5, Doc. nr 280, Minister in Romania to the Foreign Ministry, Bucharest, 2 February 1939; PA, Politische Abteilung IV: Po 2, Vol. 2, 9.37–2.39, German Legation in Bucharest to the Foreign Ministry, Tel. nr 20, 31 January 1939, signed Fabricius.
7 MAE, 71/Germania, Vol. 76 bis, pp. 79–80, To Franassovici, Romanian Embassy, Warsaw, Tel. nr 4786, 24 January 1939, signed Gafencu; ibid, pp. 91–3, Embassy in Warsaw to the Foreign Ministry, Tel. nr 313, 27 January 1939, signed Franassovici; ibid, pp. 105–6, Discussion between Minister Gafencu and Minister Fabricius on 30 January 1939.
8 Gheorghe Zaharia and Constantin Botoran, *Politica de apărare națională a României în contextul european interbelic, 1919–1939*, Bucharest, 1981, pp. 275–9.
9 MAE, 71/1920–1944, Dosare Speciale, Vol. 398, pp. 209–33, Memorandum by Gafencu, 15 April 1939.
10 Zaharia and Botoran, op. cit., p. 279. Despite the fears of a German attack, the Wehrmacht had no plans to invade Romania in 1939: Gheorghe Buzatu, *Dosare ale războiului mondial*, Iași, 1979, pp. 22–3.
11 MAE, 71/Germania, Vol. 76 bis, pp. 76–8, Romanian–German Relations. Instructions given by Minister Gafencu to Ministers Cretzeanu, Crutzescu and Christu, 23 January 1939.
12 DGFP, D, 5, Doc. nr 257, Berlin, 30 November 1938, Minute on the Conversation between the Field Marshal and King Carol of Romania on Saturday, 26 November 1938 in Leipzig.
13 Klaus J. Bade, *Deutsche im Ausland – Fremde in Deutschland. Migration in Geschichte und Gegenwart*, Munich, 1992, pp. 36–54.

14 Georges Castellan, 'The Germans in Romania', *Journal of Contemporary History*, 6, nr 1, (1971), pp. 52–75.
15 Valdis O. Lumans, *Himmler's Auxiliaries: The Volksdeutsche Mittelstelle and the German National Minorities of Europe, 1933–1945*, Chapel Hill, 1993, pp. 109–10.
16 For the Romanian government's policies towards the minorities, see Anthony Komjathy and Rebecca Stockwell, *German Minorities and the Third Reich*, New York, 1980, esp. pp. 103–10; Elemér Illyés, *National Minorities in Romania: Change in Transylvania*, Boulder and New York, 1982, esp. pp. 86–94; and C. A. Macartney, *Hungary and Her Successors: The Treaty of Trianon and its Consequences, 1919–1937*, Oxford, 1937, pp. 284–334.
17 Illyés, op. cit., p. 93: 'the government intended the statute merely as a piece of propaganda for foreign – particularly German – consumption'. According to the 22 August 1938 Bled Agreement with Hungary, the Romanian government pledged to reach agreement on a specific statute to improve the status of the Magyar minority: C. A. Macartney and A. W. Palmer, *Independent Eastern Europe*, London, 1962, pp. 378–9.
18 MAE, 71/România, Vol. 382, pp. 331–5, Romanian Legation in Berlin to the Foreign Ministry, Tel. nr 3172, 2 October 1938, unsigned.
19 PA, Politische Abteilung IV: Po 2, Vol. 2, 9.37–2.39, German Legation in Bucharest to the Foreign Ministry, Tgb. nr 3510/38, 12 October 1938, signed Fabricius; ibid, German Legation in Bucharest to the Foreign Ministry, Tgb. nr 3510/38, 14 October 1938, signed Fabricius.
20 MAE, 71/Germania, Vol. 76, p. 37, Memo, Bucharest, 26 October 1938, signed Al. Pătraș.
21 DGFP, D, 5, Doc. nr 257, Berlin, 30 November 1938, Minute of the Conversation between the Field Marshal and King Carol of Romania on Saturday, 26 November 1938, in Leipzig.
22 MAE, 71/1920–1944, Dosare Speciale, România R.29, Vol. 398, pp. 7–9, Note, 6 January 1939, unsigned.
23 MAE, 71/România, Vol. 383, p. 5, Gafencu to the Romanian Legation in Berlin, Tel. nr 1798, 11 January 1939, signed Gafencu.
24 Grigore Gafencu, *Prelude to the Russian Campaign: From the Moscow Pact (August 21st 1939) to the Opening of Hostilities in Russia (June 22nd 1941)*, translated by Fletcher-Allen, London, 1945, pp. 66–9.
25 MAE, Mica Înțelegere, Vol. 18, pp. 253–62 (257), Summary of the Questions Discussed at the Conference of the Little Entente at Sinaia, 4–5 May 1938.
26 MAE, 71/România, Vol. 6, p. 111, *Universul*, 3 March 1939, 'Germany enters into the European Danube Commission'. Gafencu subsequently pointed out that Germany rejoined the EDC 'at the entreaty of the Romanian government...'. Gafencu, *Prelude to the Russian Campaign*, p. 68.
27 Gafencu, *Prelude to the Russian Campaign*, p. 68. See also, Dan Boțescu, 'Problema Dunării în cadrul relațiilor româno-germane în anii celui de al doilea război mondial', *Analele științifice ale universității 'Al. I. Cuza' din Iași* (serie nouă), sectiunea 3, istorie-filozofie, 21, (1975), pp. 45–50 (46).
28 MAE, 71/Germania, Vol. 76 bis, pp. 29–30, Legation in Berlin to the Foreign Ministry, Tel. nr 39029, 17 January 1939, signed Brabetzianu; ibid, pp. 35–7, Letter from the Press Attaché at the Legation in Berlin to Gafencu, nr 58, 18 January 1939, signed Ilcuș.

29 Zaharia and Botoran, *Politica de apărare națională a României în contextul european interbelic*, p. 279.
30 MAE, 71/Germania, Vol. 76 bis, pp. 76–8, Romanian–German Relations. Instructions given by Minister Gafencu to Minsters Cretzeanu, Crutzescu and Christu in a meeting taking place on 23 January 1939.
31 See, for instance, Viorica Moisuc, *Diplomația României și problema apărării suveranității și independenței naționale în perioada martie 1938–mai 1940*, Bucharest, 1971, pp. 126–50, and Donald Cameron Watt, *How War Came: The Immediate Origins of the Second World War, 1938–1939*, London, 1989, p. 175.
32 See Chapter 1. Also William S. Grenzebach, *Germany's Informal Empire in East-Central Europe: German Economic Policy Toward Yugoslavia and Romania, 1933–1939*, Stuttgart, 1988, pp. 187–8 : 'The notion of comprehensive cooperation on an economic basis was not simply a canard foisted on innocent and unwilling Romania but an idea that had an independent origin in the soil of Romania's economic and political crisis.'
33 DGFP, D, 5, Doc. nr 293, Legation in Romania to the Foreign Ministry, Bucharest, 14 February 1939, signed Clodius and Fabricius.
34 Ibid.
35 Ibid.
36 Grenzebach, op. cit., p. 193.
37 *Documente privind situația internațională și politică a României, 1939*, Institutul de studii istorice și social-politice, Buletin informativ, Vol. 3, Bucharest, 1967, Doc. nr 9, Minister in Bucharest to the Ministry of Foreign Affairs, Telegram, 6 February 1939, signed Fabricius.
38 DGFP, D, 5, Doc. nr 294, Memorandum by the Deputy Director of the Economic Policy Department, Berlin, 15 February 1939, signed Clodius.
39 DGFP, D, 5, Doc. nr 297, Legation in Romania to the Foreign Ministry, Bucharest, 17 February 1939, signed Fabricius; DGFP, D, 5, Doc. nr 298, Director of the Economic Policy Department to the Legation in Romania, Berlin, 18 February 1939, signed Wiehl.
40 See also in relation to Romania's economic relations in late 1938, R. G. D. Laffan, *Survey of International Affairs, 1938*, Vol. 3, Oxford, 1953, p. 428: 'economically [Romania] was seeking to profit by manoeuvring the two Great Power blocs into the position of competitive bidders for her oil and grain'.
41 DGFP, D, 5, Doc. nr 306, Ministerialdirektor Wohlthat to Ministerialdirektor Wiehl, Berlin, 27 February 1939: during the negotiations, all ministers, under instruction from Carol, 'willingly showed secret material from their ministries concerning data and projects'.
42 DGFP, D, 5, Doc. nr 295, Minister in Romania to the Foreign Ministry, Bucharest, 15 February 1939.
43 One exception is provided by David Kaiser, who believes that the inspiration for Tilea's declarations to the British on 17 March was Gafencu's wish to sign a political agreement in Berlin. In return for a territorial guarantee, Romania would pledge not to join any anti-German combination. See, David E. Kaiser, *Economic Diplomacy and the Origins of the Second World War: Germany, Britain, France and Eastern Europe, 1930–1939*, Princeton, 1980, p. 266. For other accounts of the 'Tilea affair' in both Romanian and English, see, A. Niri, *Istoricul unui tratat înrobitor. (Tratatul economic româno–german din martie*

1939), Bucharest, 1965, pp. 85–203; Paul D. Quinlan, 'The Tilea Affair: A Further Inquiry, *Balkan Studies*, 19, (1978), pp. 147–57; Gheorghe Buzatu, *Dosare ale războiului mondial*, Iași, 1979, pp. 11–43; Sidney Aster, *1939: The Making of the Second World War*, London, 1973, pp. 61–78; Simon Newman, *March 1939: The British Guarantee to Poland*, Oxford, 1976, pp, 109–17.

44 Arh. St., Însemnări Zilnice, Carol II, roll 21, Vol. 8, Wednesday 15 March 1939, p. 422.
45 Arh. St., Însemnări Zilnice, Carol II, roll 21, Vol. 8, Friday 17 March 1939, p. 424.
46 Quoted in Dov B. Lungu, 'The European Crisis of March–April 1939: The Romanian Dimension', *International History Review*, 7, (1985), pp. 390–414 (392).
47 PRO, FO 371/C3857/3356/18, Minute by Sir O. Sargent of his conversation with Tilea, 16 March 1939.
48 DBFP, Vol. 4, nr 395, Viscount Halifax to Sir R. Hoare, (Bucharest), 17 March 1939.
49 *The Daily Telegraph*, 18 March 1939.
50 MAE, 71/România, Vol. 76 bis, p. 212, To all Legations, Tel. nr 17798, 19 March 1939, signed Gafencu.
51 MAE, 71/Anglia, Vol. 10, pp. 95–7, Legation in London to the Foreign Ministry, 18 March 1939, signed Tilea.
52 MAE, 71/Anglia, Vol. 10, p. 100, To the Legation in London from the Foreign Minister, Tel. nr 17788, 18 March 1939, signed Gafencu; ibid, p. 102, To Minister Tilea at the Romanian Legation in London from the Foreign Minister, Tel. nr 17789, 18 March 1939, signed Gafencu.
53 DBFP, Vol. 4, nr 433, Sir R. Hoare (Bucharest) to Viscount Halifax, 20 March 1939.
54 MAE, 2 Conv. G.19, unpaginated, Note presented by Sir Reginald Hoare to Gafencu, from a telegram sent from the Foreign Office, 19–20 March 1939.
55 Watt, *How War Came*, p. 171; Foreign Relations of the United States, Diplomatic Papers, 1939, Vol. 1, pp. 79–89, The Ambassador in France (Bullitt), to the Secretary of State, Paris, 20 March 1939.
56 Grenzebach, *Germany's Informal Empire in East-Central Europe*, p. 193.
57 MAE, 71/Germania, Vol. 76 bis, pp. 57–9, Note on a conversation with Marshal Göring, 1 February 1939; PA, Politische Abteilung IV: Po 2, Vol. 2, 9.37–2.39, German Legation, Bucharest, to the Foreign Minstry, Tel. nr 20, 31 January 1939, signed Fabricius.
58 MAE, 71/Germania, Vol. 76 bis, pp. 125–6, From the Legation in Berlin to the Foreign Ministry, Tel. nr 39068, 2 February 1939, signed Brabetzianu.
59 MAE, 71/Germania, Vol. 97, pp. 126–9, Note on a Conversation taking place on 14 February 1939 between Minister Gafencu and Wohlthat at the Ministry of Foreign Affairs.
60 MAE, 71/Germania, Vol. 97, pp. 130–2, Note on a Conversation taking place on 22 Febuary 1939 between Minister Gafencu and Wohlthat at the Ministry of Foreign Affairs.
61 DGFP, D, 5, Doc. nr 298, Director of the Economic Policy Department to the Legation in Romania, Berlin, 18 February 1939, signed Wiehl.
62 MAE, 71/Germania, Vol. 76 bis, pp. 243–4, For Circulation to Embassies and Legations, Tel. nr 19.192, 23 March 1939, signed Gafencu.

63 Arh. St., Însemnări Zilnice, Constantin Argetoianu, Dosar nr 74, volume unnumbered but dated 10 March–25 May 1939, 23 March 1939, p. 364.
64 Arh. St., Însemnări Zilnice, Constantin Argetoianu, Dosar nr 74, volume unnumbered but dated 10 March–25 May 1939, 29 March 1939, pp. 388–90. The accord did not include a political guarantee, but remarked in its preamble that the two countries had concluded the treaty 'in pursuance of their peaceful aims': DGFP, D, 6, Doc. nr 78, German–Romanian Economic Treaty.
65 DGFP, D, 6, Doc. nr 131, Ministerialdirektor Wohlthat to State Secretary Weizsäcker, Berlin, 30 March 1939.
66 Ibid.
67 Following the signing of the accord, Fabricius was apparently working on a project for a Romanian–German declaration similar to the non-aggression pact signed in 1934 by Poland and Germany. During the course of 1939, the Romanian foreign ministry also drafted a 'Treaty of Friendship and Cordial Collaboration between Germany and Romania', based on the maintenance of the territorial status-quo: MAE, 2 Conv. G. 19, unpaginated, From the Legation in Berlin to the Foreign Ministry, Tel. nr 39192, 25 March 1939, signed Crutzescu; MAE, 71/Germania, Vol. 77, pp. 324–6, Project M.A.S. 1939, Traité d'amité et de collaboration cordiale entre l'Allemagne et la Roumanie.
68 MAE, 2 Conv. G.19, unpaginated, Note presented by Sir Reginald Hoare to Gafencu, from a telegram sent from the Foreign Office, 19–20 March 1939.
69 DGFP, D, 6, Doc. nr 131, Ministerialdirektor Wohlthat to State Secretary Weizsäcker, Berlin, 30 March 1939.
70 Arh. St., Însemnări Zilnice, Constantin Argetoianu, Dosar nr 74, volume unnumbered but dated 10 March–25 May 1939, 24 March 1939, pp. 376–7; DGFP, D, 6, Doc. nr 131, Ministerialdirektor Wohlthat to State Secretary Weizsäcker, Berlin, 30 March 1939.
71 DGFP, D, 6, Doc. nr 80, Minister in Romania to the Foreign Ministry, Bucharest, 24 March 1939.
72 Sidney Aster, *1939: The Making of the Second World War*, London, 1973, p. 66.
73 Ibid, p. 72.
74 DBFP, Vol. 4, nr 298, Minute by Sir O. Sargent, Foreign Office, 16 March 1939; ibid, nr 395, Viscount Halifax to Sir R. Hoare (Bucharest), Foreign Office, 17 March 1939; Aster, op. cit., p. 62.
75 MAE, 71/Anglia, Vol. 10, pp. 121–4, Legation in London to the Foreign Ministry, Tel. nr 589, 21 March 1939, signed Tilea; ibid, p. 125, Legation in London to the Foreign Ministry, Tel. nr 18815, 22 March 1939, signed Tilea: ibid, p. 126, Legation in London to the Foreign Ministry, Tel. nr 591, 22 March 1939, signed Tilea. Gafencu had also ordered Tilea to return to Bucharest on 18 and 20 March.
76 DBFP, Vol. 4, Doc. nr 297, Viscount Halifax to Sir R. Hoare, (Bucharest), Foreign Office, 16 March 1939. It is clear from Martha Bibescu's journal entry for 17 March 1939 that Tilea feared an imminent German occupation of Transylvania: Martha Bibescu, *Jurnal Politic, ianuarie 1939–ianuarie 1941*, (eds) Cristian Popișteanu and Nicolae Minei, Bucharest, 1979, pp. 50–1.
77 DBFP, Vol. 4, Doc. nr 443, Sir Reginald Hoare to Viscount Halifax, Bucharest, 20 March 1939. Tilea was also suffering from a lack of adequate guidance from Bucharest. He took up his post as minister to London on 1 February 1939, having received general instructions from Carol that his task was to tie

Romania closer to Britain both politically and economically. Tilea was given a broad mandate to use the means he felt necessary to achieve this. Having been given this general brief, Tilea was given no further precise instructions as to how to carry this out or full details of the developing situation in Romania. In a telegram to the king dated 22 March, Tilea pointed out that he had received only 'one instruction and too little precise information': Aster, *1939: The Making of the Second World War*, pp. 66–7; MAE, 71/Germania, Vol. 76 bis, pp. 240–42, Legation in London to the Foreign Ministry, Tel. nr 592, 22 March 1939, signed Tilea.

78 DGFP, D, 6, Doc. nr 131, Ministerialdirektor Wohlthat to State Secretary Weizsäcker, Berlin, 30 March 1939. Whether this 'political news' referred to a political guarantee is unclear.
79 DGFP, D, 6, Doc. nr 80, Minister in Romania to the Foreign Ministry, Bucharest, 24 March 1939.
80 Arh. St., Însemnări Zilnice, Constantin Argetoianu, Dosar nr 74, volume unnumbered but dated 10 March–25 May 1939, 29 March 1939, pp. 388–90.
81 Quoted in *Cine a Fost Armand Călinescu. Mărturii*, no editor, Bucharest, 1992, p. 63.
82 Barbu Călinescu, 'Scrisoare din Cambridge. Cifrul lui Armand Călinescu', *Magazin Istoric*, 21, nr 10 (247), October 1987, pp. 16–17.
83 PRO, FO 371/23060, C3538/3356/18/, Minute by Cadogan, 18 March 1939.
84 Letter from V. V. Tilea to N. Malaxa, dated 1 July 1946. Original of letter kindly shown to the author by Mrs Ileana Troiano, eldest daughter of Tilea. See also V. V. Tilea, *Envoy Extraordinary: Memoirs of a Romanian Diplomat*, (ed.) Ileana Tilea, London, 1998, pp. 226–7.
85 Arh. St., Însemnări Zilnice, Carol II, roll 21, Vol. 8, Monday 20 March 1939, p. 427 and ibid, Thursday 23 March 1939, p. 430.
86 Nicole Jordan, *The Popular Front and Central Europe: The Dilemmas of French Impotence, 1918–1940*, Cambridge, 1992, p. 127; Mircea Mușat and Ion Ardeleanu, *România după Marea Unire*, Vol. 2, Part II-a, Bucharest, 1988, p. 719.
87 Mușat and Ardeleanu, *România după Marea Unire*, Vol. 2, Part II-a, p. 988; Lungu, *Romania and the Great Powers*, p. 196.
88 Keith Hitchins, *Rumania , 1866–1947*, Oxford, 1994, pp. 385–6; Mușat and Ardeleanu, op. cit., pp. 95–6, 719; Al. Gh. Savu, *Dictatura Regală (1938–1940)*, Bucharest, 1970, pp. 28–61.
89 Jordan, op. cit., p. 127.
90 Armin Heinen, *Die Legion 'Erzengel Michael' in Rumänien. Soziale Bewegung und politische Organisation*, Munich, 1986, p. 456.
91 PA, Politische Abteilung IV: Po 5, Vol. 5, 2.39–6.40, German Legation in Bucharest to the Foreign Ministry, Tgb. nr 857/39, 3 March 1939, signed Fabricius: unfortunately, no records exist of Argetoianu's conversations in Germany to which he went on 14 March.
92 PA, Büro des Staatssekretärs, Rumänien, Vol. 1, 11.38–1.40, German Legation in Bucharest to the Foreign Ministry, Tel. nr 90, 17 March 1939, signed Fabricius.
93 Al. Gh. Savu, *Dictatura Regală*, p. 52. This is not to underestimate the importance of Carol's links with western companies. Anglo-French and US capital remained dominant in the Romanian economy throughout the 1930s.

94 DGFP, D, 6, Doc. nr 31, Minister in Romania to the Foreign Ministry, Bucharest, 18 March 1939.
95 Arh. St., Însemnări Zilnice, Carol II, roll 21, Vol. 8, Wednesday 22 March 1939, p. 429.
96 DGFP, D, 6, Doc. nr 31, Minister in Romania to the Foreign Ministry, Bucharest, 18 March 1939; Arh. St., Însemnări Zilnice, Carol II, roll 21, Vol. 8, Wednesday 22 March 1939, p. 429; ibid., Thursday 23 March 1939, p. 430; DGFP, D, 6, Doc. nr 92, Minister in Romania to the Foreign Ministry, Bucharest, 25 March 1939; *Foreign Relations of the United States*, 1939, Vol. 1, pp. 98–9, Ambassador in the United Kingdom (Kennedy) to the Secretary of State, London, 29 March 1939.
97 MAE, 71/1939 E9II, pp.116–21, 'The Struggle for the Balkans' John C. de Wilde, *Foreign Policy Reports*, 15, nr 19, New York, 15 December, 1939: the author denied the allegations that Gemany had forced the Balkan countries to take unwanted goods or had stalled industrialisation in those countries. The Reich 'repeatedly encouraged the cultivation of such labour-intensive crops as oil seed, flax and hemp, and urged the intensification of the livestock and dairy industries. By giving the Balkans access to an expanding market at a time when their other export outlets were contracting, Germany enabled them to buy a large amount of industrial equipment.' The author concluded that the German *Grossraumwirtschaft* 'whatever its defects, recognised the mutual economic interdependence of Germany and South-East Europe'.
98 For the full details of the treaty, see DGFP, D, 6, Doc. nr 78, German–Romanian Economic Treaty.
99 Andreas Hillgruber, *Hitler, König Carol und Marschall Antonescu. Die Deutsch–Rumänischen Beziehungen, 1938–1944*, Wiesbaden, 1965, p. 48.
100 Overy has made this point with regard to the *Reichswerke Hermann Göring* established in 1937. Göring used the *Reichswerke* as a means to exploit industries in annexed territories, such as Austrian and Czech heavy industry and arms factories. 'By the end of 1941 Göring had achieved his promise to create the largest economic enterprise in Europe. Romania was the only country with significant industrial resources in Eastern Europe not drawn into the Reichswerke orbit. The 1939 German–Romanian treaty created the framework for cooperation. Until 1941, however, the Romanian government was determined to keep as much control over its own industry as it could.' See, R. J. Overy, *War and Economy in the Third Reich*, Oxford, 1994, pp. 145–59 (159).
101 DGFP, D, 6, Doc. nr 152, Minister in Romania to the Foreign Ministry, Bucharest, 4 April, 1939; ibid, Doc. nr 398, Minister in Romania to the Foreign Ministry, Bucharest, 17 May 1939.
102 MAE, 2. Conv. G.19, unpaginated, To all Embassies and Legations, except Berlin, Tel. nr 19475, 25 March 1939, signed Gafencu.
103 Armand Călinescu and Grigore Gafencu, *Rumänien und die Mitteleuropäische Krise*, Bucharest, 1939, p. 37.
104 Grigore Gafencu, *The Last Days of Europe*, pp. 25–6.
105 Mihail Manoilescu, 'Solidaritatea economică a estului Europa', offprint from *Revista cursurilor și conferințelor universitare*, nr 3–4, (May–June 1939), pp. 3–15; Ovidiu Drăgoi, *Relațiunile economic ale României cu Germania 1934–1938*, with an introduction by Mihail Manoilescu, Bucharest, 1939, pp. 3–5.

During the parliamentary debates of late 1936, Manoilescu had spoken out in favour of Romanian–German friendship, based on Romanian neutrality towards the Reich and avoidance of any obligations towards the Soviet Union: Mihail Manoilescu, *Generația nouă și politica veche. Discurs ținut in Senat la 27 noembrie 1936 de Mihail Manoilescu*, Bucharest, 1936.
106 For National Liberal hostility to foreign capital in the 1920s, see Henry L. Roberts, *Rumania: Political Problems of an Agrarian State*, Harvard, 1951, pp. 119–21.
107 I. P. Gigurtu, *Discurs rostit cu ocazia discuției generale a adresei de răspuns la mesajul tronului in ședința Camerei Deputaților din 23 iunie 1939*, Bucharest, 1939, pp. 19–20.
108 Armand Călinescu and Grigore Gafencu, *Rumänien und die Mitteleuropäische Krise*, pp. 13–22.
109 DGFP, D, 5, Doc. nr 254, Memorandum by the Foreign Minister. Conversation of the Führer with the King of Romania in the presence of the Reich Foreign Minister, Berchtesgaden, 24 November 1938; ibid, Doc. nr 257, Berlin, 30 November 1938, Minute on the Conversation between the Field Marshal and King Carol of Romania on Saturday, 26 November 1938.
110 MAE, 71/Germania, Vol. 76 bis, pp. 38–40, To the Legation in Berlin, Tel. nr 4066, 19 January 1939, signed Gafencu.
111 Arh. St., *Însemnări Zilnice, Carol II*, roll 21, Vol. 8, Monday 13 March 1939, p. 416.
112 DGFP, D, 6, Doc. nr 2, Minister in Romania to the Foreign Ministry, Bucharest, 15 March 1939.
113 DGFP, D, 6, Doc. nr 6, Minister in Romania to the Foreign Ministry, Bucharest, 16 March 1939. On 17 March, Weizsäcker informed Fabricius that the Romanian government was to be advised that her interests were best served by avoidance of violence. Germany would not mediate between Romania and Hungary. Far-reaching Romanian wishes were not to be encouraged. See, DGFP, D, 6, Doc. nr 13, State Secretary to the Legation in Romania, Berlin, 17 March 1939.
114 DGFP, D, 6, Doc. nr 29, Minister in Romania to the Foreign Ministry, Bucharest, 18 March 1939.
115 Radu R. Rosetti, *Pagini de Jurnal*, (eds) Cristian Popișteanu, Marian Ștefan and Ioana Ursu, Bucharest, 1993, p. 73.
116 DGFP, D, 6, Doc. nr 135, Minister in Romania to the Foreign Ministry, Bucharest, 31 March 1939.
117 MAE, *Înțelegerea Balcanică*, Vol. 7, pp. 18–19, To Embassies in Paris and Warsaw and Legations in Rome, London and Berlin, Tel. nr 7403, 4 February 1939, signed Gafencu.
118 PA, Büro des Staatssekretärs, Rumänien, Vol. 1, 11.38–1.40, German Legation, Bucharest, to the Foreign Minstry, Tel. nr 54, 21 February 1939, signed Fabricius; DGFP, D, 6, Doc. nr 304, Minister in Romania to the Foreign Ministry, Bucharest, 27 February 1939. While the Balkan Entente was clearly concerned not to become completely drawn into either of the Great Power blocs against the other, there is little evidence for the view that Romania was attempting in early 1939 'to create an anti-Nazi barrier in Central Europe', centred on the Balkan Entente, as claimed by Eliza Campus in *Din politica externă a României 1913–1947*, Bucharest, 1980, p. 452.

4
From 'Equilibrium' to 'Hand in Hand with Germany', April to October 1939[1]

In the months following the signing of the March 1939 economic accord between Romania and Germany, the Romanian government strenuously resisted British attempts to incorporate Romania into an anti-German bloc in Eastern Europe. The Romanian government was determined to retain neutrality or 'equilibrium' between the Great Powers and, within this, to continue its policy of gradually improving relations with the Reich. Gafencu and Carol still entertained the hope of receiving a territorial guarantee from the Reich. Hence, in order to avoid antagonising the Germans, Carol and his government sought to avoid any reciprocal agreements with the West during the negotiations which surrounded the granting of the Anglo-French guarantee in April 1939. Likewise, the Romanians prevented their country becoming an object of negotiation between the West, Turkey and the Soviet Union during 1939. Far from being the 'victim' of the West's unwillingness to assist Eastern Europe, Romanian foreign-policy initiatives were a major factor in thwarting Britain's attempts to create an anti-German bloc in the region.[2]

One effect of the 'Tilea affair' had been to strengthen British resolve to counteract growing German influence in Eastern Europe. On 21 March 1939 the British government asked France, Poland and the Soviet Union to make a common decision regarding action they would take in the event of threats to the independence of any European state. Britain's ultimate plan was to build up a system of states bound by mutual assistance pacts against Germany in Eastern Europe. The system was to include Poland, Greece, Turkey and Yugoslavia with Romania acting as the centre of this system, and as a bridge between her Polish and Balkan

Entente allies. Britain believed this system could then possibly be strengthened through Soviet assistance.[3]

The Romanian king and foreign ministry, however, had no wish to be involved in mutual assistance plans, since they were determined to maintain the policy of equilibrium between the powers. Furthermore, a mutual assistance pact with the West would destroy the possibility of a German guarantee of Romania's territorial integrity which Carol and Gafencu still hoped to receive. Consequently, on 20 March Gafencu informed London and Paris that the Romanian government did not regard a mutual assistance pact as opportune since it wished to avoid provocation of Germany. A mutual assistance pact, Gafencu argued, was felt to expose Romania to possible German military action. The Romanian government also regarded Soviet support as provocative to Germany and as compromising Romania's alliances with anti-Soviet Poland and Yugoslavia. Instead, Gafencu advocated 'that the western powers, through their own initiative, [should] let it be known categorically that they will not allow a change of European frontiers, and that they will help us to defend our frontiers with all their military power'.[4]

Britain and France responded to Romania on 31 March, the day on which they guaranteed Poland.[5] The western governments informed Gafencu that they were willing to defend Romania if she resisted any attack on her and provided that the Polish–Romanian alliance, which was directed against an attack by the Soviet Union, was transformed into an *erga omnes* agreement against any aggressor. The western governments hoped that this could then form the basis for the creation of a larger bloc to include Greece and Turkey, with possible Soviet assistance.[6]

Romanian historians have tended to place the blame solely on Poland for the failure to transform the Romanian–Polish alliance into an *erga omnes* form.[7] In fact, Gafencu, ever mindful of the need to maintain equilibrium between Germany and the West, was equally loth to transform the alliance, fearing thereby to provoke Germany or to become involved in growing German–Polish tensions over the fate of Danzig. As Gafencu observed in a foreign-ministry memo, while Germany had no points of conflict with Romania, she had several with Poland. An *erga omnes* agreement could thus force Romania to intervene on Poland's behalf against Germany, while providing no reciprocal advantage for the Romanians. Gafencu concluded that 'the transformation of the Polish–Romanian alliance into an *erga omnes* alliance is obviously aimed against Germany and gives the whole agreement the character of a new attempt to encircle Germany'.[8]

The Romanian foreign ministry envisaged western help in terms of a unilateral guarantee which would not tie Romania to the western camp, or oblige Romania to intervene on behalf of her neighbours. In this way, the Romanians could retain links with Germany and use a western guarantee as a bargaining tool for requesting a similar guarantee from Germany. Cretzianu, secretary-general at the Romanian foreign ministry, was to visit Paris and London in early April. In his instructions to Cretzianu, Gafencu pointed out the need to prevent any link being made between a western guarantee and an extension of the Polish–Romanian alliance, in order not to give 'the impression that we wish to encircle Germany'. Gafencu suggested instead two systems: a 'northern system' linking Poland and the West and a 'southern system' linking Romania to the West through a unilateral declaration. 'This system', argued Gafencu, 'would have the advantage that it could be extended, Germany participating in the ranks of the guaranteeing states, while Yugoslavia could enter that of the guaranteed states.'[9]

Gafencu reiterated these points again in his discussion with Sir Reginald Hoare on 11 April. A British unilateral declaration, explained Gafencu, would strengthen Romania without provoking Germany, which would also be free to give such a declaration to Romania. Although Romania wanted Britain and France to have a presence in the region, Germany should not be excluded. The government, concluded Gafencu, wanted all the Great Powers to be interested in the maintenance of Romania's independence.[10] At the same time as Romania was negotiating with Britain, Gafencu assured Fabricius that Romania had no wish to join a British led combination against Germany. While Romania would not turn down a unilateral offer of defence from the West, Gafencu pointed out that a German declaration would be considered more useful to Romania.[11]

As the Romanian government had wished, the Anglo-French guarantee of 13 April 1939 was a unilateral guarantee by the West to protect Romania's borders against aggression provided Romania defended herself in the event of attack. The Romanians were not bound by any reciprocal pledges to help either Britain or her allies. The military clauses of the Polish–Romanian alliance remained directed against an attack by the Soviet Union. The unilateral guarantees to Poland and Romania meant that the British attempt to create a system of mutual assistance against Germany in Eastern Europe had failed.[12] Gafencu and Carol's plans had thus succeeded so far: Romania had retained her neutrality between Germany and the West. Gafencu now renewed his attempts, which had been stalled as a result of the 'Tilea affair', to induce Germany to guarantee Romania's borders.[13]

Gafencu's visit to Berlin from 18 to 20 April 1939 was used as another opportunity to broach the question of the guarantee. King Carol instructed Gafencu 'not to make commitments to anybody, but if we can obtain from the Germans a guarantee like the Anglo-French, it would be very good'.[14]

During discussions with Ribbentrop on 18 April, Gafencu pointed out that Romania had rejected any bilateral agreements with Britain as well as any arrangements in which the Soviet Union would take part. The acceptance of the British guarantee was not directed against any power, since Romania 'would accept guarantees from other countries'. Gafencu emphasised King Carol and the Romanian government's 'readiness to come to an understanding with Germany'.[15] During his meeting with Göring on the following day, Gafencu pointed out that during the economic negotiations with Wohlthat earlier in the year, the economic accord was 'bound in my mind to an agreement or declaration with a political character through which Germany would recognise our state. We are ready at any time to perfect our security system through a German guarantee.'[16]

These Romanian requests for a guarantee received no immediate response from the German leaders. On the contrary, Gafencu was warned by both Ribbentrop and Göring that any further Romanian involvement in Britain's 'encirclement' of Germany would damage relations between the two countries. Göring added that in this case, the Reich would have no interest in restricting the revisionist claims of Romania's neighbours.[17]

Hitler was somewhat milder in his reactions, pointing out to Gafencu that Romania's acceptance of the western guarantee would be represented in Britain as evidence of the country's commitment to the anti-German front. Nevertheless, he 'could understand Gafencu's statement that he could not reject the gesture'. Hitler also reassured Gafencu regarding Hungary. The Reich, he affirmed, was not interested in border alterations in favour of Hungary, 'for the Hungarians were no kin of ours'. The Führer concluded that commercial relations would continue to bind Germany and Romania together.[18]

Despite this mixed response from German leaders, Gafencu continued to harbour hopes of a German guarantee. As late as 7 July, with Romanian–German relations complicated by negotiations between Turkey and the West, Gafencu repeated his wish for a German guarantee.[19]

Following Gafencu's discussions in Berlin in April, the Romanian government were anxious to avoid any expansion of the western guarantee, especially one which might include the Soviet Union, in order not to provoke the Germans. In April negotiations had opened between the West, Turkey and the Soviet Union for a possible mutual assistance pact to include support for the Balkan countries. Gafencu pointed out to members of the Romanian government the dangers of rumoured negotiations between France and the Soviet Union through which the Soviets would give Romania material support. Such an accord, said Gafencu, 'would compromise the action of clarification and détente which I have carried out in Berlin'.[20] During his visit to London in late April, Gafencu explained to British representatives the importance of the concept of European 'equilibrium'. Gafencu added that his government believed Germany would not allow Hungarian revisionist claims on Romania to be realised 'so long as Romania did not enter into close relations with Soviet Russia and so long as she could continue to be considered as a bastion against bolshevism'.[21] On 29 April, Armand Călinescu, recently appointed minister president, ordered the Romanian ambassador in Turkey to inform the Turkish foreign ministry of Romania's wish not to be drawn into any mutual assistance system which included the Soviet Union. Gafencu and Călinescu were agreed that 'the participation of the Soviet Union in the guarantee given us by Britain and France would not strengthen our position but compromise our relations with Germany....'.[22] On his return to Bucharest from his April tour of foreign capitals, Gafencu stressed to Fabricius that he had informed all governments that Romania would enter no combinations against Germany and would not be party to any agreements with the Soviet Union.[23]

Despite Gafencu's post-war claims, there is little evidence of his supposed desire to have Romania linked to a Soviet security system, which would have destroyed his efforts both to establish closer links with Germany, and to extract a territorial guarantee from her.[24] Even in August 1939, only a few weeks before the outbreak of the war in Europe, King Carol was still reluctant to pursue a mutual assistance pact with the Soviets. The king feared that such a pact would not only provoke the Germans, but was also impossible while the Soviet Union refused to recognise Romanian sovereignty over Bessarabia.[25]

In the summer of 1939, negotiations opened between Britain, France and Turkey for a mutual assistance pact. During these negotiations, the Romanian government continued to pursue the policy of equilibrium between the Great Powers. Consequently, Gafencu sought to avoid any mention of Romania or the Balkan Entente in these negotiations which might have provoked German reprisals.

On 12 May the Anglo-Turkish declaration was published. Under its terms, Britain and Turkey pledged to undertake negotiations for a long-term pact of mutual assistance. Until such time as a pact was concluded, the two countries agreed to reciprocal support in the event of war or aggression in the Mediterranean. According to article 3 of the declaration, if Britain and France came to the aid of Romania or Greece in accordance with the 13 April guarantees, Turkey would help make this aid effective by opening the Straits to British ships. Under paragraph 6 of the declaration, Britain and Turkey 'recognize that it is also necessary to ensure the establishment of security in the Balkans and they are consulting together with the object of achieving that purpose'.[26] Turkey's pledge to help Britain in enforcing the April guarantees and, in particular, the reference in paragraph 6 to the need to establish Balkan security, threatened to destroy attempts by Romania and the Balkan Entente, of which Romania was then president, to remain neutral between the Great Powers. German officials made it clear to the Romanians that they regarded the Anglo-Turkish declaration as putting an end to Turkey's neutrality, thus casting a shadow over the status of the Balkan Entente as a whole.[27]

Gafencu was particularly worried that any weakening of Balkan Entente unity would drive Yugoslavia further towards the Axis. During talks with Yugoslav Foreign Minister Marcović in May, Gafencu tried to convince him of the need to remain within the Balkan Entente. Marcović pointed out that the proposed Anglo-Turkish accord would itself weaken the Balkan Entente, since it drew one of the Entente members (Turkey) into the western security system and proposed to draw in the others. Marcović agreed with Gafencu that the Balkan Entente must maintain its complete independence so as not to give an impression of pursuing a policy hostile to the Axis.[28]

In late May Gafencu informed Britain and France of the importance of maintaining Balkan Entente independence from the Great Powers. Resisting British attempts to draw Romania and the Balkan Entente into a mutual assistance system, Gafencu pointed out that relations between the Balkan Entente countries and the West should not be deepened beyond the unilateral Anglo-French guarantees to Romania and Greece.[29]

During his visit to Ankara on 12 June, Gafencu sought to persuade the Turkish foreign minister, Saracoğlu, to ensure the exclusion of paragraph 6 of the Anglo-Turkish declaration from the final accord. This would ensure that there would be no reference to the Balkan Entente or Balkan security.[30] Speaking afterwards to von Papen, German minister in Turkey, Gafencu said he now hoped that paragraph 6 would be excluded from the final Anglo-Turkish accord. He also assured von Papen that he was endeavouring to get paragraph 6 deleted from the forthcoming Franco-Turkish declaration.[31]

Unfortunately for Gafencu, the Franco-Turkish declaration for mutual assistance in the Mediterranean published on 24 June not only included article 3, which obliged Turkey to help Britain and France in the execution of their guarantees to Romania and Greece, but also paragraph 6 to ensure stability in the Balkans. It thus caused considerable difficulties for Romania in her relations with Germany. Although the Turkish government claimed that the declaration left the independence of the Balkan Entente untouched, neither Gafencu nor German officials were entirely convinced.[32] An angry Fabricius said he feared that Gafencu was being drawn into the western security system, albeit against his will, and that it was 'high time that he should at last publicly define his attitude towards us'.[33]

Tension between Germany and Romania became worse a few days later after the German minister in Turkey, von Papen, informed Fabricius that Britain wished to have a pledge of Turkish support to help defend Romania's Balkan borders included in the final accord between Turkey and the western powers. As a result of this, Fabricius accused the Romanians of having finally entered the British 'encirclement' policy against Germany. Gafencu tried to defend his country's position by arguing that Britain had not asked Turkey for a new guarantee of Romania's frontiers but simply to help Britain in the execution of the April Anglo-French guarantee. This was in any case only applicable if Romania was attacked and defended herself with arms. Hence, Gafencu argued, if there was no aggression against Romania, the whole system would not have to come into force. He repeated his wish for a German guarantee.[34] Following these discussions, King Carol ordered Ambassador Tătărescu in Paris to inform the French and British governments that the proposals for their final treaty with Turkey was 'uncomfortable' for Romania.[35]

Despite Gafencu's protestations, the Germans remained suspicious of Romanian intentions. Articles in the German press began to come out in support of Bulgarian revisionist claims. On 12 July Fabricius used this to exert further pressure on Gafencu. The Reich's friendly attitude towards Romania had not changed, Fabricius explained, but any allusion to Romanian security in the final accord between Turkey and the West could leave the impression that Romania had entered the British sphere of influence. Gafencu replied that Romania had taken no pledge to support any action against Germany and again hinted at Romania's willingness to receive a guarantee from Germany.[36]

The treaty between Britain, France and Turkey was finally signed on 19 October, after the outbreak of the war in Europe. The treaty included article 3 but excluded paragraph 6.[37] Gafencu repeated to Fabricius, who had complained about the inclusion of article 3, that it referred to the unilateral Anglo-French guarantees to Romania and Greece of which Germany was already aware. As such, these were not new obligations but simply the affirmation of pledges taken well before the start of the war. The accord, therefore, did not affect Romania's neutral status. Nevertheless, Fabricius maintained that the Reich feared that an anti-German eastern front was being created with Romanian help.[38] In an attempt to ensure the Germans that Romania had not entered the British camp, Minister President Călinescu officially informed Fabricius that in the event of a British occupation of the oilfields, Romania would defend herself against the British with arms.[39] The Romanians, however, remained under German pressure. On 20 October Fabricius demanded, albeit unsuccessfully, that Romania renounce the Anglo-French guarantee.[40]

Unfortunately for the Romanians, increasing tension with Germany with regard to the Anglo-Turkish treaty had coincided with diplomatic changes in Eastern Europe which made it even more necessary for Romania to retain German goodwill. The signing of the Nazi–Soviet Pact on 23 August was greeted with alarm in Romania, and led to an increasing sense of political and military isolation from the West.[41] It was clear that Germany and the Soviet Union were now the undisputed arbiters of the fate of Eastern Europe. In particular, the Romanians feared that under the terms of the pact, Germany and the Soviet Union had come to an agreement over Bessarabia, whereby Germany would agree to the seizure of the province as the price of Soviet friendship. At the same time, the likelihood of a large-scale European war made the possibility of western military aid to Romania increasingly remote owing to the country's strategic position. The Romanian government continued to hope that by maintaining German goodwill, the Reich would be prepared to act as an arbiter with, and possibly even as a barrier against, the Soviet Union.[42]

In their discussions of the Nazi–Soviet Pact with German officials both Gafencu and Minister President Călinescu pointed out that, over the years, Romanian foreign ministers had remained true to their pledges to German leaders not to enter into any alliances or agreements with the Soviet Union. They claimed that as a direct result of this, Romania had not concluded a non-aggression pact with the Soviets. Romanian politicians thus now sought to use the previous unofficial pledges of neutrality they had given to German leaders as leverage to try to win German support for the maintenance of Romania's territorial integrity.

As Gafencu hinted to the German air attaché, Gerstenberg, on 29 August, Romania had been loyal towards Germany and he hoped that 'we will not have to suffer the consequences of this loyalty'.[43]

Gafencu also tried to influence German officials in Romania's favour by arguing that it was strategically necessary to Germany that Romania should remain in her present borders. In his discussions with the German chargé d'affaires, Stelzer, on 23 August, Gafencu pointed out that a powerful, independent Romania was necessary to the Reich in order to keep the mouth of the Danube free and open to German shipping.[44] This was an argument that was to be constantly repeated by the Romanians in their discussions with German leaders and officials over the coming months.

Despite the increasing importance of the Reich for Romania in the late summer of 1939, the Romanian government was still faced with a problem of how to define its diplomatic position once war broke out between Germany and the West on 3 September. Many in the government feared that a formal declaration of neutrality might jeopardise Romania's right to invoke western help under the Anglo-French guarantee. Many also believed that Britain, with the resources of her empire, could ultimately emerge victorious over the Germans. An official Romanian declaration of neutrality might compromise Romania's position at any future peace conference.[45] The Romanian government's desire to maintain the policy of equilibrium between the Great Powers thus suggested a cautious attitude towards an official declaration of neutrality. At the same time, Romanian politicians continued to give the Germans many unofficial indications of Romania's neutrality in the event of war, while, initially at least, resisting German pressure for an official declaration. On 27 August, Gafencu assured Fabricius of Romanian neutrality in the event of a German–Polish war, even if the western powers were to intervene. A Bulgarian or Hungarian attack alone would force Romania out of her neutrality. Romania would also continue to fulfil her economic pledges to the Reich.[46] The following day, Carol gave assurances to air attaché Gerstenberg to the effect that he had no formal alliance with the British. Carol also claimed he had rejected British plans to sabotage the oilfields in the event of war. He promised Gerstenberg that he would give the Reich 'tangible proofs' of Romania's neutrality.[47]

Carol subsequently decided to send the pro-German industrialist Ion Gigurtu to Berlin to explain to the Germans that Romania would remain true to her unofficial declarations of neutrality and her economic pledges.[48] By 6 September, however, the Romanian government had decided on a formal declaration of neutrality. The rethinking of Romania's public position caused Ion Gigurtu's trip to Berlin to be delayed from 3 to 9 September.[49] The exact reason for Romania's change of policy is unclear. Doubtless, Yugoslavia's formal declaration of neutrality on 5 September affected Romania's position on the issue. At the same time, Hungarian forces had been positioned on the Romanian border and a Hungarian attack on Romania seemed increasingly likely. On 5 September, Ribbentrop intervened in Budapest, warning the Hungarians not to attack Romania under any circumstances.[50] It may well be that this show of support for Romania by the Reich encouraged Romania to give the formal declaration of neutrality which Germany required.[51] On 6 September the Crown Council voted for formal neutrality. Nevertheless, there were voices which favoured a pro-German orientation and the question of a possible German guarantee was again raised.[52]

On 9 September, Gigurtu arrived in Berlin and transmitted the king and government's decision to observe strict neutrality to members of the German foreign ministry. Gigurtu tried to convince German officials that Romanian neutrality had in fact been agreed two weeks before the outbreak of war and that Romania's favourable attitude towards Germany had begun some three to four years previously. Romania, Gigurtu claimed, was now bound to the Reich as a result of changes in the international situation or, as he put it, 'through the power of events'.[53]

In view of the growing fears in the Romanian government that the Soviet Union and Germany had come to an agreement on the annexation of Bessarabia, Gigurtu stressed both to Field Marshal Göring and German foreign ministry officials that Germany had need of Romania in her current borders both for defensive and economic reasons. In other words, Greater Romania was necessary to provide Germany with economic provisions and to act as a powerful, neutral buffer state between Germany and the Soviet Union at the mouth of the Danube. Gigurtu also alluded to the negative effects which Hungarian and Bulgarian revisionism could have on the stability of the region.[54] During his discussion with Göring on 9 September, Gigurtu also placed great emphasis on Romania's need for a powerful Germany in order to protect her against Soviet revisionism.[55]

Romanian fears of Soviet military intervention in Romania were greatly increased by the Soviet entry into Poland which began on 17 September and the subsequent massing of Soviet troops on the Romanian border.[56] The defeat and partition of Poland and the consequent worthlessness of the Polish–Romanian treaty, meant that Romania had no ally to help her against an attack by the Soviets. It was now clear to the

Romanian government that the Soviets were a greater threat to Romanian security than the Germans. Even Călinescu, who had long regarded the Reich as at least as much of a danger as the Soviets, noted in his diary for 19 September that 'the march forward of the Russians changes the situation. The German danger is fading. We must turn around our military positions and concentrate our troops in the Siret valley.'[57]

The extent to which the Soviet Union's military presence on the Polish–Romanian border affected the Romanian government's perception of Germany as its potential protector, was starkly revealed in a request made by Gafencu to Fabricius following the Soviet entry into Poland. Gafencu indicated that his government had hoped that Polish territory adjoining the Romanian frontier would be occupied by the Germans rather than the Soviets. Since this had not taken place, Gafencu enquired whether the German government would be disposed to set up a buffer state, in the form of an independent Ukraine, as a barrier between Romania and the enlarged Soviet Union.[58] During his final meeting with German foreign ministry officials in Berlin, Ion Gigurtu expressed his government's fears that the Soviet invasion of Poland would lengthen the Romanian–Soviet border. He also requested the creation of a common German–Romanian border in occupied Poland.[59] Germany's importance as a possible protector against the Soviets now even brought the Romanians into potential difficulties with the western powers. Late in September, the French ambassador to Bucharest informed Gafencu that France's aim in the present war was the complete defeat of Germany. Gafencu replied that, 'France has [therefore] set herself to the contrary of Romania's interests. For if Germany is destroyed, bolshevism will come to Central Europe and Romania will be lost.'[60]

In view of the Soviet threat, the Romanian government was prepared to make a number of new economic concessions to the Germans. In mid-August, Minister President Călinescu had already intervened personally to ensure the flow of petroleum to Germany. This had previously been stalled as a result of German delays with arms deliveries.[61] Following the outbreak of war, Călinescu was prepared to make even greater concessions. On 16 September he asked Germany to supply Romania with large quantities of war material from surplus booty taken in Poland. In exchange, Romania would supply petroleum and grain on a larger scale than before. Călinescu was prepared to continue these supplies for several years, 'thereby contributing decisively towards meeting [German] needs in the event of a war of even several years' duration'.[62] This request formed the basis of the May 1940 'Oil for Arms' Pact, which was crucial in delivering sufficient petroleum supplies to the Reich to sustain the German war effort.[63] As with the March 1939 economic accord, it was the Romanians who made the initial proposals which resulted in this major economic concessions to the Germans. The Romanian government regarded such concessions as essential in order to retain German support against a potential Soviet threat.[64]

Călinescu's willingness to make major economic concessions to Germany renders it unlikely that high-ranking German officials connived in his murder by the Iron Guard on 21 September.[65] Indeed, there is evidence that Călinescu may have been prepared by then to make even greater concessions to the Reich in exchange for a territorial guarantee. Shortly before his death, Călinescu sent the ethnic German senator, Hans Hedrich, on a mission to Berlin. The full nature of Hedrich's 'mission' remains unclear, but according to a German source, Hedrich claimed that before his death, Călinescu had offered the German government the whole of Romania's oil production in exchange for a border guarantee.[66] While Hedrich may have exaggerated the extent of Călinescu's offer, it seems clear that Călinescu's death was hardly in the interests of the Reich. Moreover, the creation of an openly pro-German government at this stage of the war would have exposed the Romanian oilfields to possible Allied attack.

German officials, on the other hand, blamed the murder on the British secret service and Polish circles who wished to destroy Romania's neutrality policies, which Călinescu supported, in favour of Romania's entry into the war on the Allied side.[67] While this theory may be discarded, it is worth noting again that Romanian neutrality was more damaging to western interests than to those of Germany in the autumn of 1939. German sources reported Anglo-French pressure on the Romanian government in late August to force Călinescu's resignation.[68]

Although high-ranking German complicity in Călinescu's death is unlikely, the Iron Guard assassins may have had the backing of SS circles close to Heinrich Himmler. According to Radu Lobey, the director of Călinescu's cabinet, following the Nazi–Soviet Pact, many Romanians began to think in terms of reconciliation with Germany in order to ensure their influence in any future German-oriented government. Amongst these Lobey lists the court minister, Ernest Urdăreanu, the industrialist Nicolae Malaxa, Mihail Moruzov, the head of the secret police, and Gabriel Marinescu, the Bucharest police chief. According to Lobey, it was these four, together with Guardists led by Horia Sima, who had been under SS influence in Berlin, who had plotted Călinescu's death.[69] Whatever the truth of this assertion, Călinescu's actual murderers were indeed members of the Iron Guard recently returned to Romania from asylum in Germany. It was the pro-German Urdăreanu who promised German officials that the Romanian government would quieten any rumours that there was a link between Călinescu's murder and German connections with the Iron Guard.[70]

The death of Călinescu, who had been the Romanian government's most important pro-westerner up until the Soviet invasion of Poland, strengthened the position of the overt pro-Germans around the king. These had long argued that the Soviet Union was more of a danger to Romanian interests than Germany. On 25 September Court Minister Urdăreanu informed Fabricius that due to Romanian fears for Bessarabia, not only was Romania 'ready to lean more heavily towards Germany' but that 'the whole of Romania looked expectantly towards Germany'.[71] On 28 September, a new government was established under the presidency of Constantin Argetoianu.[72]

Unfortunately for the Romanians, just as they were seeking to court Germany as their protector, differences between the two countries arose owing to Romania's relations with her former Polish ally.

On 12 September, Foreign Minister Ribbentrop demanded that the Romanian government should halt the transit of all war materials passing through Romania to Poland. Two days later, the Romanian cabinet decided that while the general provisions of international law forbade Romania from preventing the passage of war materials, precautions would be taken to ensure that large amounts of war material did not reach Poland.[73]

Further complications arose over the question of Polish rights of asylum in Romania. On 14 September, under German pressure, the Romanian cabinet decided on a formula for their treatment of Polish refugees entering Romania. If the Polish government and High Command of the Army crossed into Romania, they were to be interned. If civilians wished to leave Romania for a foreign country, this could not be denied, but they were to be forbidden from any political activity whilst in Romania.[74] On the night of 17/18 September, Polish President Moscicki, together with the head of the army, Marshal Rydz Smigly, and members of the Polish government were allowed to enter Romania in flight from the Red Army.[75] In accordance with the cabinet decision of 14 September, the Romanian government interned the Polish refugees. Fabricius was, therefore, able to thank the Romanian government for what his government regarded as a clear-cut application of neutrality.[76]

Nevertheless, despite the Romanian government's pledge to intern military personnel, it became increasingly clear to the Germans that, as the weeks went by, Poles were being allowed to leave Romania. On 12 October, the German chargé d'affaires, Stelzer, complained to Cretzianu, secretary general at the foreign ministry, that numbers of Polish officers were being allowed to leave Romania for France.[77] Further tension was created by Carol's request on 11 October that Germany should give its consent for President Moscicki to leave Romania for Switzerland for health reasons. Germany was adamantly opposed to the president's departure.[78] Despite German objections, and Gafencu's promise to permit Moscicki's departure from Romania only after consultation with the Reich, the Romanian cabinet decided on 24 December 1939 to allow the president and his family to leave for Switzerland.[79] Justifying his government's action to an angry Fabricius, who threatened to leave his ministerial post, Gafencu pointed out that Moscicki had resigned office two months previously and had abstained since then from any political action. Gafencu argued that the decision to allow Moscicki to leave should be regarded solely as an act of charity.[80] Ribbentrop's anger was assuaged by the intervention of Minister Clodius, who stressed the Romanian government's loyalty in the policy of economic collaboration with Germany, 'with all the political consequences which this collaboration will bring'.[81]

Despite these isolated acts of loyalty towards its former Polish ally, the Romanian government's alliance system had effectively broken down by late 1939, making the country internationally isolated and even more dependent upon German goodwill for its survival. The Little Entente had already become effectively redundant following the 1938 Munich agreement. With the defeat and partition of Poland in September 1939, the Romanians had lost their only ally against a possible Soviet attack. The western powers, although still considered vital for Romania's future, were militarily distant following the outbreak of the European war. Additionally, the Anglo-French guarantee against an attack by Germany or her allies seemed, in view of the fate of guaranteed Poland, more or less worthless. Of Romania's pre-war alliances, the Balkan Entente alone survived and was to be the core of Gafencu's proposals for a 'bloc of neutrals' in the autumn of 1939.

Notes

1 Following the signing of the Nazi–Soviet Pact in August 1939, Foreign Minister Gafencu informed Fabricius that he wished 'to go hand in hand with [Germany]...': DGFP, D, 7, Doc. nr 361, Minister in Romania to the Foreign Ministry, Bucharest, 27 August 1939.

2 Moisuc has argued that Romania was the victim of the West's neglect of South-East Europe in 1939: see, *Diplomația României și problema apărării suverănitați și independenței naționale în perioada martie 1938–mai 1940*, Bucharest, 1971, p. 173; D. Cameron Watt has argued that Gafencu's policies in 1939 upset British plans for an anti-German bloc in the region: 'Misinformation, Misconception, Mistrust: Episodes in British Policy and the Approach of War, 1938–1939', in (eds), Michael Bentley and John Stevenson, *High and Low Politics in Modern Britain: Ten Studies*, Oxford, 1983, pp. 214–55.

3 David Britton Funderburk, *Politica Marii Britanii față de România, 1938–1940. Studii asupra stratagiei economice și politice*, Bucharest, 1983, p. 104; Dov B. Lungu, *Romania and the Great Powers, 1933–1940*, Durham and London, 1989, pp. 177–8.

4 MAE, 71/1920–1944, Dosare Speciale, Vol. 398, pp. 209–33 (221), Memorandum put together by Grigore Gafencu, 15 April 1939. See also, PRO, FO 371/C3876/3356/18, Memorandum left by the Romanian Minister following a conversation with Sir A. Cadogan on 23 March 1939.

5 Lungu, op. cit., pp. 107–8.

6 MAE, Dosare Speciale, Vol. 398, pp. 209–33 (224–5), Memorandum by Grigore Gafencu, 15 April 1939.

7 See, for example, Moisuc, *Diplomația României*, p. 176.

8 MAE, 71/România, Vol. 503, pp. 37–8, Note by Minister Gafencu, 31 March 1939.

9 MAE, 71/România, Vol. 503, pp. 86–7, Instructions given by Gafencu to Al. Cretzianu on 7 April 1939 in view of his mission to London and Paris.

10 MAE, 71/România, Vol. 503, pp. 92–3, Note on a Conversation of 11 April 1939 between Gafencu and Sir Reginald Hoare at the Foreign Ministry. According to the British version of this conversation, Gafencu stated that the western guarantees to Poland and Romania should be kept separate, and that it would be 'a good move to try, with the approval of Britain and France, for such a guarantee [from Germany] to reinforce and complete the Anglo-French declaration': PRO, FO 371/C5105/3356/18, Sir R. Hoare (Bucharest), Tel. nr 109, 11 April 1939.

11 PA, Büro des Staatssekretärs, Rumänien, Vol. 1, 11.38–1.40, German Legation in Bucharest to the Foreign Ministry, Tel. nr 156, 4 April 1939, signed Fabricius; ibid, German Legation in Bucharest to the Foreign Ministry, Tel. nr 173, 11 April 1939, signed Fabricius; DGFP, D, 5, Doc. nr 173, Minister in Romania to the Foreign Ministry, Bucharest, 7 April 1939.

12 The French had also exerted pressure on the British to guarantee Romania as the price of France's guarantee of Greece: Watt, 'Misinformation, Misconception, Mistrust', pp. 247–9.

13 Arh. St., Însemnări Zilnice, Carol II, roll 21,Vol. 8, 13 April 1939, pp. 451–2: following the receipt of the Anglo-French guarantee, Carol noted the need to retain neutrality between the Great Powers. Romania's acceptance of the guarantee cannot be seen as part of a pro-western policy on the part of the Romanian foreign ministry. The intention was to counterbalance this with a similar declaration from the Germans.

14 Arh. St., Însemnări Zilnice, Carol II, roll 21, Vol. 8, 15 April 1939, p. 453.

15 DGFP, D, 6, Doc. nr 227, Memorandum by an Official of the Foreign Minister's Secretariat. Record of the Conversation between the Reich Foreign

Minister and Gafencu, the Romanian Foreign Minister in Berlin on 18 April 1939; MAE, 71/Germania, Vol. 77, pp. 29–33, Legation in Berlin (Minister Gafencu) to the Foreign Ministry, Tel. nr 39227, 19 April 1939, signed Gafencu.
16. MAE, 71/Germania, Vol. 77, pp. 24–8, Conversation between Grigore Gafencu, Foreign Minister, and Göring on 19 April 1939.
17. DGFP, D, 6, Doc. nr 227, Memorandum by an Official of the Foreign Minister's Secretariat. Record of the conversation between the Reich Foreign Minister and Gafencu, the Romanian Minister, in Berlin on 18 April 1939; MAE, 71/Germania, Vol. 77, pp. 24–8, Conversation between Grigore Gafencu, Foreign Minister, and Göring on 19 April 1939.
18. DGFP, D, 6, Doc. nr 234, Conversation between the Führer and Gafencu in the Presence of the Reich Foreign Minister, State Secretary Meissner and the Romanian Minister, 19 April 1939; MAE, 71/Germania, Vol. 77, pp. 29–33, Legation in Berlin (Minister Gafencu) to the Foreign Ministry, Tel. nr 39227, 19 April 1939, signed Gafencu. Argetoianu noted in his diary that as well as Gafencu, Gheorghe Brătianu, Vaida-Voevod and Sidorovici, leader of the king's youth movement, the Guard of the Country (Straja Țării), also visited Berlin to attend Hitler's 50th birthday celebrations. Hitler apparently also informed Voevod that Germany would not support Hungary against Romania: Arh. St., Însemnări Zilnice, Constantin Argetoianu, Dosar nr 74, volume unnumbered but dated 10 March–25 May 1939, 21 April 1939, p. 495.
19. PA, Büro des Staatssekretärs, Rumänien, Vol. 1, 11.38–1.40, German Legation in Bucharest to the Foreign Ministry, Tel. nr 287, 7 July 1939, signed Fabricius.
20. MAE, 71/Germania, Vol. 77, pp. 45–51, Legation in Berlin, (Minister Gafencu) to the Foreign Ministry, Tel nr. 39233, 20 April 1939, signed Gafencu.
21. PRO, FO 371/C6140/3356/18, Foreign Office Minute, Visit of the Romanian Foreign Minister to London. Meeting with Lord Halifax, Secretary of State for Foreign Affairs and Sir A. Cadogan, Permanent Under-Secretary of State, 25 April 1939.
22. MAE, 71/Germania, Vol. 77, p. 95, Călinescu to the Romanian Embassy in Ankara, Tel. nr 27487, 29 April 1939, signed Călinescu.
23. PA, Büro des Staatssekretärs, Rumänien, Vol. 1, 11.38–1.40, German Legation in Bucharest to the Foreign Ministry, Tel. nr 215, 8 May 1939, signed Fabricius.
24. Gafencu later claimed that with regard to British efforts to link the countries of Eastern Europe with the Soviet Union: 'I was sorry I could give no effective encouragement to the efforts of Lord Halifax to consolidate the guarantees which Britain had given my country': Grigore Gafencu, *The Last Days of Europe: A Diplomatic Journey in 1939*, translated by Fletcher-Allen, London, 1947, p. 103.
25. MAE, 71/Turcia, Vol. 61, pp. 189–204 (195–8), Notes on a talk between His Majesty King Carol II and His Excellency The President of the Republic of Turkey, Ismet Inönu, Istanbul, 14 August 1939.
26. Funderburk, *Politica Marii Britanii față de România*, p. 147; DGFP, D, 6, Doc. nr 513, Ambassador in Turkey to the Foreign Ministry, Ankara, 12 June 1939.
27. MAE, 71/Germania, Vol. 77, pp. 127–8, Embassy in Belgrade to the Foreign Ministry, Tel. nr 1695, 16 May 1939, signed Cadere.

28 MAE, Înțelegerea Balcanică, Vol. 7, pp. 147–8, Gafencu to the Romanian Legation in Ankara, Tel. nr 29349, 8 May 1939, signed Gafencu; ibid, pp. 227–31, Text of talks held between Marcović and Gafencu at Orsova, 21 May 1939.
29 MAE, Înțelegerea Balcanică, Vol. 7, pp. 168–73, 20 May 1939, Instructions given by Minister Gafencu to Alexandru Cretzianu, Secretary General at the Ministry of Foreign Affairs, regarding conversations to take place in Geneva with Lord Halifax and Mr Bonnet during the May session of the Council.
30 MAE, Înțelegerea Balanică, Vol. 7, pp. 265–8, From Minister Gafencu in Istanbul, unnumbered telegram, 14 June 1939, signed Gafencu.
31 PA, Büro des Staatssekretärs, Rumänien, Vol. 1, 11.38–1.40, Minister in Ankara to the Foreign Ministry, Tel. nr 189, 12 June 1939, signed von Papen; the German minister believed 'that Gafencu has conducted himself here in accordance with our expectations'.
32 MAE, Înțelegerea Balcanică, Vol. 7, pp. 312–13, Embassy in Ankara to the Foreign Minister, Tel. nr 39350, 24 June 1939, signed Stoica.
33 DGFP, D, 6, Doc. nr 567, Minister in Romania to the Foreign Ministry, Bucharest, 25 June 1939.
34 MAE, 71/Germania, Vol. 77, p. 200, Note of a conversation held on 4 July between Minister Gafencu and German Minister Fabricius in the Foreign Ministry; PA, Büro des Staatssekretärs, Rumänien, Vol. 1, 11.38–1.40, German Legation in Bucharest to the Foreign Ministry, Tel. nr 287, 7 July 1939, signed Fabricius.
35 PA, Büro des Staatssekretärs, Rumänien, Vol. 1, 11.38–1.40, German Legation in Bucharest to the Foreign Ministry, Tel. nr 294, 11 July 1939, signed Fabricius.
36 MAE, 71/Germania, Vol. 77, pp. 206–8, Note on a conversation of 12 July 1939 between Minister Gafencu and German Minister Fabricius at the Ministry of Foreign Affairs.
37 Article 3 of the Treaty stated: 'so long as the guarantees given by France and the UK to Greece and Romania by their respective declarations of 13 April 1939 remain in force, Turkey will cooperate effectively with France and the UK and will lend them all aid and assistance in her power…': DGFP, D, 8, Doc. nr 296, Memorandum by the Director of the Political Dept, Berlin, 24 October 1939.
38 MAE, 71/1939 E9, Vol. 92 (-71/1939 E9 II 1-), pp. 52–5, To the Legation in Berlin, Tel. nr 66022, 20 October 1939, signed Gafencu.
39 PA, Deutsche Gesandschaft Bukarest, IA 4, Vol. 6, 1939–1940, German Legation in Bucharest to the Foreign Ministry, Tel. nr 768, 19 October 1939, no signature.
40 Arh. St., Însemnări Zilnice, Carol II, roll 22, Vol. 10, Friday 20 October 1939, p. 39.
41 Florin Constantiniu, *Între Hitler și Stalin. România și Pactul Ribbentrop–Molotov*, Bucharest, 1991, p. 87.
42 Armin Heinen has pointed out that following the Nazi–Soviet Pact, the Romanian government was increasingly inclined to turn to the Germans for support, believing that the Reich was in control of Romania's fate: 'Der Hitler–Stalin-Pakt und Rumänien', in (ed.) Erwin Oberländer, *Hitler–Stalin-Pakt 1939. Das Ende Ostmitteleuropas?*, Frankfurt, 1989, pp. 98–113.

43 MAE, 71/Germania, Vol. 77, pp. 307–9, Note on a conversation of 29 August 1939 between Minister Gafencu and Colonal Gerstenberg, German Military Attaché, at the Foreign Ministry. On 31 August, Călinescu also informed Fabricius that it was out of loyalty to Germany that Romania had been prevented from signing a non-aggression pact with the Soviets: ibid, pp. 314–18, Interview between the Minister President and Fabricius at the Presidential Council, 31 August 1939.
44 MAE, 71/Germania, Vol. 77, pp. 273–6, Note on a Conversation of 23 August 1939 between Minister Gafencu and Stelzer, German Chargé d'Affaires, at the Foreign Ministry.
45 Lungu, *Romania and the Great Powers*, p. 197; Gh. Zaharia, 'Cu privire la politica externă a României în prima etapă a celui de-al doilea război mondial', *Analele institutului de studii istorice și social-politice de pe lîngă C. C. al P.C.R.*, 12, nr 5, (1966). pp. 73–5.
46 DGFP, D, 7, Doc. nr 361, Minister in Romania to the Foreign Ministry, Bucharest, 27 August 1939. As early as March 1936, the then minister to Berlin, Comnen, had told Rosenberg that Romania would remain neutral in any future clash between Poland and Germany: Seppo Kuusisto, *Alfred Rosenberg in der nationalsozialistischen Aussenpolitik, 1933–1939*, Helsinki, 1984, p. 225. On 6 May 1939, Carol informed Fabricius that, provided she was not herself attacked, Romania would remain neutral in any war. A few weeks later, Călinescu assured Fabricius that Romania was prepared to fulfil her economic obligations. 'Even in the event of possible hostilities', Călinescu confirmed that Romania 'would fulfil her obligations to Germany under long-term delivery agreements, as she would remain absolutely neutral in a possible conflict'. For this information, see MAE, 71/Germania, Vol. 77, pp. 98–9, Embassy in Belgrade to the Foreign Ministry, Tel. nr 1463, 30 April 1939, signed Cadere; PA, Büro des Staatssekretärs, Rumänien, Vol. 1, 11.38–1.40, German Legation in Bucharest to the Foreign Ministry, Tel. nr 213, 6 May 1939, signed Fabricius; DGFP, D, 6, Doc. nr 376, Minister in Romania to the Foreign Ministry, Bucharest, 13 May 1939. Far from wanting Romania to become a potential pro-Axis belligerent, which would expose her oilfields to western bombing, the Reich seems to have continued to regard Romanian neutrality as compatible with its interests in 1939: C. A. Macartney and A. W. Palmer, *Independent Eastern Europe*, London, 1962, p. 407.
47 DGFP, D, 7, Doc. nr 386, Minister in Romania to the Foreign Ministry, Bucharest, 28 August 1939.
48 Arh. St., Însemnări Zilnice, Carol II, roll 21,Vol. 8, Thursday 31 August 1939, p. 581.
49 PA, Büro des Staatssekretärs, Rumänien, Vol. 1, 11.38–1.40, German Legation in Bucharest to the Foreign Ministry, Tel. nr 424, 2 September 1939, signed Fabricius; MAE, 71/Germania, Vol. 78, p. 12, Legation in Berlin to the Foreign Ministry, Tel. nr 39484, 9 September 1939, signed Crutzescu.
50 Frank Marzari, 'Some Factors Making for Neutrality in the Balkans in August-September 1939', *East European Quarterly*, 3, nr 2, (1969), pp. 179–99 (199).
51 Gheorghe Tătărescu later pointed out that Romania had declared formal neutrality because 'Romania cannot engage in battle other than for her own interests. Romanian blood cannot flow except for national interests':

Gheorghe Tătărescu, *Mărturii pentru istorie*, (ed.) Sanda Tătărescu-Negropontes, Bucharest, 1996, p. 235.

52 Chief amongst the advocates of a pro-German orientation were Argetoianu and Vaida-Voevod. Fabricius's report of the meeting seems to suggest that the Council was divided on the question of orientation and that it was Carol's vote in favour of official neutrality which decided the matter: PA, Büro des Staatssekretärs, Rumänien, Vol. 1, 11.38–1.40, German Legation in Bucharest, Tel. nr 469, 7 September 1939, signed Fabricius; MAE, 71/România, Vol. 7, pp. 172–80, Meeting of the Crown Council, Cotroceni, convened by His Majesty, 6 September 1939.

53 MAE, 71/Germania, Vol. 78, pp. 21–5, Legation in Berlin to the Foreign Ministry, Tel. nr 39491, 11 September 1939, signed Crutzescu; PA, Büro des Staatssekretärs, Rumänien, Vol. 1, 11.38–1.40, Note, Berlin, 19 September 1939, signed Woermann; MAE, 71/Germania, Vol. 78, pp. 97–99, Memorandum, signed Gigurtu, Bucharest, 25 September 1939.

54 MAE, 71/Germania, Vol. 78, p. 89, *Hamburger Fremdenblatt*, Sunday 23 September 1939; ibid, pp. 97–9, Memorandum, signed Gigurtu, Bucharest, 25 September 1939.

55 MAE, 71/Germania, Vol. 78, pp. 21–5, Legation in Berlin to the Foreign Ministry, Tel. nr 39491, 11 September 1939, signed Gigurtu.

56 Florin Constantiniu, *Între Hitler și Stalin*. p. 88.

57 Armand Călinescu, *Însemnări Politice, 1916–1939*, (ed.) Al. Gh. Savu, Bucharest, 1990, 19 September 1939, p. 432.

58 PA, Büro des Staatssekretärs, Rumänien, Vol. 1, 11.38–1.40, From the German Legation in Bucharest to the Foreign Ministry, Tel. nr 601, 20 September 1939, signed Fabricius.

59 PA, Büro des Staatssekretärs, Rumänien, Vol. 1, 11.38–1.40, Note, Berlin, 19 September, signed Woermann.

60 PA, Büro des Staatssekretärs, Rumänien, Vol. 1, 11.38–1.40, German Legation in Bucharest to the Foreign Ministry, Tel. nr 667, 29 September 1939, signed Fabricius.

61 MAE, 71/Germania, Vol. 77, pp. 273–6, Note on a conversation held on 23 August 1939 between Minister Gafencu and Stelzer, German Chargé d'Affaires, at the Foreign Ministry.

62 DGFP, D, 8, Doc. nr 74, Minister in Romania to the Foreign Ministry, Bucharest, 16 September 1939.

63 Lungu, *Romania and the Great Powers*, p. 199.

64 British representatives in Bucharest noted that 'Soviet military intervention has tended to weaken Romania's will or ability to resist German [economic] pressure': PRO, FO 371/R8883/247/39, From the Bucharest Chancery to the Southern Department, 16 October 1939.

65 For this argument, see for example, Alexandru Cretzianu, *The Lost Opportunity*, London, 1957, pp. 32–3.

66 Arh. St., S.U.A., roll 39, frame 1786358, Note, AUSL, nr 9492/39g, 22 September 1939. The author has been unable to establish the location of the original document, but believes it is held at the Bundesarchiv – Militärarchiv, Freiburg i. Br.; MAE, 71/Germania, Vol. 78, p.84, From the Legation in Berlin, Tel. nr 39531, 22 September 1939, signed Crutzescu.

67 PA, Büro des Staatssekretärs, Rumänien, Vol. 1, 11.38–1.40, DNB Representative, nr 262, 21 September 1939; ibid, German Legation in Bucharest to the Foreign Ministry, Tel. no nr, 21 September 1939, signed Fabricius.
68 Arh. St., S.U.A., roll 39, frame 1786413, AUSL. Chef Amtsge. nr 8870/39g Ausl. Ic., Foreign Policy and Military News, 23 August 1939. The author has been unable to establish the location of the original document, but believes it is held at the Bundesarchiv – Militärarchiv, Freiburg i. Br.
69 Radu Lobey, 'Un Asasinat Uitat', *Le Monde*, 21–22 September 1969, in *Cine a fost Armand Călinescu. Mărturii*, no editor, Bucharest, 1992, pp. 125–8.
70 DGFP, D, 7, Doc. nr 120, Minister in Romania to the Foreign Ministry, Bucharest, 22 September 1939; PA, Politische Abteilung IV: Po 5, Vol. 5, 2.39–6.40, German Legation in Bucharest to the Foreign Ministry, unnumbered telegram, 22 September 1939, signed Fabricius.
71 PA, Büro des Staatssekretärs, Rumänien, Vol. 1, 11.38–1.40, German Legation in Bucharest to the Foreign Ministry, Tel. nr 636, 25 September, signed Fabricius.
72 According to the Swiss minister to Bucharest, Argetoianu's appointment represented 'a victory for Germany': *Cine a fost Armand Călinescu*, p. 157.
73 DGFP, D, 8, Doc. nr 55, Foreign Minister to the Legation in Romania, Berlin, 12 September 1939; ibid, Doc. nr 64, Minister in Romania to the Foreign Ministry, Bucharest, 14 September 1939.
74 DGFP, D, 8, Doc. nr 64, Minister in Romania to the Foreign Ministry, Bucharest, 14 September 1939.
75 Gheorghe Zaharia, 'România în preajma și la începutul celui de-al doilea război mondial', in (ed.) Viorica Moisuc, *Probleme de politică externă a României, 1918–1940*, Bucharest, 1977, pp. 388–426 (404–8).
76 DGFP, D, 8, Doc. nr 100, An Official of the Foreign Minister's Secretariat to the Legation in Romania, Berlin, 19 September 1939.
77 MAE, 71/Germania, Vol. 78, pp. 138–40, Note of a conversation of 12 October 1939 between Al. Cretzianu, Secretary General, and Stelzer, Counsellor at the German Legation, at the Foreign Ministry. Apparently, Polish officers were being issued with passports at the Polish embassy in Bucharest. Officers were leaving for France through Yugoslavia and Greece. According to Zaharia, 100,000 Poles were given transit through Romania, of whom 60,000 were officers. For this information see, Gheorghe Zaharia, 'România în preajma și la începutul celui de-al doilea război mondial', in (ed.) Moisuc, *Probleme de politică externă a României*, pp. 388–426.
78 DGFP, D, 8, Doc. nr 100, An Official of the Foreign Minister's Secretariat to the Legation in Romania, Berlin, 19 September 1939, footnote.
79 DGFP, D, 8, Doc. nr 488, Minister in Romania to the Foreign Ministry, Bucharest, 24 December 1939.
80 MAE, 71/Germania, Vol. 78, pp. 239–41, To the Legation in Berlin, Tel. nr 80051, 26 December 1939, signed Gafencu.
81 DGFP, D, 8, Doc. nr 491, Foreign Minister to the Legation in Romania, Berlin, 28 December 1939; MAE, 71/Germania, Vol. 78, p. 243, To Legation in Berlin, Tel. nr 80105, 28 December 1939, signed Gafencu; ibid, pp. 248–50, Legation in Berlin to the Foreign Ministry, Tel. nr 39697, 29 December 1939, signed Crutzescu.

5
Germany's Transformation to a 'Fairy Godmother', Autumn 1939 to June 1940[1]

Despite Romania's declaration of official neutrality on 6 September 1939, the following months were to see the Romanian government increasingly regarding Germany as the counterweight to growing Soviet influence in the Balkans. King Carol's plan to mediate between Germany and the West in the autumn of 1939 was conceived in the hope of a quick end to the war in Europe. Carol hoped that Germany and the western countries would then be free to stand together against further bolshevik expansion. With the failure of these peace plans, the Romanian government became involved in schemes for a 'Balkan bloc' and a 'bloc of neutrals' in South-East Europe during the autumn of 1939. The Romanians believed that through such blocs they would convince Germany, suspicious of Romanian links with the West, of the genuineness of Romania's neutrality. Carol's government also envisaged that these blocs would create a barrier to German, and more importantly, to Soviet encroachments into South-East Europe. With the Soviet Union now in occupation of Polish territory bordering Romania, King Carol and his government regarded the Soviets as a threat not only to Romania's territorial integrity, but also to her monarchical system. The Soviets were thus regarded as a far greater danger to Romania than the Germans who had no territorial claims on Romania and whose favour could be maintained by economic concessions.

Since the mid-1930s, Carol had hoped for a reconciliation between Germany and the West, which would ensure that Romania would not be forced to choose between either power bloc. Since Carol regarded bolshevism as the greatest danger to Romania and Europe, he continued to hope for peace between the Reich and the western powers during the early months of the war. He was thus heartened by the peace proposals put to the West by Hitler on 27 September 1939, despite the fact that Hitler demanded recognition of a German sphere of influence in South-East Europe.[2] In mid-October Carol recorded in his diary that 'the best international solution today would be a provisional peace between the allies and Germany and a change of front against the communist danger, because if Germany is defeated and the Soviets advance into Europe it will bring about the destruction of our European civilization and the capitalist-bourgeois countries'.[3]

Carol was disappointed by Neville Chamberlain's rejection of Hitler's peace plans. Consequently, Carol tried to prompt other neutral states to intervene between the powers and made contact with the neutral Belgian government with this aim in mind.[4] Carol was encouraged by offers of mediation by the kings of Belgium and the Netherlands and by George VI's offer to accept any proposals leading to a 'just peace'. On 13 November, Carol indicated to Fabricius that he had himself decided to act as a mediator for peace between the West and Germany. The following day, Carol sent Fabricius by plane to Berlin with his offer of mediation and a request to Hitler to put forward his proposals. The German minister believed that Carol was motivated more by fear of the Soviet Union than by attachment to the West. 'If Germany should be engaged in a long war with the western powers', wrote Fabricius to the foreign ministry, 'Romania will fall victim to the aspirations of the Soviet Union which, for the king, would signify the loss of his throne.' With Hitler's refusal of Carol's offer of mediation, however, the war seemed set to continue.[5]

Simultaneously with Carol's plans for peace between Germany and the West, the Romanian foreign ministry became involved in plans for the creation of a bloc of neutral states in South-East Europe.[6] The Romanians hoped that the Soviet Union would not be disposed to attack a Romania at peace with her revisionist Hungarian and Bulgarian neighbours and protected by a bloc which had the backing of Italy, and possibly also of Germany and Britain.[7]

The initial plan for a Balkan bloc was motivated by Romanian fears that Bulgarian revisionist claims might be exploited by the Soviet Union. The Balkan bloc was to include the Balkan Entente countries, together with Bulgaria, under Italian leadership. On 19 September 1939, Gafencu and the Yugoslav Foreign Minister, Marcović, decided to invite Bulgaria to join the Balkan Entente. Bulgaria was to assume the obligations which this entailed, in exchange for receiving a certain amount of territory from each Balkan Entente country.[8]

Gafencu's intention was to consolidate this enlarged Balkan Entente under Italian leadership. On 21 September, in the wake of the Soviet occupation of Polish territory, Gafencu announced to the Italian government in Rome his wish for an Italian-led, anti-bolshevik bloc. The neutral Balkan countries, Gafencu told the Italians, looked to Italy to protect them against the Soviet danger. Both Mussolini and the Germans initially welcomed the plan. Mussolini was flattered by the idea of being the leader of a neutral South-East Europe, while the Germans saw an Italian-led Balkan bloc as a means to prevent the opening of a second front in the Balkans.[9]

The initial Balkan bloc scheme, however, foundered on Bulgaria's refusal to enter the Balkan Entente. With the European diplomatic situation in such a state of flux, the prospect of large-scale territorial revision had become a distinct possibility. The Bulgarian government had no wish to see its room for manoeuvre limited by joining the Balkan Entente.[10]

Nevertheless, Romanian schemes to draw the countries of South-East Europe into a bloc of neutral states under Italian leadership continued. On 14 October, Carol recorded in his diary that closer links between Romania and Italy were regarded favourably by both Germany and Britain. At this stage, the king still entertained hopes of peace between the Reich and Britain and envisaged their joint backing for an Italian-led bloc in South-East Europe.[11] From mid-October 1939, the Romanian government was also concerned to draw Hungary, as well as Bulgaria and Italy, into the new configuration. A new plan drawn up by Gafencu in late October for an Italian-led bloc of neutrals was thus to comprise the Balkan Entente countries, along with Bulgaria and Hungary. Gafencu hoped that, despite the failure of the initial Balkan bloc, Italian leadership would draw in revisionist Hungary and Bulgaria.[12] The overriding considerations in Gafencu's new plan for a bloc of neutrals was not only the need to create a bulwark against Soviet expansion but also to conciliate Germany. The latter was particularly necessary as the publication of the Anglo-Turkish treaty on 19 October 1939 had created tension between Germany and Romania.

On 20 October, Fabricius complained to Gafencu about the inclusion of article 3 in the Anglo-Turkish treaty which obliged Turkey to help Britain and France if these were called on to execute their guarantees to Greece and Romania. This, claimed Fabricius, meant that an eastern front was being created against Germany and that Turkey was, therefore, no longer a neutral. Following this discussion, Gafencu informed the German foreign ministry that the Romanian government's intention was to create an independent, neutral bloc in South-East Europe. In order to reassure Germany that Turkey continued to be a neutral country, Gafencu confirmed that Turkey would be part of the bloc.[13] The bloc of neutrals was thus, in part, an attempt by Gafencu to conciliate Germany and to distance the Balkan Entente countries from the British policy of 'encirclement' of Germany, which Reich officials believed the Anglo-Turkish treaty represented. The Romanian government hoped that by conciliating the Reich in this way, it could enlist Germany in Romania's defence against the Soviet Union.

Unfortunately, Mussolini chose to reject Italian leadership of any bloc of neutrals. On 17 October, he decided that Italian neutrality was not in keeping with the country's status as a Great Power. Although Italy confirmed this position to the Germans on 16 November, she did not officially inform the Balkan countries of her decision for a full month.[14] Romania, therefore, continued her attempts to set up the bloc of neutrals despite Italian indifference and growing German doubts.

On 30 October, Gafencu unveiled the details of his proposed project for a bloc of neutrals.[15] The scheme, however, immediately ran into problems. On 2 November, the Romanian embassy in Ankara reported that Turkey herself, the main object of the bloc, was undecided as to whether to join. Greece no longer regarded her Turkish ally as a true neutral, while Yugoslavia feared she would be forced to make territorial concessions to Italy and Hungary. Meanwhile, Hungary and Bulgaria regarded satisfaction of their revisionist claims as a prerequisite for joining the bloc.[16]

German hostility to the plan was also hardening in the wake of Italy's decision not to lead the bloc. On 7 November the German minister in Turkey, von Papen, informed the Romanian ambassador to Turkey, Stoica, that the bloc could only go ahead if Turkey were excluded and its members did not follow Anglo-French policy.[17] On 23 November, Bossy, the Romanian ambassador to Rome, reported a conversation with his German counterpart, Mackensen. The latter regarded the bloc as being directed against Germany, since Turkey was 'playing the game of the West'. As Hungary, Bulgaria and Italy had no wish to join the bloc, Mackensen believed it would be best 'if the question were buried'.[18] Bowing to German wishes, Gafencu informed Fabricius on 28 November that 'knowing now that Italy and Germany did not welcome the neutral bloc, he was withdrawing his proposals'.[19]

The outbreak of the Soviet–Finnish 'Winter War' at the end of November offered further evidence of Soviet expansionist tendencies and renewed Gafencu's determination to build up a bloc of neutrals against possible Soviet expansion into South-East Europe.[20] Moreover, since Romania had still not received official notification of the Italian decision not to lead the bloc, Gafencu continued to try to coax the Italians. Gafencu hoped that Italian leadership would convince the Germans that the bloc was truly neutral and would not follow western policy. Gafencu informed the Italian chargé d'affaires on 4 December that the Romanian government had interrupted the creation of the bloc 'due to German reserves'. Romania now wished to prove that the bloc was not aimed against any country. Gafencu said that he believed that 'an action on the part of Italy would have the great advantage that it would remove any suspicions on Germany's part'.[21] Even after Italy's official refusal to lead the bloc on 16 December, it was still necessary for Count Ciano to rebuff the ever hopeful Romanians. On 30 December, Ciano informed the Romanians that since Italy had good relations with all Balkan countries, there was no need of a bloc 'which will raise suspicions in Berlin'.[22]

An additional reason for Gafencu's fervent espousal of the bloc of neutrals in the autumn of 1939 was the gradual recognition among members of the Romanian government that the Anglo-French guarantee would not operate in the event of a Soviet attack on Romania. The final text of the Anglo-Turkish treaty of 19 October contained a 'Russian clause' whereby Turkey would not have to participate in action against the Soviet Union. This meant that in the event of a Soviet attack on Romania, British and French vessels would be unable to enter the Black Sea to help Romania.[23] Clearly, the Romanian government had anticipated that the Anglo-Turkish treaty would contain such a clause. On 18 October, Weizsäcker, state secretary at the German foreign ministry, had enquired of the Romanian minister to Berlin, Radu Crutzescu, whether Britain would help Romania if she was attacked by the Soviets. Crutzescu had replied that 'in Bucharest no one speaks of the English guarantee any more'.[24]

The threat posed by the Soviet Union to Romania following the conclusion of the Anglo-Turkish treaty was pointed out by the US minister to Bucharest. The minister reported that, 'whereas the terms of the Franco-British-Turkish pact may be considered as a diplomatic defeat for Germany and as erecting a definite barrier against German aggression... it leaves the door wide open to aggression from Russia. There is no echo here of the jubilation in the allied countries over this pact... Russia presents a much greater danger to this part of the world than does Germany.' The minister went on to point out that neither Britain, France nor Turkey would be prepared to fight the Soviets for Romania. The minister concluded that unless the proposed 'Balkan–Danube bloc can be created promptly ... Russian aggression is just a question of whether and when'.²⁵ The British provided confirmation of their position on 2 November 1939, when Sir Reginald Hoare informed Gafencu that 'when we gave you the [Anglo-French] guarantee, no one could foresee an aggression on the part of the Soviet Union and today we can see no material possibility of fulfilling our guarantees against Russian aggression'.²⁶

It was therefore clear by late autumn, with Italy's refusal to lead a neutral bloc and Britain's interpretation of the Anglo-French guarantee, that Germany alone might be disposed to help Romania in her problems with the Soviet Union. During the autumn of 1939, the Romanian government became increasingly fearful of a Soviet attack on Romania in order to annex Bessarabia. The Soviet Union's re-establishment of diplomatic relations with Budapest in September 1939 and her offer of a mutual assistance pact to Bulgaria in October suggested, moreover, that the Soviet Union would support Hungarian and Bulgarian revisionism against Romania. On 12 November, Gafencu recorded in his diary that he believed the Russian advance to the Baltic and into Poland heralded a further round of expansion. He wondered whether Germany would be prepared to help Romania and, if so, under what conditions.²⁷ In December 1939, with the Soviet–Finnish war under way, Molotov proclaimed that Soviet foreign-policy was also directed towards South-East Europe and the Black Sea.²⁸ By now, the Romanian government was receiving ceaseless information regarding aggressive Soviet intentions against Romania and expected a military break-through into Bessarabia in the spring of 1940.²⁹

The Romanian foreign ministry renewed its efforts to win German support in its problems with the Soviet Union in the autumn of 1939 by stressing the Reich and Romania's common anti-bolshevism and opposition to the spread of pan-slavism. Romanian officials frequently reminded the Germans of previous conversations in which these ideological themes had been stressed. On 4 November 1939, Gafencu made it clear to Fabricius that Romania was determined to fight if the Soviet Union attacked Bessarabia. Moreover, 'it is the wish of the king and the Romanian government', said Gafencu, 'that Germany should come out of the war unweakened and strong because only a strong Germany can be a certain guarantee against bolshevism and pan-slavism, whose first victim would be Romania'.³⁰ On the same day, the Romanians unsuccessfully requested that the Germans should arrange a non-aggression pact for them with the Soviets.³¹

Over the following month, Gafencu continued to point out to Fabricius the common danger to Germany and Romania of Russian expansion.

Soviet claims on Bessarabia, Gafencu explained, were part of a plan to conquer the territories which separated the Soviet Union from the Danube Basin and the Straits. German passivity in the face of these attempts would open the road to the spread of bolshevism in the Danube Basin and would be fatal for both Romania and Germany. Gafencu reminded Fabricius of the talks to this effect which he had had in the past with German leaders.[32] A few days later, Gafencu requested German intervention in Moscow on Romania's behalf with regard to Bessarabia.[33]

News of German reactions to the Soviet claims on Bessarabia began to reach Romania in December 1939. During a conversation early that month, Fabricius admitted to Gafencu that he did not know exactly what the Soviet Union's intentions were towards Romania. If war broke out in the West, however, and German forces were deployed there, Fabricius believed it would be impossible to prevent the Soviets 'from realising some plans'. Fabricius went on to explain that in the event of the diversion of German troops to the West, and since the Reich currently had friendly relations with the Soviets, Romania would only be able to count on Germany's 'goodwill' and not on her military support against the Soviets.[34]

Yet despite Germany's acceptance of Soviet claims on Bessarabia, the Romanian legation in Berlin reported on 18 December that 'Germany has given a free hand to the Russians over Bessarabia, but will never consent to Romania falling completely under Soviet influence'.[35] Under the terms of the Nazi–Soviet Pact, the Reich had accepted Soviet interest in Bessarabia. Nevertheless, Ribbentrop had pointed out to the Soviets Germany's economic interests in the area, which implied the need for political and territorial stability in the region.[36] In wanting to prevent Soviet aggression against Romania beyond Bessarabia, German and Romanian government policies coincided and made collaboration possible. As Gheorghe Tătărescu, who replaced Constantin Argetoianu to become minister president once again on 24 November 1939, later pointed out: 'Through talks with Reich representatives, I could ascertain that Germany, although abandoning Bessarabia to the Soviet "sphere of influence", sought to avoid a Russian aggression being aimed against Romania and in this respect her political activity coincided with our political activity.'[37]

The reappointment of Tătărescu as minister president fitted well with Carol's neutrality policy. Having been minister president during the years of Titulescu's foreign ministry in the early 1930s, Gheorghe Tătărescu had been associated with Romania's previously pro-western foreign-policy line. At the same time, he had long been working for closer economic collaboration with the Reich. On 27 November, Tătărescu insisted to Fabricius that his previous appointment as ambassador to Paris did not mean that Romania was committed to a pro-western foreign-policy line. As Tătărescu explained, 'the foundation of [my] policy is that the danger which threatens Romania comes from Russia, and that the only country which can help Romania is Greater Germany ... Romania has known for a long time that the French and English guarantee has no value and that salvation comes from Germany.' Tătărescu declared to Fabricius that his intention as minister president was to support Romania's policy of official neutrality while increasing economic collaboration with Germany.[38] The new government also contained a number of ministers, known to be favourable to Germany, who were placed in key economic positions in order to further this policy. These including Ion Gigurtu as minister of public works and communication and General Gheorghe Argeşanu, who was made minister of national economics.[39]

The new Tătărescu-led cabinet had every reason to step up the rate of economic cooperation with the Reich, especially in the area of petroleum deliveries. Since September 1939, Britain had been engaged in 'economic warfare' in Romania against Germany. In particular, this meant depriving the Germans of as much petroleum as possible in order to limit Germany's capacity to continue the war. Britain had a number of means at her disposal to do so in the winter of 1939–40.

First, Britain could limit the amount of petroleum sold to Germany. Some three-quarters of Romanian petroleum production was controlled by Anglo-French capital. Romania's largest petroleum company, Astra Română, controlled by the Royal Dutch Shell Group, for instance, represented 25% of the total Romanian oil industry. In contrast, German-owned companies controlled a mere 0.86% of crude oil output.[40] German petroleum imports were, therefore, made up of surpluses produced by western-owned companies. During the early months of the war, Britain began to limit supplies sold to Germany and bulk-buy much of the surplus produced by British-owned companies in Romania. In September 1939, for example, Shell agreed to limit sales to Germany.[41] By December 1939, Britain had built her purchases up to 140,000 tons per month, while German purchases were falling sharply.[42] By November, the German foreign ministry had begun complaining to the Romanians of progressive drops in petroleum deliveries. While a minimum of 100,000 tons per month was required for the war effort, a mere 70,000 tons had been delivered in October and less that 60,000 tons in November. The German foreign ministry ordered the legation in Bucharest to come to an agreement with the Romanian government whereby Romania would commit herself to guarantee deliveries.[43]

The Germans sought to pressurise the Romanians by arguing that, as a neutral state, Romania should not tolerate the waging of economic war on its territory. The Tătărescu government responded quickly, especially as the onset of the Soviet–Finnish war on 30 November made the threat of Soviet aggression against Romania all the more plausible.[44] On 4 December, Germany became a direct participant in the Romanian oil industry by her purchase of shares in 'Petrolbloc'.[45] Two days later, Minister President Tătărescu informed the Germans that the government would guarantee German petroleum purchases of 130,000 tons per month in exchange for arms. He explained that Romania wished to have her armed forces up to strength by the early spring of 1940 when it was believed that the Soviet Union would launch an attack on Bessarabia.[46] In December, the Romanian government also imposed a quota system for petroleum sales on all countries in order to prevent Britain, in particular, from buying up huge quantities of petroleum to halt its sale to Germany.[47] Romanian policy here revealed an increasing tendency to satisfy German demands at the expense of links with the West.[48]

Another means by which the British sought to deprive Germany of petroleum was by direct sabotage of deliveries bound for the Reich. The Germans were already experiencing considerable transportation difficulties with supplies of petroleum from Romania. The British naval blockade of the Mediterranean meant that petroleum bound for Germany could no longer be transported from the Black Sea and through the Straits. Germany was thus forced to import oil via the Danube river, which was frozen during the winter of 1939–40.[49] Subsequent flooding of the oil-producing region in the spring of 1940 as the ice melted also impeded deliveries. The other means of transporting petroleum to the Reich was on Romania's primitive railway system, which consisted of a single track only between Predeal and Brașov, and was vulnerable to British sabotage. This ranged from lighting fires at oil installations to 'putting sand in the grease boxes of tank cars'.[50] In addition, the British government began a policy of chartering tugs and barges on the Danube to prevent them being used by the Germans to transport petroleum. Britain and France already owned 16% of the Danube barge fleet at the start of the war. By the end of 1939, Britain had chartered barges of the Anglo-Danubian Transport Corporation, the Yugoslav Danube fleet and the Belgian Danube fleet.[51] In February 1940, the British government set up the Goeland Transport and Trading Company in order to purchase and charter all manner of vessels on the Danube and in the Black and Aegean Seas which could possibly be used by the Germans on the Danube.[52] The German backlash against British sabotage was, however, not long in coming.

During the winter of 1939–40, the Romanian military secret service (Serviciului Special de Informații or SSI) began to collaborate with its German counterpart, the Abwehr. Links between the SSI under General Mihail Moruzov and Admiral Canaris's Abwehr had first been established in early 1937 in order to exchange information regarding the Red Army. The links were taken up again in the summer of 1939, through the mediation of the pro-German Court Minister Urdăreanu in order to counteract British sabotage of the Romanian oilfields.[53]

In the autumn of 1939 an organisation consisting of Romanian and German agents was created for security of the petroleum zone in the Prahova valley and along the course of the Danube. Agents were also recruited from amongst Romanian-speaking ethnic Germans. King Carol and Moruzov assured the free entry of German agents into Romania. Moruzov even bought an estate near Ploești to help shelter these agents. Nevertheless, despite these measures, during November and December 1939 the German legation consistently complained to the Romanian foreign ministry of acts of sabotage on petroleum trains bound for Germany. Hence, in December the Romanians agreed to militarise the oilfields to secure them from western sabotage.[54] On 7 December, the Romanian government sent motorised police units to the petroleum areas to prevent further sabotage.[55] A series of explosions in the Prahova valley in early December brought Canaris himself unexpectedly to Bucharest on Hitler's express orders to prevent sabotage.[56]

Anti-sabotage measures were strengthened by the appointment of Manfred von Killinger as inspector of German diplomatic missions in the Balkans in December 1939. His purpose was to impede the work of 'secret enemy organisations', operating in South-East Europe.[57] In addition, Hermann Neubacher, former Mayor of Vienna, was sent in January 1940 by the German foreign ministry to Bucharest as special representative for economic questions. His task was to ensure that economic agreements between the two countries were fully exploited and to counteract enemy sabotage of petroleum deliveries.[58]

It seems likely that the appointment of the pro-German Vaida-Voevod as the president of the government party, the National Renaissance Front, in January 1940 was undertaken to offset the negative impression given to the Germans by the shortfall in petroleum deliveries. It was certainly regarded as such in London where British foreign office officials questioned whether Voevod's appointment was 'not a preparation for further inclinations towards Germany'.[59]

By the spring of 1940, Romanian–German economic cooperation and anti-sabotage activities began to bear fruit. The Romanian government's agreement to the provisional 'Oil for Arms' Pact with the Reich on 6 March 1940 represented an important economic concession to the Germans at the expense of the West. Under this agreement Romania bartered 200,000 tons of oil for weapons seized by the Germans in Poland and from Czechoslovakia. The pact shattered the higher prices for petroleum which had been set by Britain in the autumn of 1939 to prevent Germany, whose foreign currency reserves were low, from buying more petroleum. The agreement thus ensured that the price for petroleum and the war materials to be exported to Romania would be calculated at pre-war prices.[60] Since the world price of petroleum was 150% above the pre-war price now secured, the deal represented a substantial gain for the Reich as well as for the Romanian government which was determined to arm against the Soviet threat.[61] This successful deal had been negotiated by Hermann Neubacher.

A major success in Romanian–German collaboration against British sabotage was the prevention of the British attempt to blow up the Iron Gates on 1 April 1940. The British had hoped thereby to make the Danube unnavigable to German barges taking petroleum to the Reich.[62] Following the incident, Carol ensured that all the materials which the British had stored on a lighter for the proposed explosion were sequestered and the British agents expelled.[63] The German foreign ministry was apparently satisfied by the loyalty shown by Romania in handling the affair.[64] In the following days, Gafencu secured the agreement of the British and French ministers to Bucharest that no further acts of sabotage would be carried out. Gafencu feared such acts could lay Romania open to German counter-measures or a Soviet attack.[65]

The Romanian government's sense of reliance on Germany increased with the conclusion of the Soviet–Finnish war on 12 March 1940 which left the Soviets free to secure their control in other areas of Eastern Europe. As Carol observed in his diary, the small countries of Eastern Europe which felt threatened by the Soviet Union were becoming increasingly sympathetic towards Germany. Carol noted that even Minister President Tătărescu, long a believer that the West would ultimately be victorious over the Reich, had come round to the view that Romanian foreign policy should be oriented towards Germany. For the time being, however, the king himself, together with Foreign Minister Gafencu, held that Romania should continue to maintain neutrality between the Great Powers.[66] In a document drawn up in late March 1940, Gafencu defended the neutralist position. Unconvinced that there would be a decisive German military victory in Europe, Gafencu believed that Romanian neutrality should be maintained in case the war was won by the West or resulted in a compromise peace. Romanian neutrality would thus give the government a stronger hand at the post-war negotiating table.[67]

While outwardly maintaining the policy of neutrality, however, the Romanian government was prepared to make even more economic concessions to Germany in the spring of 1940. In his discussion with Fabricius on 30 March, Minister President Tătărescu emphasised Romania's fear of the Soviet Union and that 'it was precisely this political consideration that had primarily caused Romania to go to the utmost limits to accommodate us in economic matters'. Following the spring thaw, the Danube river was now navigable, and Tătărescu pledged to compel British and French oil companies to fulfil deliveries of petroleum supplied to the Reich. As token of his pledge, Tătărescu confirmed that he had already assured the full quotas for April and May. Tătărescu further pointed out that Britain had been exerting great pressure on Romania to prevent deliveries of petroleum to Germany and had placed an embargo on ships carrying raw materials bound for Romania from Britain. Intervention by Tătărescu had compelled Britain to lift the embargo.[68]

As Fabricius reported to the German foreign ministry on 1 April, although there was still great sympathy for France, in 'so-called "Society"', the king and his ministers realised that protection against the Soviets could only be achieved through alignment with Germany. Fabricius added, however, that since 'for the most part this line of policy is dictated by the head and not by the heart', the policy of alignment with Germany against the Soviet Union could only be sustained 'as long as faith in the victory of German arms, or at least in the maintenance of German hegemony in Europe endures'.[69]

In early April 1940, the German army was successfully sweeping through Northern Europe. On 9 April Germany occupied Denmark and Norway. On 15 April, King Carol informed his cabinet that petroleum deliveries to Germany must be maintained regardless of any possible opposition by western-owned companies. Arrangements were also to be made to catch up with arrears created over the winter months. Court Minister Urdăreanu confirmed to Fabricius on 15 April that Romanian economic policy was entirely dictated by political concerns, for Carol believed that only a strong Germany could protect Romania from the Soviet Union.[70]

On 10 May Germany began her successful offensive in Western Europe. Carol informed Fabricius on 15 May 'that Romania's future depended solely upon Germany'. In recognition of this, the king had decided to send his childhood, pro-German, friend Romalo as the new minister to Berlin.[71] On 27 May, the day before the capitulation of neutral Belgium, the Romanian government signed the 'Oil for Arms Pact' with the Reich. The pact finalised the preliminary arrangements of the 6 March pact and ensured that German armaments and Romanian petroleum were to be exchanged at pre-war prices. As Hermann Neubacher observed, the pact finally 'frustrated the attempts of the enemy powers to throttle German petroleum purchases by extraordinary price increases. . . . '.[72] As a result of the pact, two-thirds of the petroleum from western-owned companies was now delivered to Germany.[73]

During the spring of 1940, and simultaneously with the policy of economic concessions to Germany, Carol sought reconciliation with the pro-German Iron Guard. Carol's motivations were twofold. First, Carol, like most Romanians, believed that the Guard had the full backing of the Germans. Hence, coming to terms with the Guard would serve to bring rapprochement with the Reich itself that much closer. This was especially important by late May and June 1940 when German victories in the West forced Carol to discard the policy of equilibrium in favour of open friendship and collaboration with Germany. Secondly, the Guard's inclusion in Carol's government would increase public support for his regime since the Guard was the country's most popular nationalist movement. As Carol recorded in his diary on 18 April, he believed the nationalist Guardists would 'be of use in applying their motto: God, Nation and King'.[74]

The Romanian-based Guard proved relatively easy to reconcile with Carol's regime. Their leader, Vasile Noveanu, the former Guardist leader in Arad, had been intent upon agreement with Carol as the means of saving the movement since the death of Codreanu in 1938.[75] By early March 1940, the pro-German Court Minister Urdăreanu had received a Guardist delegation willing to give a pledge of support to the king.[76] On 26 April, Carol issued an amnesty for the Guard.[77]

The most important Guardists elements had fled into exile in Germany following Carol's crackdown on the Guard after the murder of Codreanu in November 1938 and again following the assassination of Călinescu in September 1939. These were based in Berlin under the leadership of the Transylvanian Horia Sima, and proved a tougher nut to crack. A delegation from the Romanian government arrived in Berlin in early May 1940. Sima made reconciliation with Carol dependent upon a Romanian alliance with the Reich. In keeping with the foreign-policy declarations made by Codreanu in late 1937, a Guardist manifesto of 2 May claimed that only the Axis could give Romania support against Slav imperialism and Hungarian and Bulgarian revisionism.[78]

German military successes over the next few weeks were to push Carol into agreement with Guardist foreign-policy demands. On 26 May, Sima, newly returned from Germany to Romania, had a discussion with General Moruzov, head of the military secret service. Moruzov pointed out to Sima the king's desire for a change in Romania's foreign-policy position and his wish for Guardist collaboration with the regime. Between 28 May and 7 June, Sima had meeting with Guardists throughout Romania in order to bring about the final reconciliation between the movement and the government.[79]

It was the capitulation of Belgium on 28 May which brought about an official change in Romanian policy towards Germany. The Belgian policy of neutrality had provided the model for Romania's own neutrality. Belgium's failure to avoid the consequences of the war in Western Europe thus caused dismay in Romania. The king had continued to support Gafencu's neutralist viewpoint until the eve of Belgium's capitulation, in the belief that a German victory in the European war would not necessarily be final if, for instance, the United States were to enter the war.[80] The days following the Belgian capitulation witnessed a move by Carol and his government away from the policy of neutrality towards all the Great Powers in the direction of one of seeking specific political collaboration and rapprochement with the Reich. Up to now the Romanian government had largely perceived collaboration with Germany as imposing economic commitments. From late May onwards, however, collaboration was also seen in terms of strengthened political links. On the night of 27 May, as the Belgian army lay encircled by the Germans, Foreign Minister Gafencu had a discussion with Minister President Tătărescu and Court Minister Urdăreanu at which the king presided. Tătărescu and Urdăreanu argued that Romanian foreign policy should 'be adapted to realities'. They sought to convince Gafencu that Romania should make an official request in Berlin for support against the Soviet Union. Carol now supported Tătărescu and Urdăreanu against Gafencu's neutralist position. Later on the evening of 27 May, Tătărescu informed Fabricius of the government's wish for 'stronger political links with the Axis'.[81] On the following day, Minister President Tătărescu made an official declaration to Fabricius, pointing out Romania's wish for 'active collaboration with Germany in all domains'.[82]

As Manfred von Killinger, inspector of German diplomatic missions in the Balkans, reported to Berlin on 29 May during a visit to Bucharest, pro-German personalities around the king were gaining ground. These pro-German elements were now led by General Moruzov whose military secret service was collaborating with the Abwehr. Von Killinger confirmed that the task of the pro-Germans was made all the easier due to Carol's hopes that Germany would be able to restrain the Soviet Union.[83] There are even suggestions that Carol unofficially proposed a military alliance with the Reich through the mediation of General Moruzov during von Killinger's trip to Bucharest in late May.[84]

As a consequence of the change of government policy to one of 'unconditional rapprochement' with Germany, Grigore Gafencu resigned from his post as foreign minister on 1 June. He was replaced by Ion Gigurtu.[85] The appointment of Gigurtu was a reflection of the increasing pro-German orientation of Romanian foreign policy. His elevation to the foreign ministry was greeted warmly in Rome and Berlin since, in addition to his economic links with Germany, as a member of the former National Christian Party, he was known as both a nationalist and an antisemite.[86]

On 2 June, Fabricius replied to Tătărescu's 28 May declaration which had called for active Romanian–German collaboration. Fabricius suggested that in order to have 'closer friendship with Germany' Romania should make concessions to the Soviet Union on the Bessarabian question.[87]

The reaction of the Romanian government to Fabricius's suggestion, however, was to seek to ingratiate itself with the Germans. At the same time, Romanian officials continued to justify the maintenance of their country's territorial integrity by its strategic and economic importance to the Reich. The Romanians hoped that in this way they would be able to avoid any discussion of territorial claims on Romania by her neighbours, pending the 'general peace conference' which they assumed would follow the conclusion of the European war.[88]

Hence, on 3 June, Tătărescu indicated to Fabricius that he realised Romania 'would have to satisfy certain revisionist claims of her neighbours'. He went on to hint, nonetheless, at the importance for Germany of Romania within her current borders as a barrier against bolshevism. A few days later, Tătărescu and the new foreign minister, Ion Gigurtu, assured Fabricius that Romania would hold discussions with the Soviets in order to find a peaceful solution to the Bessarabian question. Romania, they claimed, would also try to come to terms with her Bulgarian and Hungarian neighbours.[89] Nevertheless, the Tătărescu government did not make an official reply to Fabricius's 2 June statement until as late as 20 June. In this reply, Tătărescu claimed that Romania was opening talks to clarify relations with the Soviets. At the same time, he once again laid stress on the importance of Romania's territorial integrity for Germany as a barrier against bolshevism through direct reference to Romania's 'mission to guard the Dneister and mouth of the Danube'.[90] Since the Dneister was the border between Romanian Bessarabia and the Soviet Union, the implication was clear: Romania had no intention of ceding any of Bessarabia. On the following day, Tătărescu informed Fabricius that Romania 'wished to return to the policy of Carol I; this meant cooperation in all fields'. If the Soviets demanded Bessarabia, however, 'Romania would have to draw [Germany's] attention to the danger thus threatening the Balkans'.[91] Meanwhile, in discussions in Berlin on 18 June, Minister Romalo informed German foreign ministry officials that Romania's 'political and economic interests drive us towards a policy of collaboration with the Reich'. Romalo went on to stress that 'any change in [Romania's] borders would weaken her economic power and hence her value to the Reich'.[92]

Indeed, only hours before the delivery of the Soviet ultimatum to Romania regarding Bessarabia on 26 June, the Romanian government was still insisting to the Germans on the importance of the country's territorial integrity.[93] As Fabricius pointed out to his ministry on 26 June, 'I have the impression that the Romanians are protracting the negotiations with the Russians in the hope of an early German victory, and because they believe that our interest in cooperation in the Danube region and peace in the South-East is so great that after ending the present war in the West, we might still after all be interested in keeping the Russians out of the Balkans.'[94]

In fact, since Fabricius's declaration of 2 June in which he had suggested that the Romanians open negotiations with the Soviets, the Romanian government had not even begun discussions with the Soviet Union on the territorial question.[95] The king was convinced that government collaboration with the Iron Guard, rather than flexibility on the Bessarabian question, was the surest way of retaining German support. He continued, therefore, to court Horia Sima and the Iron Guard.[96]

On 13 June Sima gave his consent to full-scale reconciliation between the Guard and the royal government.[97] Following this, Carol accepted Sima's proposals for fundamental changes in the structure and organisation of the National Renaissance Front.[98] On 19 June, Fabricius reported that the head of the secret police, Nicky Stefanescu, and two Guardists were travelling to Germany to bring about the final reconciliation of the German-based Guardists with Carol. The king now planned an 'integration of the Iron Guard into the government which is to be formed and which is to be clearly marked as pro-German'.[99] On 21 June, one day before the fall of France, Carol refounded the National Renaissance

Front as the Party of the Nation into which the Guard was to be integrated.[100] Commentating on Carol's decision to bring the Iron Guard into the party, Fabricius noted that 'there is no doubt that this is the first great step that the king has undertaken in the practical execution of his policy of rapprochement with us'.[101]

The internal changes in Carol's government had, however, no impact on the fate of Bessarabia. With the fall of France on 22 June the possibility of any western influence being exerted on Romania's behalf ended. Neither could the Reich, with its resources deployed in Western Europe, help protect Romania against Soviet claims to Bessarabia.[102] On the evening of 26 June Molotov presented the Romanian minister to Moscow, Davidescu, with an ultimatum for the surrender of Bessarabia and the northern Bukovina. A twenty-four hour time-limit was initially set for 10pm on 27 June for the Romanian evacuation of these areas. Fabricius, who received from Ribbentrop the news of the ultimatum on the night of 26 June, immediately conveyed Ribbentrop's advice to Foreign Minister Gigurtu to accept the Soviet conditions.[103] Notwithstanding this advice, Carol was at first determined to fight for Bessarabia. At 8.30 am on 27 June, Foreign Minister Gigurtu sent for Fabricius and reported to him that Carol was determined to defend Bessarabia. Gigurtu asked that in the event of war between Romania and the Soviet Union, the Axis powers should prevent Hungary and Bulgaria from using the opportunity to launch an attack on Romania. Fabricius advised Gigurtu against waging what he termed 'a hopeless war' for Bessarabia, but pointed out that the Soviet claim to the northern Bukovina was entirely new to him.[104]

The king himself summoned Fabricius for a personal audience at 10 am on the morning of the same day. Carol stated that during his visit to Germany in November 1938, 'he had been given to understand clearly that a rapprochement with the Reich excluded a rapprochement with the Soviets'. As a result of this, claimed Carol, Romania had not officially clarified her relations with Russia. Carol now asked for assistance from Germany 'because [Germany] had a certain responsibility for the present situation'. Fabricius once again advised Carol to yield to the Soviet demands.[105] The Crown Council which met at 12 noon on 27 June, however, voted by a narrow margin to reject the Soviet ultimatum.[106]

In the afternoon of 27 June, therefore, Molotov stepped up the pressure on Romania. He announced that Soviet troops would cross the Romanian border early on the morning of 28 June if the Romanian government did not concede to Soviet demands.[107] Nevertheless, at 5 pm on 27 June, in his discussion with Manfred von Killinger, who was again in Bucharest, Carol made it clear that he was still determined to fight the Soviets.[108]

Seeking to exploit his previous discussions with German leaders, Carol claimed that in 1938 he had promised Hitler and Göring that he would fight against bolshevism and that he had fulfilled this promise. The king also sought once again to point out the importance for the Reich of Romania remaining within her present borders. He added that if the Soviets penetrated into South-East Europe, the Balkans would be bolshevised leading to the loss of German economic interests in the region. Carol was even prepared to offer the Germans all the petroleum they needed if they would ensure that Hungary and Bulgaria would remain neutral in any conflict between the Soviets and Romania. Like Fabricius before him, von Killinger advised the king not to commit his country to a war which, he believed, Romania could not win. Von Killinger argued that war would lead not only to the loss of Bessarabia, but also to the destruction of the oil wells.[109]

By the time the Crown Council reconvened that evening, the majority of councillors were prepared to accept the Soviet ultimatum. It was by now perfectly clear that neither Germany nor Italy would help Romania and that Romania alone could not win a war against the Soviet Union.[110] Early on 28 June, the Romanian government informed the Germans that they had accepted the Soviet terms unconditionally. The government asked the Reich to exert its influence in Moscow in order to lengthen the evacuation time limit from two to four days for the areas ceded. The Romanians suggested that the German government should intercede in Moscow to prevent Cernăuți, a heavily German-populated city in the northern Bukovina, passing under Soviet control. The Romanian government stressed that in accepting the ultimatum, it was 'relying on German advice and thereby wanted to prove that it wished to follow the path of close collaboration'. Proof of this wish was to be seen in the new cabinet formed on 28 June which included such 'German-friendly' politicians as Constantin Argetoianu as foreign minister, Cancicov as minister for economics, as well as Gigurtu, Vaida-Voevod, Horia Sima and two other Guardists.[111]

Despite these appeals to Germany, the Romanian minister in Moscow was forced to accept the Soviet demand for Cernăuți at 11 am on 28 June. Although the German minister in Moscow had interceded with the Soviets to try to extend the time limits for evacuation, he had been unable to sway the Soviet government.[112]

Writing in July 1940 in the wake of the Bessarabian ultimatum crisis, Gheorghe Tătărescu, who had been advocating more reliance on Germany since the spring of 1940, sought to justify Romania's new pro-

German orientation. Although after the First World War, Romania had been in the anti-revisionist camp, none of Romania's alliances had been directed against Germany, Tătărescu claimed. Indeed, from 1936 onwards a policy had been initiated 'of strengthening relations with Germany and Italy', particularly in economic policy. Tătărescu went on to explain that the Soviet ultimatum had been accepted because to resist would have opened the way to the possible destruction of the entire Romanian army. Romania's duty now, Tătărescu concluded, was to readapt herself, internally and externally, to the New European Order.[113]

Notes

1 Despite Gafencu's post-war claims that Britain abandoned the Balkans to Germany, 'he himself was evidently prepared to stage-manage the transformation-scene that thus so swiftly changed the German Demon King into a Fairy Godmother': C. A. Macartney and A. W. Palmer, *Independent Eastern Europe*, London, 1962, p. 421.
2 Hitler's other proposals included a recreation of reduced Polish and Czechoslovak states; Corsica and Tunisia to be ceded to Italy; and recognition of a Soviet sphere of influence in the Baltic. Hitler also pledged to recognise France's eastern border: see, Arh. St., Însemnări Zilnice, Carol II, roll 22, Vol. 10, Sunday 1 October 1939, p. 22.
3 Arh. St., Însemnări Zilnice, Carol II, roll 22, Vol. 10, Saturday 14 October 1939, p. 32.
4 PA, Büro des Staatssekretärs, Rumänien, Vol. 1, 11.38–1.40, German Legation in Bucharest to the Foreign Ministry, Tel. nr 737, 13 October 1939, signed Fabricius.
5 Nicolae Jurcă, 'O inițiativă românească de pace necunoscută la începutul celui de al doilea război mondial', *Magazin istoric*, serie nouă, 25, nr 9 (294), (September 1991), pp. 33–5 (34). See also Andreas Hillgruber, *Hitler, König Carol und Marschall Antonescu. Die Deutsch-Rumänischen Beziehungen, 1938–1944*, Wiesbaden, 1965, pp. 60–2.
6 Although the terms 'Balkan bloc' and 'bloc of neutrals' are often used interchangeably, the 'bloc of neutrals' represented an elaboration of the earlier plan for a 'Balkan bloc'. For this, and much of what follows, see Frank Marzari, 'Projects for an Italian-Led Balkan Bloc of Neutrals, September–December 1939', *Historical Journal*, 13, nr 4, (1970), pp. 767-88.
7 Dov B. Lungu, *Romania and the Great Powers, 1933–1940*, Durham and London, 1989, pp. 202–5. Lungu points out that the 'bloc of neutrals' was designed as a bulwark against both the Soviet Union and Germany, but in reality Romania most feared the Soviets. While Germany could be appeased by economic concessions, the Soviet Union sought the return of Bessarabia: ibid, p. 205.
8 Following the outbreak of war, Britain and France hoped that the Balkan countries would make a collective stand for neutrality. Romania was under pressure from Britain to concede territory to Bulgaria in order to create a

Balkan bloc. See Zivko Avramovski, 'Attempts to form a Neutral Bloc in the Balkans (September-December 1939)', *Studia Balcanica*, 4, (1971), pp. 123–52 (128–30) and Marzari, 'Projects for an Italian-Led Balkan Bloc of Neutrals', p. 769. See also, Ion Calafeteanu, 'România și blocul neutrilor (octombrie–decembrie 1939)', *Revista română de studii internaționale*, 6, nos 2–3 (16–17), (1972), pp. 267–300, esp. 269–70.

9 Lungu, *Romania and the Great Powers*, pp. 205–6; Marzari, 'Projects for an Italian-Led Balkan Bloc of Neutrals', pp. 770–2.
10 Marzari, 'Projects for an Italian-Led Balkan Bloc of Neutrals', p. 778.
11 Arh. St., Însemnări Zilnice, Carol II, roll 22, Vol. 10, Saturday 14 October 1939, p. 32.
12 Gheorghe Buzatu, *Dosare ale războiului mondial*, Iași, 1979, p. 52.
13 MAE, 71/1939 E9, Vol. 92 (-71/1939 E9 II 1-), pp. 52–5, To the Legation in Berlin, Tel. nr 66022, 20 October 1939, signed Gafencu.
14 Marzari, 'Projects for an Italian-Led Bloc of Neutrals', pp. 774, 785–7.
15 Gafencu's proposals for the bloc included: absolute neutrality during the present conflict; treaty of non-aggression amongst bloc members; benevolent neutrality if a member is attacked; reduction to normal level of troops on common frontiers; direct contact between the foreign ministers of member-states; and economic cooperation. See Gh. Zaharia and Ion Calafeteanu, 'The International Situation and Romania's Foreign Policy Between 1938 and 1940', *Revue roumaine d'histoire*, 18, nr 1, (1979), pp. 83–105 (98–9).
16 Hungary and Bulgaria would, in any case, not have been prepared to join without Italy: Arh. St., P. C. M., Dosar nr 276/1939, pp. 109–10, Embassy in Ankara to the Foreign Ministry, 2 November 1939, signed Capitaneanu.
17 Buzatu, *Dosare ale războiului mondial*, p. 57.
18 MAE, 71/1939 E9, Vol. 92 (-71/1939 E9 II 1-) pp. 273–4, Legation in Rome to the Foreign Minister, Tel. nr 6635, 23 November 1939, signed Bossy.
19 DGFP, D, 8, Doc. nr 392, Minister in Romania to the Foreign Ministry, Bucharest, 28 November 1939. As Buzatu has pointed out, 'the opposition manifested by Germany towards the idea of the "bloc of neutrals" was one of the main causes of the Romanian government's decision to renounce the project' : *Dosare ale războiului mondial*, p. 58.
20 (eds) Gerhard Schreiber, Bernd Stegemann, Detlef Vogel, *Das Deutsche Reich und der Zweite Weltkrieg*, Vol. 3, Stuttgart, 1984, p. 352.
21 MAE, 71/1939 E9, Vol. 92 (-71/1939 E9 II 1-), pp. 300–2, Note on a conversation of 4 December 1939 between Minister Gafencu and Cappecce, Italian Chargé d'Affaires.
22 MAE, 71/1939 E9, Vol. 92 (-71/1939 E9 II 1-), p. 386, Legation in Rome to the Foreign Ministry, Tel. nr 7439, 30 December 1939, signed Bossy. By early 1940, it was clear that the Balkan Entente had effectively lost its freedom of action. On 12 January 1940, Gafencu informed Fabricius of the future Balkan Entente conference to be held on 2 to 4 February in Belgrade. He asked Fabricius 'for any instructions, in case we have any particular wishes': PA, Deutsche Gesandschaft Bukarest, IA 28, Vol. 3, 1939–40, German Legation in Bucharest to the Foreign Ministry, Tel. nr 43, 12 January 1940, signed Fabricius. The February conference was the last meeting of the Balkan Entente.
23 Arh. St., P. C. M., Dosar nr 276/1939, p. 28, Embassy in Ankara to the Foreign Ministry, Tel. nr 1947, 9 October 1939, signed Stoica; ibid, pp. 38–9, Ambas-

sador Stoica in Istanbul to the Foreign Ministry, Tel. nr 1966, 13 October 1939.
24 PA, Büro des Chef des Auslandsorganisation (A. O.), Rumänien, Vol. 114, 1937–1940, Circular, St. S., nr 824, Berlin, 18 October 1939, signed Weizsäcker.
25 *Foreign Relations of the United States*, 1939, Vol. 1, pp. 464–5, The Minister in Romania (Gunther) to the Secretary of State, Bucharest, 23 October 1939.
26 MAE, 71/1939 E9, Vol. 2 (-71/1939 E9 I general-), p. 46, To the Romanian Legation in London, Tel. nr 68914, 3 November 1939, signed Gafencu.
27 Grigore Gafencu, *Însemnări politice, 1929–1939*, (ed.) Stelian Neagoe, Bucharest, 1991, 12 November 1939, p. 342.
28 H. W. Koch, 'Hitler's Programme and the Genesis of Operation Barbarossa', in (ed.) H. W. Koch, *Aspects of the Third Reich*, London, 1985, pp. 285–322 (293). For Soviet attitudes towards Romania, see Stephen Fischer-Galați, 'Smokescreen and Iron Curtain: A Reassessment of Territorial Revisionism vis-à-vis Romania since World War 1', *East European Quarterly*, 22, nr 1, (March 1988), pp. 37–53.
29 PA, Politische Abteilung IV: Po 1, Vol. 1, 5.1938–7.1940, German Legation in Bucharest to the Foreign Ministry, Tgb. nr 5965 –IA4–, 4 November 1939, signed Fabricius; MAE, 71/Germania, Vol. 78, pp. 196–9, Note of a Conversation of 4 December 1939 between Minister Gafencu and Fabricius, German Minister, at the Ministry of Foreign Affairs.
30 PA, Politische Abteilung IV: Po 1, Vol. 1, 5.1938–7.1940, German Legation in Bucharest to the Foreign Ministry, Tgb. nr 5965 –IA4–, 4 November 1939, signed Fabricius.
31 Lungu, *Romania and the Great Powers*, p. 213; on 21 October Carol proposed to his ministers that the Germans be asked to support Romanian non-aggression pacts with Hungary and the Soviet Union: Arh. St., Însemnări Zilnice, Carol II, roll 22, Vol. 10, Saturday 21 October 1939, p. 39.
32 MAE, 71/Germania, Vol. 78, pp. 196–9, Note of a Conversation of 4 December 1939 between Minister Gafencu and Fabricius, German Minister, at the Ministry of Foreign Affairs.
33 MAE, 71/Germania, Vol. 78, pp. 205–7, To the Legation in Berlin, Tel. nr 76167, 7 December 1939, signed Gafencu; PA, Büro des Staatssekretärs, Rumänien, Vol. 1, 11.38–1.40, German Legation in Bucharest to the Foreign Ministry, Tel. nr 975, 8 December 1939, signed Fabricius; DGFP, D, 8, Doc. nr 427, Minister in Romania to the Foreign Ministry, Bucharest, 8 December 1939.
34 MAE, 71/Germania, Vol. 78, pp. 196–9, Note of a conversation of 4 December 1939 between Minister Gafencu and Fabricius, German Minister, at the Ministry of Foreign Affairs.
35 MAE, 71/Germania, Vol. 78, pp. 232–3, Legation in Berlin to the Foreign Ministry, Tel. nr 2730, 18 December 1939, signed Guranescu.
36 (eds) Gerhard Schreiber, Bernd Stegemann, Detlef Vogel, *Das Deutsche Reich und der Zweite Weltkrieg*, Vol. 3, Stuttgart, 1984, p. 353.
37 Gheorghe Tătărescu, 'Politica noastră externă', dated 1 May 1943, in Gheorghe Tătărescu, *Mărturii pentru istorie*, (ed.) Sanda Tătărescu-Negropontes, Bucharest, 1996, pp. 242–67 (254).
38 PA, Büro des Staatssekretärs, Rumänien, Vol. 1, 11.38–1.40, German Legation in Bucharest to the Foreign Ministry, Tel. nr 917, 27 November 1939, signed Fabricius.

39 Argeşanu had also been minister president from 21 to 27 September before the appointment of Argetoianu.
40 Elisabeth Barker, *British Policy in South-East Europe in the Second World War*, London, 1976, p. 32; Maurice Pearton, *Oil and the Romanian State*, Oxford, 1971, pp. 229, 237.
41 Barker, *British Policy in South-East Europe in the Second World War*, p. 33. See also, Philippe Marguerat, *Le IIIe Reich et le pétrole roumain, 1938–1940*, Leiden, 1977, pp. 168–74.
42 Ivor Porter, *Operation Autonomous: With the S.O.E. in Wartime Romania*, London, 1989, p. 41.
43 DGFP, D, 8, Doc. nr 402, Director of the Economic Policy Department to the Legation in Romania, Berlin, 30 November 1939, signed Wiehl.
44 Lungu, *Romania and the Great Powers*, p. 218.
45 Frank Marzari, 'The Bessarabian Microcosm: September 1939–February 1940', *Canadian Slavonic Papers*, 12, nr 2, (1970), pp. 128–41 (131–2).
46 DGFP, D, 8, Doc. nr 422, Legation in Romania to the Foreign Ministry, 6 December 1939.
47 Barker, *British Policy in South-East Europe in the Second World War*, p. 33.
48 As Maurice Pearton has pointed out, industrial and commercial companies that were legally owned by British nationals were, nevertheless, 'Romanian-registered institutions subject to Romanian jurisdiction'. The Tătărescu government was, therefore, fully entitled to oppose British measures. See, Pearton, 'British Policy towards Romania: 1939–1941', in (ed.) Rebecca Haynes, *Occasional Papers in Romanian Studies*, no. 2, London, 1998, pp. 59–92 (67).
49 Barry Crosby Fox, 'German Relations with Romania, 1933–1944', unpublished PhD thesis, Dept of History, Western Reserve University, September 1964, p. 104
50 Ivor Porter, *Operation Autonomous*, pp. 41–2; Hillgruber, *Hitler, König Carol und Marschall Antonescu. Die deutsch–rumänischen Beziehungen, 1938–1944*, Wiesbaden, 1965, p. 67.
51 Fox, op. cit., p. 104.
52 Pearton, 'British Policy towards Romania, 1939–1941', pp. 71–2.
53 For links between the S.S.I. and Abwehr, see Cristian Troncotă, 'Din istoria serviciilor secrete. S.S.I. – Abwehr 1937–1940', *Magazin istoric*, serie nouă, (July 1994), pp. 13–17; ibid, (August 1994), pp. 73–7; ibid, (September 1994), pp. 28–32; Cristian Troncotă, *Eugen Cristescu. Asul serviciilor secrete româneşti*, Bucharest, 1994, pp. 139–47.
54 Lungu, *Romania and the Great Powers*, p. 219; as Lungu notes, in conformity with the policy of neutrality between the powers, the Romanian government was also in negotiation with western representatives over the destruction of the oil wells in the event of a German invasion; DGFP, D, 8, Doc. nr 502, Memorandum by the Director of the Economic Policy Department, Berlin, 3 January 1940.
55 MAE, 71/Germania, Vol. 78, pp. 188–9, Note from the German Legation in Bucharest to the Foreign Ministry, nr 72125, 28 November, unsigned; ibid, p. 202, Legation in Berlin to the Foreign Ministry, Tel. nr 39665, 6 December 1939, signed Crutzescu; ibid, p. 203, To the Legation in Berlin, Tel. nr 76130, 7 December 1939, signed Gafencu.
56 Troncotă, *Eugen Cristescu*, p. 227.

57 DGFP, D, 8, Doc. nr 495, The Foreign Minister to Legations in Hungary, Romania, Bulgaria, Greece and Yugoslavia, Berlin, 30 December 1939. Von Killinger had been a member of the *Freikorps*, an SA leader and early friend of Hitler. He was appointed minister in Slovakia in 1940 and minister in Romania from January 1941, when he replaced Fabricius.
58 DGFP, D, 8, Doc. nr 533, The Foreign Minister to the Legation in Romania, Berlin, 13 January 1940. Neubacher had been an underground leader of the NSDAP in Austria from 1933 to 1938. He was to become an important 'go-between' for the Iron Guard with the Romanian government in 1940–41.
59 MAE, 71/România, Vol. 353, p. 161, Legation in London to the Foreign Ministry, Tel. nr 98, 29 January 1939, signed Tilea.
60 Lungu, *Romania and the Great Powers*, pp. 217, 220: while the appearance of neutrality was maintained by similar concessions made to France, the pact represented 'a disguised retreat from neutrality'.
61 DGFP, D, 9, Doc. nr 21, Legation in Romania to the Foreign Ministry, Bucharest, 29 March 1940, signed Clodius and Fabricius.
62 For details of the often hilarious 1 April adventure see, DGFP, D, 9, Doc. nr 116, Minister Killinger to the Foreign Minister, Bucharest, 14 April 1940, and Maurice Pearton, 'British Policy towards Romania, 1939–1940', pp. 77–85.
63 MAE, 71/Germania, Vol. 79, pp. 139–46, Note, 13 July 1940. Report submitted to the Führer by von Killinger regarding meetings in Bucharest, 26–27 June 1940.
64 MAE, 71/Germania, Vol. 78, pp. 375–8, Legation in Berlin to the Foreign Ministry, Tel. nr 40121, 17 April 1940, signed Crutzescu; although the Germans would have preferred it 'if the Giurgiu incident had not been deemed simply a customs offence', the speed with which the Romanian authorities reacted was appreciated.
65 MAE, 71 Germania, Vol. 78, pp. 323–6, Note of a conversation of 29 March, 2 and 4 April 1940 between Minister Gafencu and Ambassador Thierry and Sir Reginald Hoare at the Foreign Ministry.
66 Arh. St., Însemnări Zilnice, Carol II, roll 22, Vol. 11, Sunday 17 March 1940, p. 178; ibid, Wednesday 20 March 1940, pp. 180–1.
67 MAE, 71/România, Vol. 275, pp. 436–43, Note following a Conversation with Clodius, 26 March 1940, signed Gafencu.
68 DGFP, D, 9, Doc. nr 27, Legation in Romania to the Foreign Ministry, Bucharest, 30 March 1940, signed Clodius and Fabricius.
69 DGFP, D, 9, Doc. nr 33, Legation in Romania to the Foreign Ministry, Bucharest, 1 April 1940, signed Clodius and Fabricius.
70 DGFP, D, 9, Doc. nr 117, Legation in Romania to the Foreign Ministry, Bucharest, 15 April 1940, signed Clodius and Fabricius.
71 PA, Handelspolitische Abteilung, Handakten Carl August Clodius, Rumänien, Vol. 4, 4.40–7.40, German Legation in Bucharest to the Foreign Ministry, Tel. nr 712, 15 May 1940, signed Fabricius. According to the Italian press, Romalo 'has never hidden his ardent sympathy for Germany': MAE, 71/România, Vol. 8, pp. 263–4, *Agenția Rador*, 2 June 1940, Press Service reporting from Rome.
72 DGFP, D, 9, Doc. nr 338, The Special Representative for Economic Questions at the Legation in Romania to the Foreign Ministry, Bucharest, 28 May 1940. See also, Hermann Neubacher, *Sonderauftrag Südost 1940–1945. Bericht eines*

fliegenden Diplomaten, Göttingen, 1957, pp. 38–43 for the account of his appointment and work up to the signing of the May 1940 pact.
73 Hans-Erich Volkmann, 'NS-Aussenhandel im "geschlossenen" Kriegswirtschaftsraum (1939–1941)', in (eds) Friedrich Forstmeier and Hans-Erich Volkmann, Kriegswirtschaft und Rüstung, 1939–1945, Düsseldorf, 1977, pp. 92–134 (112).
74 Arh. St., Însemnări Zilnice, Carol II, roll 22, Vol. 11a, Thursday 18 April 1940, pp. 213–14.
75 Horia Sima, Sfârşitul unei domnii sângeroase, Timişoara, 1995, p. 31.
76 Arh. St., Însemnări Zilnice, Carol II, roll 22, Vol. 11, Monday 4 March 1940, p. 195.
77 Arh. St., Însemnări Zilnice, Carol II, roll 22, Vol 11a, Thursday 18 April 1940, pp. 213–14; Hillgruber, Hitler, König Carol und Marschall Antonescu, p. 70.
78 MAE, 71/1920–1944, Dosare Speciale, România R25, Vol. 395, pp. 232–3, Unsigned Legionary Manifesto, Berlin, 2 May 1940. The manifesto was clearly the work of Sima. See his identical letter, dated 2 May 1940 in Sima, Sfârşitul unei domnii sângeroase, p. 44.
79 Sima, Sfârşitul unei domnii sângeroase, pp. 104, 108–9.
80 Arh. St., Însemnări Zilnice, Carol II, roll 22, Vol. 11a, Wednesday 15 May 1940, pp. 239–40; ibid, Monday 20 May 1940, p. 242.
81 Grigore Gafencu, Jurnal iunie 1940–iulie 1942, (eds) Ion Ardeleanu and Vasile Arimia, Bucharest, no date, pp. 18–19.
82 MAE, 71/Germania, Vol. 78, pp. 466–7, Communication made by Tătărescu, President of the Council of Ministers, to Fabricius, German Minister, on 28 May 1940, in the presence of Foreign Minister Gafencu and Ernest Urdăreanu, Minister of the Palace.
83 DGFP, D, 9, Doc. nr 346, Minister Killinger to the Foreign Minister, Berlin, 29 May 1940.
84 MAE, 71/1939 E9 II General, Vol. 90, pp. 367–70, Mission of von Killinger to Bucharest, May 1940; 71/Germania, Vol. 82, pp. 101–5, Note, 25 May 1940, Interview with von Killinger; ibid, pp. 106–9, Note on the Mission of von Killinger to Bucharest in May 1940, 28 February 1941, signed Al. Cretzianu. See also Cretzianu's letters in February and March 1941 to Tătărescu, Gafencu and Al. Romalo and their replies in ibid, pp. 110–12. During his trial in 1946, General Antonescu claimed that Carol had requested an alliance with Germany as early as April or May 1940: (ed.) Marcel-Dumitru Ciucă, Procesul Mareşalului Antonescu. Documente, Vol. 1, Bucharest, 1995, p. 200. In early May, Carol had requested German help to build up the defences on Romania's border with the Soviet Union. The defences were to be camouflaged as help for 'road building': Andreas Hillgruber, Hitler, König Carol und Marschall Antonescu. p. 71.
85 Raoul Bossy, Aminitiri din viaţa diplomatică (1918–1940),(ed.) Stelian Neagoe, Vol. 2, Bucharest, 1993, p. 268; Grigore Gafencu, Jurnal, pp. 18–19; DGFP, D, 9, Doc. nr 393, Minister in Romania to the Foreign Ministry, Bucharest, 6 June 1940, footnote 2.
86 MAE, 71/România, Vol. 8, pp. 263–4, Agenţia Rador, 2 June 1940, Report from the Press service in Rome; MAE, 71/România, Vol. 8, p. 316, Dresdner Neueste Nachrichten, 18 June 1940.

87 MAE, 71/Germania, Vol. 78, p. 463, Verbal communication made by the German Minister to the President of the Council of Romania and Foreign Minister on 2 June 1940, as a response to the communication of 28 May.
88 Gheorghe Tătărescu, 'Politica noastră externă', dated 1 May 1943, *Mărturii pentru istorie*, pp. 242–67 (250).
89 DGFP, D, 9, Doc. nr 393, Minister in Romania to the Foreign Ministry, Bucharest, 6 June 1940.
90 MAE, 71/Germania, Vol. 79, pp. 53–4, Résumé de la communication faite par Son Excellence le Président du Conseil à Son Excellence le Ministre d'Allemagne en date du 20 Juin 1940.
91 DGFP, D, 9, Doc. nr 515, Minister in Romania to the Foreign Ministry, Bucharest, 21 June 1940.
92 MAE, 71/Germania, Vol. 79, pp. 43–5, Legation in Berlin to Minister Gigurtu, Tel. nr 2408, 18 June 1940, signed Romalo.
93 MAE, 71/ Germania, Vol. 79, pp. 64–6, Minister Gigurtu and Minister Fabricius at the Foreign Ministry, 26 June 1940.
94 DGFP, D, 9, Doc. nr 19, Minister in Romania to the Foreign Ministry, Bucharest, 26 June 1940.
95 Gafencu, *Jurnal*, p. 40.
96 On 24 May, the then Foreign Minister Gafencu had a discussion with an official at the German legation regarding the Reich's attitude towards the Guard. The official pointed out that it was Romania's willingness to make concessions to the Soviet Union, rather than the Iron Guard question, which was decisive in German–Romanian relations. For this, see: PA, Politische Abteilung IV: Po 1, Vol. 1, 5.1938–7.1940, Note, Bucharest, 24 May 1940, unsigned. The Romanians do not appear to have absorbed this advice.
97 Sima, *Sfârșitul unei domnii sângeroase*, p. 116; Arh. St., Însemnări Zilnice, Carol II, roll 22, Vol. 11a, Wednesday 12 June 1940, p. 264.
98 Arh. St., Însemnări Zilnice, Carol II, roll 22, Vol. 11a, Thursday 13 June 1940, p. 265.
99 PA, Politische Abteilung IV: Po 5, Vol. 5, 2.39–6.40, German Legation in Bucharest to the Foreign Ministry, Tel. nr 941,19 June 1940, signed Fabricius.
100 Armin Heinen, *Die Legion 'Erzengel Michael' in Rumänien. Soziale Bewegung und politische Organisation*, Munich, 1986, p. 421.
101 PA, Politische Abteilung IV: Po 5, Vol. 5, 2.39–6.40, German Legation in Bucharest to the Foreign Ministry, Tel. nr 959, 21 June 1940, signed Fabricius.
102 In June 1940 only six German divisions were deployed facing the Soviet Union, while thirty-six Soviet divisions were deployed on the Romanian border and some hundred more in West Russia: Heinz Höhne, *Canaris*, London, 1979, p. 457.
103 MAE, 71/Germania, Vol. 79, p. 63, Verbal Note by the German Minister communicated to the Foreign Minister on the night of the 26 June 1940.
104 DGFP, D, 9, Doc. nr 29, Minister in Romania to the Foreign Ministry, Bucharest, 27 June 1940, 11 am. The Nazi–Soviet Pact had made no mention of Soviet interests in the Bukovina. The Soviets demanded the northern Bukovina for strategic reasons since it brought the passes of the southern Carpathians under Soviet control. This gave the Soviet Union access into

the Hungarian Plain. See, Ion Gheorghe, *Rumäniens Weg zum Satelliten-Staat*, Heidelberg, 1952, p. 51.
105 DGFP, D, 10, Doc. nr 33, Minister in Romania to the Foreign Ministry, Bucharest, 27 June 1940, 4 pm; ibid, Doc. nr 28, Telephone message to be transmitted to Minister Fabricius, 27 June 1940, 10.30 am, from Ribbentrop. Romania had also consulted the Italians, who had likewise advised the Romanians to yield. The Italians feared that a conflict in the Balkans would deprive them of economic resources, especially petroleum. For this information, see Galeazzo Ciano, *The Ciano Diaries, 1939–1943*, (ed.) Hugh Gibson, New York, 1946, 28 June 1940, p. 270.
106 Arh. St., Însemnări Zilnice, Carol II, roll 22, Vol. 11a, Thursday 27 June 1940, pp. 275–80.
107 DGFP, D, 10, Doc. nr 32, Ambassador in Moscow to the Foreign Ministry, 27 June 1940, 4.40 pm.
108 MAE, 71/Germania, Vol. 79, pp. 139–46, Note, 13 July 1940, Report submitted to the Führer by von Killinger regarding Meetings in Bucharest, 26–27 June 1940. On 27 June, the German foreign ministry confirmed Fabricius's instructions of the night before, i.e. that the Reich advised Romania to accept the ultimatum: MAE, 71/Germania, Vol. 79, p. 71, Legation in Berlin to the Foreign Ministry, Tel. nr 40293, 27 June 1940, signed Romalo.
109 MAE, 71/Germania, Vol. 79, pp. 139–46, Note, 13 July 1940, Report submitted to the Führer by von Killinger regarding Meetings in Bucharest, 26–27 June 1940.
110 Arh. St., Însemnări Zilnice, Carol II, roll 22, Vol. 11a, Thursday 27 June 1940, pp. 275–80.
111 DGFP, D, 10, Doc. nr 44, Legation in Romania to the Foreign Ministry, Bucharest, 28 June 1940, signed Fabricius.
112 DGFP, D, 10, Doc. nr 49, Ambassador in the Soviet Union to the Foreign Ministry, Moscow, 28 June 1940. The Soviets also demanded Herța in the Bukovina on the basis of the rough pencil line drawn by Molotov on the map of the Bukovina which he handed to the Romanian ambassador. The pencil line represented a seven-mile band of territory and led to confusion as to which places fell on the Soviet side. For this, see Dennis Deletant, 'A Shuttlecock of History: Bessarabia', *South Slav Journal*, 10, nr 4, (1987–8), pp. 1–14.
113 Gheorghe Tătărescu, *Evacuarea Basarabiei și a Bucovinei de nord*, Craiova, July 1940.

6
Carol and the Axis, June to September 1940

King Carol's decision to enter into political collaboration with Germany had been prompted by the capitulation of neutral Belgium on 28 May 1940. By late June, Romania had lost Bessarabia and the northern Bukovina to the Soviet Union, France lay defeated and the fate of Britain was uncertain. As a result, Carol attempted to speed up the process of establishing formal political relations with the Reich. He believed that only loyalty to Germany could now save Romania from further Soviet attack. Carol's decision was reflected in the creation of the pro-German government headed by Ion Gigurtu as minister president on 4 July 1940. The following weeks were to see many attempts by Carol to enter into close collaboration, and even alliance, with the Reich. As well as protection from the Soviet Union, through working closely with Germany, the Romanian government hoped to avoid the realisation of Hungarian and Bulgarian revisionist claims against Romania. The price of German friendship, however, proved to be high. Hitler required the Romanian government to enter into direct negotiations with the country's revisionist neighbours.

Minister Fabricius regarded the elevation of the 'German-friendly' Constantin Argetoianu as foreign minister on 28 June 1940, as heralding a new era in German–Romanian relations.[1] During a discussion on 29 June, Argetoianu assured Fabricius that he had taken the office on the definite understanding that Carol would openly adopt a policy of cooperation with the Axis. He described his foreign policy as one of 'open and conspicuous collaboration, with Romania declaring herself unambiguously as Germany's friend'.[2] A letter from Hitler to Carol received the same day, however, did not bode well for Carol's plans for collaboration. In his letter, the Führer condemned Romania's alleged complicity in British policies during 1939 and her acceptance of the Anglo-French guarantee.[3]

The coldness of Hitler's tone was probably responsible for the government decision of 1 July to renounce the Anglo-French guarantee. On the same day, Carol informed Fabricius of his wish to have a political agreement with Germany. Carol had in mind 'a policy of alliance like that of King Carol I with the Triple Alliance'. Lacking such protection, stated Carol, 'Romania is incapable of any action and is subject to Soviet Russian influence'.[4] On the following day, having failed to reach Hitler by telephone, Carol asked Fabricius to transmit directly to the Führer his decision to renounce the Anglo-French guarantee and to seek closer collaboration with Germany through an alliance. Carol pointed to apparent Soviet intentions to cross their new frontier in Bessarabia to gain control of the Romanian oil fields as a reason for requesting German protection. In the first of several requests, the king asked for a German military mission to be sent to Romania.[5]

According to Horia Sima, who had been in the government since 28 June together with two other Guardists, the idea of a German military mission to Romania originated within the German legation itself. Sima was apparently invited to meet von Ritgen, press attaché at the legation, on 30 June. Von Ritgen claimed that Germany wished to protect Romania against further Soviet attacks. A request for a military mission, von Ritgen suggested, should come from the Romanian government itself. Such a mission would provide the best means of defence for Romania and give proof of Romania's desire to change her alliances. Sima then conveyed this news to the king. Other sources, however, suggest that the military mission originated in the joint plans of the Romanian military secret service under General Moruzov and the Abwehr to combat British sabotage of the oilfields.[6]

Wherever the idea of a military mission originated, it was clearly favoured by King Carol. On 12 July, Carol again requested 'the open or concealed assignment for training purposes of officers who are tank and air force experts, together with the necessary equipment'.[7] In a letter of 16 July to Hermann Göring, Ion Gigurtu also requested a military mission on the king's behalf. In exchange, Gigurtu pledged to fulfil all Germany's economic war needs, including doubling petroleum deliveries.[8] According to German sources in Bucharest, Carol believed that once the Romanian army was properly trained, it could serve as a right-wing to the German army in any war against the Soviet Union.[9]

In the midst of these requests, on 4 July Carol had established a new government under Ion Gigurtu, with Mihail Manoilescu as foreign minister. German officials greeted Manoilescu's appointment warmly. Although his first sympathy in foreign policy was known to be Italy and

Fascism, he was friendly to both Germany and the Iron Guard. His appointment therefore fitted with Carol's decision to build a government to include the Guard.[10] Horia Sima was moved from the ministry of national education and became minister for cults and arts. His two Guardist colleagues, Vasile Noveanu and Augustin Bideanu, remained in the cabinet as minister for public wealth and sub-secretary of state at the ministry of finance respectively. Nicifor Crainic, a ideological Guardist 'fellow-traveller' became minister of propaganda.[11]

In his post-war memoirs, Mihail Manoilescu argued that the Gigurtu government 'did not follow a policy of subordination to Germany, only one of adaptation'.[12] The Gigurtu government was clearly less integrated into the Axis than the National Legionary government created in September 1940. Nevertheless, the foundations for Romania's alliance with Germany, sealed by Romania's adherence to the Tripartite Pact in November 1940, were laid down during the term of the Gigurtu government.

Gigurtu and his colleagues surpassed themselves in obsequious declarations as they tried to ingratiate themselves with Axis officials.[13] Thus, on 4 July, Gigurtu made a government declaration in which he pointed out that integration into the Axis was not only a result of political realism but corresponded with the government's 'political and ideological conceptions'.[14] Further declarations of loyalty were made over the next few weeks. On 9 July, Gigurtu declared that a pro-Axis foreign policy was not a 'momentary convenience' but a return 'to the old traditions of our state', in particular, that of nationalism. Gigurtu also resorted to the economic arguments, which had long been used by the Romanians, in favour of closer cooperation between the two countries. On 6 July he informed the German newspaper, *Berliner Börsenzeitung*, that Romania would be incorporated into the New European Order through the utilisation of her natural wealth. He believed Romanian agricultural production could only be improved through 'strong collaboration with Germany'.[15] On 14 July, Foreign Minister Manoilescu informed representatives of *Deutsche Nachrichten Büro* that Romania's departure from the League of Nations was a concrete step on the road to 'links of friendly collaboration of undying value'.[16]

During the early weeks of the Gigurtu government, Carol sought an alliance with Germany through the mediation of Victor Moldovanu, secretary general of the government mass party, the Party of the Nation. During a discussion between General Moruzov and Manfred von Killinger on 26 June, the development of links between the newly-formed

Party of the Nation and the NSDAP had already been agreed.[17] Moldovanu was subsequently sent to Berlin twice by Carol during July 1940, but his initial brief clearly covered more than a mere discussion of interparty links. His first trip began on 3 July.[18] On 9 July, Carol recorded in his diary that news received from Moldovanu in Berlin 'seems to show that we are on the road to an alliance with Germany more quickly than we thought'.[19] On the following day, Foreign Minister Manoilescu informed the Romanian legation in Berlin that he required 'the precise points of the possible accord and with whom we are to conclude it', before the government could authorise the 'official concluding of the accord'.[20] On the same day, Court Minister Urdăreanu proposed that the king should visit Hitler in Germany. A telegram was clearly sent to Germany to this effect but the Reich's lack of response led to what Manoilescu described as a 'stagnation in our whole diplomatic action'.[21]

On 18 July, Moldovanu was sent for a second time to Berlin to make contact with leaders of the Reich government and with NSDAP party leaders.[22] On 23 July, Manoilescu ordered Moldovanu not to enter into discussions of a political nature but 'to limit himself to studying the organisation of the National Socialist Party in his capacity as secretary general of the Party of the Nation'.[23] This change of policy was probably due to the realisation that as far as the Reich was concerned a German–Romania alliance had to be preceded by a negotiated territorial settlement between Romania and her Hungarian and Bulgarian revisionist neighbours.

By late July, the Romanian government had received many indications of how urgently the Reich government required Romania to negotiate with the revisionist states. On 4 July, Minister Fabricius stressed to King Carol Hitler's wish for a peaceful settlement of territorial disputes in the Balkans. Fabricius attempted to ascertain whether Carol was prepared to negotiate with, and cede territory to, Hungary and Bulgaria.[24]

The Romanian government, however, hoped that by close collaboration with Germany, it could avoid having to make territorial concessions. The government favoured instead a population exchange between Hungary and Romania.[25] During discussions with Minister President Gigurtu and Foreign Minister Manoilescu on 6 July, Carol took the decision to begin negotiations with Hungary and Bulgaria on the basis of population exchange. Later that day, Carol informed Fabricius of this decision. Carol added that he hoped the Führer would help Romania by preventing Hungarian demands going 'beyond the bounds of national justice and political reason'.[26] Not for the first time, Carol clearly hoped that Germany would act as an arbiter in Romania's interests. As a result, it was to take until mid-August for the Romanian government to begin the first direct discussions with Hungary and Bulgaria.

On 15 July, Hitler again wrote directly to King Carol regarding the question of revision. He pointed out that he considered concessions to Hungary and Bulgaria as the prerequisite for closer German–Romanian collaboration. Hitler went on to note that although Romania's offer of friendship was welcomed, until very recently the Romanian attitude had been 'quite hostile'. He added ominously that although Germany had no territorial interest in the Balkans, she had ties of friendship in the area 'amongst which those with Hungary and Bulgaria had existed and been cultivated for a long time'.[27]

On 26 July, Carol responded to Hitler's letter, arguing that population transfer was the solution to Romania's disputes with her neighbours. Romania, wrote Carol, was already suffering internal problems as a result of the loss of Bessarabia and the northern Bukovina. Further territorial losses, Carol believed, could lead to a complete breakdown of the Romanian state. Carol once again asked that the Axis' governments should exert their influence in Romania's negotiations with Hungary and Bulgaria, since the Romanian government had 'little faith in the moderation of our neighbours'. Once the territorial disputes had been settled, Carol concluded that he hoped for a territorial guarantee and large-scale political collaboration with the Reich.[28]

The Romanians were happy to discover that the Führer was in agreement with their thesis that population transfer should be the solution to their problems with Hungary. On 26 July Gigurtu and Manoilescu met Hitler at the Berghof.[29] During the meeting, Gigurtu admitted that the Romanian government was unlikely to come to an agreement with Hungary while the latter's claim continued to be based on vast territorial cessions by Romania. His government, Gigurtu confirmed, was prepared to cede only some 14,000 square kilometres of the 123,000 square kilometres which Romania had received from Hungary in 1920. Population exchanges should, therefore, be made parallel to any territorial cessions. Gigurtu repeated the Romanian requests for a military mission and territorial guarantee on behalf of the Romanian government.

Hitler agreed that the solution to the dispute should be reached through a population exchange which would 'lead to the 100 per cent satisfaction of all with regard to nationality'. Hitler also gave his consent for a census and plebiscite to be held in the contested Hungarian-speaking Szekler region in south-east Transylvania to determine whether the Szeklers wished to belong to Hungary or Romania. The areas of Transylvania inhabited by ethnic Germans, the Führer maintained, should remain within the Romanian state. Hitler concluded by confirming that following the resolutions of the territorial disputes, the Axis would be prepared to give Romania a territorial guarantee. He rejected Gigurtu's plea for a German arbitration of the Romanian–Hungarian dispute.[30]

Gigurtu and Manoilescu's private meeting with German Foreign Minister Ribbentrop later on 26 July was less cordial. Unlike Hitler, Ribbentrop appeared to support large-scale territorial concessions by Romania to Hungary rather than population exchange. Ribbentrop said that Germany was in sympathy with Hungarian and Bulgarian revisionism. The 'great period of treaty revision had arrived' and minor border rectifications would not suffice, stated Ribbentrop.[31]

On 31 July, only days after Gigurtu and Manoilescu's meeting with Hitler, the Romanians were notified of Hitler's wish that the whole of southern Dobruja (also known as the Cadrilater), within its 1913 boundary, should be returned to Bulgaria.[32] Manoilescu was taken aback, since he had hoped to save the strategically important coastal town of Balcic, together with Silistra on the Danube, which controlled the only highway between Bucharest and the port of Constanţa on the Black Sea. Fabricius sought Manoilescu's agreement to these losses by arguing that a positive response to Hitler's 'suggestion' would 'demonstrate that the new course in Romania was completely orientated towards the Axis'.[33] Manoilescu retorted that Hitler's decision might well set a precedent for the more important negotiations with Hungary over Transylvania. Just as Hitler's great authority had validated Bulgarian claims to the Cadrilater, so he might choose to endorse Hungarian claims to Transylvania if a Hungarian delegation convinced him of the justice of its cause. Fabricius assured Manoilescu that Hitler was inclined to be benevolent towards Bulgaria but was 'more reserved and cold' towards Hungary. Sacrifices made towards Bulgaria, claimed Fabricius, would win the Führer's goodwill in the more difficult Hungarian question.[34]

The Romanian government, therefore, decided to open negotiations with Bulgaria in the belief that they would gain the goodwill of the Axis in their dealings with Hungary. The Romanians, however, did not give up their attempt to retain Balcic and Silistra. On 3 August, in a meeting with the Bulgarian prime minister and foreign minister, the Romanian ambassador to Sofia agreed to cede the southern Dobruja to Bulgaria but requested that Romania should retain Balcic and Silistra. The Bulgarians, now assured of Hitler's backing, refused.[35]

In early August, Minister Romalo in Berlin, made one last attempt to win German foreign ministry support for Romania to retain Balcic and

Silistra. Romalo was advised by the foreign ministry that Romania's request would damage future talks with Hungary and that Romania should dispense with the Bulgarian question as soon as possible.[36] German support for Bulgarian revisionism in southern Dobruja reflected Romania's increasingly restricted freedom of maneouvre in her foreign relations and her gradual incorporation into the Reich's foreign-policy strategies. Formal negotiations between Romania and Bulgaria opened on 19 August at Craiova.

Meanwhile, both the Romanian and Hungarian governments attempted to obtain German intervention in the Romanian-Hungarian territorial dispute. Despite the German government's persistent refusal to intervene, both governments continued to request German arbitration.[37]

Negotiations between Romania and Hungary officially began at Turnu Severin on 16 August 1940.[38] Both delegations were headed by Transylvanians: royal councillor Valer Pop for Romania and András Höry for Hungary. There was an immediate clash over the terms of negotiation. The Hungarian delegation insisted on negotiating on the basis of territorial cession; the Romanians on that of population transfer. The Romanians consistently refused to accept Hungary's claim to some 69,000 square kilometres, or two-thirds, of Transylvania, together with a population of 3,900,000 of which 2,200,000 were Romanian. A further problem arose due to the Hungarian demand for the unconditional surrender of the Szekler region, which was well away from the Hungarian border, in south-east Transylvania. The cession of the Szekler region to Hungary would have pushed the Hungarian border to a point just north of Brașov and thus into the very heart of Romania. On 19 August, the Romanian negotiator, Pop, officially rejected the Hungarian demands and proposed instead a population exchange. He added that some frontier rectifications in Hungary's favour could be made in order to give more space for the Hungarian population displaced from Transylvania. Since this proposal was unacceptable to the Hungarian delegation, Höry and Pop agreed to return to their respective governments for new instructions. Meanwhile, both Hungarian and Romanian officials attempted to press the Germans into arbitrating in the dispute. The German foreign ministry upheld Hitler's position of non-intervention.[39]

During the pause between negotiations, both Höry and Pop were told by their respective governments to stand firmly by their original terms of negotiation. During the Crown Council meeting on 23 August, Carol and his councillors approved unanimously the decision to continue the negotiations on the basis of the ethnic principle and population exchange. It was hardly surprising, therefore, that when negotiations resumed at Turnu Severin on 24 August, the positions of the two delegations remained irreconcilable. As a result, the Hungarian delegation formally closed negotiations.

In the days following the close of negotiations, the Romanian government continued to request German arbitration in the dispute, arguing that Hitler himself had approved the policy of population exchange and ethnic homogenisation.[40] The Romanian position was also put forward by Minister President Gigurtu in a personal letter to Ribbentrop of 27 August. Gigurtu pointed out that although the Romanian government had ceded Bessarabia on German advice and was negotiating with Bulgaria along the lines recommended by Hitler, the question of Transylvania was of quite a different order. Gigurtu pleaded that it was regarded as the birth-place of the Romanian nation and consequently as an integral part of the Romanian state. Nevertheless, the Romanian government was willing to negotiate with the Hungarians based on the principle of population exchange, even if this necessitated some cession of territory. Gigurtu refused to renounce the Szekler region since this lay in the geographic heart of Romania, but was prepared to accept a degree of autonomy for the area. Gigurtu concluded his letter with the warning that the loss of territory in Transylvania might lead to the collapse of the Romanian state itself.[41]

Having consistently refused to arbitrate in the Romanian–Hungarian territorial dispute, Axis policy underwent a complete reversal in late August. On 29 August, the Romanian and Hungarian foreign ministers were invited to Vienna by Ribbentrop and Ciano for what proved to be an unconditional arbitration by the Axis of the Transylvanian dispute. The despair which Manoilescu felt during his conversations with Ribbentrop and Ciano is reflected in the numerous telegrams which he sent to Bucharest during the day. He described the situation as 'worse than expected', since the Axis required Romania to accept an unconditional arbitration which would affect between 25,000 and 68,000 square kilometres of Romanian territory. Although an exchange of population was both possible and desirable, Ribbentrop had confirmed that it would not be obligatory. In exchange for coming to a settlement with both Hungary and Bulgaria, Romania would receive a territorial guarantee from the Axis covering all her frontiers. Following the settlement, Manoilescu was told that it would also be possible to meet Romania's other wishes, such as the dispatch of a German military mission. Manoilescu once again attempted to argue to Ribbentrop and Ciano that the award should be made on the basis of the ethnic principle. In reply, Ribbentrop threatened that if King Carol did not accept the arbitration, a combined attack by Hungary and the Soviet Union was likely to ensue in which Romania would be completely destroyed.[42]

Manoilescu, nonetheless, made one more attempt to avoid the worst outcome of the arbitration. On the evening of 29 August, he requested the consent of his government to put forward a proposal previously discussed in Bucharest. Under this plan, Romania would cede Hungary 3,000 square kilometres of Transylvania including a number of border towns and a population of 350,000. Additionally, the Romanian government would request that the Axis' armies enter the area ceded and remain there until the end of the war, when a final solution could be reached.[43] Fearing that a combined Soviet and Hungarian attack was imminent, however, the Romanian Crown Council which met on the night of 29/30 August decided to accept the Axis arbitration. The councillors recognised that Romania's diplomatic isolation and military weakness made it unlikely that she could survive such an attack.[44] In his reply to Manoilescu on 30 August, Gigurtu therefore directed him to accept the arbitration but also to request that the territorial guarantee should be immediate and that the German and Italian armies should enter the territory to be ceded as a guarantee of safety for the Romanian population.[45] These requests reflect the extent to which the Romanian government now saw the Reich as its protector against her neighbours, even to the extent of allowing the long-term presence of Axis troops on Romanian soil.

The 30 August Vienna Award ceded 43,591 square kilometres to Hungary, together with a population of some two and a half million, of whom over a million were Romanian. The Hungarian territorial gains, which included Cluj and the Szekler area, brought the new Hungarian–Romanian border to just north of Braşov, far into the heart of Romania.[46] The Romanian government also undertook a pledge to put the Romanian ethnic German minority 'on a footing of equality with the members of the Romanian national community in every respect....'. The Vienna Award also included the long-awaited territorial guarantee of Romania by the Axis.[47]

Given the massive territorial loss suffered by Romania, it is hardly surprising that Romanian historians have tended to regard the Vienna Award as the culmination of a cynical plot against Romania by Germany in complicity with Horthyist Hungary.[48] In their post-war accounts of the Vienna proceedings, both Mihail Manoilescu and Valer Pop, the chief Romanian negotiator at the Turnu Severin negotiations, stress that during the negotiations with Hungary, the Romanian delegation believed that Hitler was in agreement with their thesis that negotiations should be based on the ethnic principle, leading to population exchange. The resulting arbitration, which overturned the ethnic principle, is therefore portrayed as an example of German perfidy.[49]

Romanian accusations of bad faith on the part of Germany, however, overlook the complete deadlock in negotiations with Hungary by 24 August. A strain had also appeared in the negotiations with the Bulgarians at Craiova by 27 August. Manoilescu and Pop were correct in stressing that they believed that by ceding the whole of southern Dobruja to Bulgaria, they would earn Axis goodwill in the Transylvanian question. The fact that Romania was, nonetheless, forced to cede northern Transylvania is therefore portrayed as another example of Hitler's broken word. By Manoilescu and Pop's own admission, however, Romania did not formally agree to cede southern Dobruja to Bulgaria until as late as the night of 29/30 August, under the pressure of the arbitration.[50] The Romanian delegation had clearly been stalling in the negotiations with Bulgaria, hoping that they might still be able to retain Balcic and Silistra. Indeed, the Romanians continued to hope that the German government would be convinced of their argument that the Reich's interests required Romania's complete territorial integrity.

Nevertheless, Manoilescu and Pop are right to point out that Hitler had originally been in favour of population transfer as the solution to the Transylvanian question. Hitler had put forward this view during his meeting with Gigurtu and Manoilescu on 26 July. Indeed, as early as 5 July, Fabricius informed former Foreign Minister Gafencu that 'the Führer does not wish that regions inhabited by compact masses of Romanians should be ceded, because the quarrel would reopen'.[51] Hitler seems to have remained personally sympathetic to the Romanian position. During his discussions with Ciano and Ribbentrop on 28 August, he pointed out that he believed Romania's ethnic claim to Transylvania to be justified since two-thirds of the population were Romanian. As he put it, 'the territorial claim that was psychologically extremely popular in the Hungarian nation was confronted by an ethnographical claim which was surely incontestable'. Hitler was by no means wholly sympathetic to the Hungarian revisionist cause. Referring to the Vienna Award of November 1938 in which the Axis had awarded southern Slovakia to Hungary, Hitler said that 'Hungary really ought to compromise, for she had not earned anything through her own efforts but owed her revisionist victories solely to Fascism and National Socialism'.[52] Indeed, Hitler appears to have been reluctant to encourage Hungarian claims on Transylvania following the 1938 First Vienna Award and he maintained this position right up until August 1940, since he regarded Romania to be of greater military value than Hungary.[53]

Minister Fabricius was also in agreement with the Romanian thesis that negotiations with Hungary should be based on the ethnic principle and population transfer. On 26 August, he informed the Hungarian minister to Bucharest that 'he was endorsing the Romanian proposal presented at Turnu Severin and that he held this to be the only solution to the dispute'.[54] Reporting to Berlin on the same day about the breakdown of the negotiations at Turnu Severin, Fabricius pointed out the particular problem caused by Hungary's insistence that the Szekler areas in south-east Transylvania should be ceded to Hungary. Fabricius proposed that the new Hungarian–Romanian border should leave the Szekler area well inside Romania.[55] Following a conversation with Fabricius on 5 July, former Foreign Minister Gafencu recorded that the Germans approved a plan under which Romania would only have to cede the eastern Tisza basin valley area, running along the line of the towns of Arad, Oradea and Satu Mare, near the Hungarian border.[56] Clearly, initial German plans did not foresee large-scale territorial cessions by Romania. Moreover, during his meeting with Manoilescu and Gigurtu on 26 July, Hitler had categorically informed the Romanians that he wished the ethnic German minority to remain within the Romanian state. Yet Hitler consented to an arbitration which transferred a large number of ethnic Germans to Hungary and contravened the ethnic principle which he himself had recommended. The explanation for the German decision can be found by examining the international context in which the Vienna Award took place.

The background to Hitler's decision to arbitrate in Romania's territorial disputes with her neighbours was the Reich's increasingly tense relationship with the Soviet Union. Soviet power and influence in Eastern Europe had increased during the spring and early summer of 1940. Prior to the seizure of Bessarabia and the northern Bukovina in late June, the Soviets had begun the incorporation of the Baltic states into the Soviet Union. With Nazi–Soviet collaboration looking increasingly uneasy in 1940, and Britain still undefeated in the West, Hitler began to fear that the British might have entered into negotiations with the Soviets.[57]

On 31 July 1940, Hitler took the decision to postpone Operation Sea Lion against Britain and to attack and destroy the Soviet Union as soon as possible. This would prevent a possible alliance between the Soviet Union and the Anglo-Saxon powers and the opening of a second front in Eastern Europe. At the same time, Hitler needed peace in South-East Europe in order to ensure that Germany's economic needs continued to be fulfilled. The steady flow of petroleum from Romania, in particular, was essential for the Reich's war machine. Hitler decided, therefore, that a settlement must be reached between Hungary and Romania to prevent a war between the two countries. This settlement would then be followed by an Axis guarantee to Romania. Plans for the potential dispatch of troops to secure Romania's borders had already been formulated as early as 15 August.[58]

The need to bring Balkan territorial disputes to a swift conclusion was prompted not only by these wider military considerations, but also by Hitler's growing apprehension of Soviet links with Hungary and Bulgaria. On the day that he demanded Bessarabia and the northern Bukovina from Romania, Soviet foreign minister Molotov declared to the Germans that 'certain Hungarian requests were considered reasonable by the Soviet government....'. Molotov added that 'the Bulgarian demands for the Dobruja and for access to the Aegean Sea were considered justified by the Soviet government, which had recognised them'.[59] In early July, the Soviets informed the Germans that their government 'had not forgotten that at one time all three estuaries of the Danube were in Russian possession'.[60] This implied that the Soviets might be prepared to use Bulgarian demands to further their own expansion into the Danube. It was as a result of this Soviet stress on friendship with Bulgaria and support for Bulgaria's claims that Hitler decided to intervene in the Romanian–Bulgarian dispute. Hence Hitler gave his backing to the Bulgarian demand for the whole of southern Dobruja in late July.[61]

The Soviets also continued to support Hungarian revisionist demands. On 5 July Hungarian Foreign Minister Csáky reported to the Germans that Molotov 'considered Hungary's demands on Romania quite as just as the Russian demand for Bessarabia'.[62] On 7 July, in a discussion with Count Ciano and Ribbentrop, Hitler discussed the possibility of a Hungarian attack on Romania. He believed that in the event of such a war, the Soviets would use the occasion to cross the Danube, establish a connection with Bulgaria, and move on into Turkey and the Near East. Hitler suspected that Hungary would be inclined to attack Romania jointly with the Soviets, since ties between the two countries had recently been strengthened. Hitler feared that such a war would cut Germany and Italy off from vital supplies of petroleum.[63] Nevertheless, having put pressure on Hungary and Romania to enter into negotiations, Hitler clearly hoped that the dispute could be solved without Axis arbitration.

Hitler's immediate decision to arbitrate in the Romanian–Hungarian dispute in late August was due to Hungarian and Soviet military actions during the days following the breakdown of negotiations at Turnu Severin on 24 August. The German minister to Budapest reported on that day that he believed 'that Hungary will start military operations next week unless the Axis intervenes'.[64] The minister was rather optimistic regarding Hungary's timing of an attack. The Germans were, in fact, forced to prevent a Hungarian military strike against Romania only one day later, on the night of 25/26 August.[65] Despite the check, the Hungarians continued to threaten military action against Romania. On 26 August, Hungarian Foreign Minster Csáky told the German minister in Budapest that he was under pressure from Regent Horthy and the military to strike against Romania.[66] The Hungarian minister to Berlin informed the German foreign ministry the following day that 'the Hungarian government feels impelled to consider the idea of a military solution against Romania'.[67]

Meanwhile, the Soviet threat to Romania was gaining momentum. Border incidents occurred on the Romanian–Soviet border between 23 and 25 August. A Soviet parachute regiment and other divisions were identified at Chişinău. The Romanian General Staff anticipated an imminent Soviet attack from the northern Bukovina.[68] The Soviet danger reached a high-point on the night of 29/30 August, when the Soviets accused Romania of hostile actions on the frontier.[69] At the same time, Hungary appeared to be forging ever closer links with the Soviets. Following the breakdown of the negotiations at Turnu Severin, the Hungarian minister to Moscow had spoken with Molotov. The latter had reaffirmed that 'the Soviet government recognised the Hungarian claims on Romania and agreed to their realisation'.[70] Hungary was apparently even prepared to cede Ruthenia to the Soviets as the price of their support.[71] It was as a result of this threat of combined military action against Romania that Hitler decided both to take certain military measures and to intervene in the Transylvanian dispute. German neutralisation of Hungary required that Hungary be granted at least partial fulfilment of her claims.

On 26 August Hitler ordered forces stationed in the Polish General Gouvernement to be strengthened. Ten divisions were to be transferred to the east and two armoured divisions to the south-east of the General Gouvernement. The forces were arranged 'in such a manner that quick intervention to protect the Romanian oil districts would be guaranteed if necessary'.[72] It was only on 28 August, however, that Hitler decided on a non-negotiable arbitration.[73]

During a meeting with Ciano and Ribbentrop, Hitler pointed out that Hungarian war threats vitally affected the interests of both Italy and

Germany. War in Romania might lead to the permanent destruction of the Romanian oil wells on which both Axis countries were heavily dependent. In the event of war the Soviets would take the opportunity to intervene and would, as Hitler correctly predicted, 'advance the boundary line of their interests as far as circumstances permitted'. Hitler decided during this meeting that at the appropriate time during the planned discussions with the Romanians and Hungarians at Vienna, a joint German–Italian map should be submitted to both the parties for acceptance. The map was to show the new Hungarian–Romanian frontier in Transylvania and was not to be the subject of discussion. In return Romania would be given a territorial guarantee.[74]

In the event, it was Ribbentrop and Ciano, rather than Hitler, who drew up the Award.[75] This factor had a further adverse outcome for Romania. As he had revealed in his discussion with Gigurtu and Manoilescu on 26 July, Ribbentrop believed in substantial territorial concessions by Romania. More crucially, the new Hungarian–Romanian border had strategic importance for the Germans. By pushing the border of Hungary, which was at this point more closely tied to the Axis than Romania, to the ridge of the east Carpathians, the Germans had created a barrier behind which their army could prepare for war against the Soviet Union. Most importantly, the new border brought the German army to within striking distance of the Prahova valley, where the Romanian oil wells were situated, thus helping to ensure their safety. The German High Command had apparently been instrumental in imposing the final shape on the Vienna Award.[76]

The Vienna Award, sealed by the Axis' territorial guarantee to Romania, gave concrete expression to the Reich's interests in Romania. As former Foreign Minister Gafencu pointed out, the guarantee signified that 'German influence began at the line of the Prut and the Lower Danube at which Russia had halted, and that no other foreign influence would henceforth be tolerated'.[77] Had there been room for doubt before August 1940, it was now quite clear that Romania was inextricably bound up in the power struggle between Germany and the Soviet Union. As Hitler declared on 31 August, the Soviet Union had to learn that 'Germany has a vital influence in Romania and will stop short of nothing to safeguard them... Romania is inviolable'.[78] By 2 September, Hitler had already decided to send tanks and air protection to Romania under the Axis guarantee. He was only prevented from executing this decision by the political crisis which broke out the following day in Romania.[79]

The popular unrest which erupted in various parts of Romania on 3 September was a direct result of the loss of northern Transylvania. This led to Carol's abdication on 6 September and the granting of dictatorial powers to General Ion Antonescu. The General formed an alliance with the Iron Guard and the so-called National Legionary State was proclaimed on 14 September 1940.

It is common among Romanian historians to regard the Antonescu and Iron Guard regime as having been brought to power by the Germans, who were suspicious of Carol's past links with the West. According to this view, the Antonescu regime then completed Romania's subordination to the Axis.[80] It is certainly true that Fabricius at the German legation encouraged Antonescu to demand dictatorial powers from King Carol. Antonescu was favoured by the Germans owing to his willingness to fulfil the stipulations of the Vienna Award.[81] The unrest against Carol was, however, popular and spontaneous and not fomented by Germany.[82] Despite the support it enjoyed amongst certain Nazi Party circles in Berlin, the Iron Guard was not pushed into the new government by German pressure.[83] The high political profile which the Guard enjoyed by September 1940 was, in fact, a direct result of Carol placing them in government in the summer of 1940.

The process which culminated in General Antonescu's signing of the Tripartite Pact on 23 November 1940, had been set in motion by King Carol in the summer of 1940. The renunciation of the Anglo-French guarantee, the creation of a cabinet more agreeable to Germany, reconciliation with the Iron Guard, and the request for a military mission, were all regarded by Carol as precursors to an alliance and to political collaboration with the Reich.[84] Carol hoped thereby to save Romania from the clutches of the Soviet Union and of her other rapacious neighbours. The basis of Antonescu's collaboration with the Reich was the same antibolshevism and fear of the Soviet Union which had drawn Carol into the arms of Germany in the first place. The diplomatic events leading up to the Axis' arbitration of the Vienna Award at the end of August 1940 showed that Romania was already being integrated into Reich foreign policy even before the establishment of the Antonescu regime on 6 September. Despite, therefore, the apparent break in the continuity of Romanian foreign policy occasioned by Carol's abdication on 6 September, General Antonescu's alliance with Germany had its origins in the foreign policy conducted by King Carol II in the summer of 1940.

Notes

1. MAE, 71/Germania, Vol. 79, pp. 74–6, Minister Argetoianu and Fabricius, German Minister, at the Foreign Ministry, 28 June 1940. Argetoianu was well-known in Germany due to his links with the Dresdner Bank. He had studied in Germany and had a fluent command of the language. Argetoianu had held various cabinet posts during the 1920s and 30s and had been a royal councillor from March 1938. He was also president of the Bucharest office of the Romanian Bank and president of the oil-companies Steaua Română and Petrolbloc (which had German-held shares). He was also a member of the board of various industrial companies, including the Reşiţa Iron Works, which had German connections.
2. MAE, 71/Germania, Vol. 79, p. 77, Note of a talk with Fabricius after having spoken to the Minister President, 29 June 1940, signed Argetoianu; DGFP, D, 10, Doc. nr 57, Minister in Romania to the Foreign Ministry, Bucharest, 29 June 1940.
3. DGFP, D, 10, Doc. nr 56, Adolf Hitler to King Carol II of Romania, Führer's Headquarters, 29 June 1940.
4. DGFP, D, 10, Doc. nr 68, Minister in Romania to the Foreign Ministry, Bucharest, 1 July 1940. Romania joined the Triple Alliance of Germany, Austria-Hungary and Italy on 30 October 1883. These allies agreed to come to each other's aid if attacked by Russia.
5. Arh. St., Însemnări Zilnice, Carol II, roll 22, Vol. 11a, Tuesday 2 July 1940, p. 287; DGFP, D, 10, Doc. nr 80, Minister in Romania to the Foreign Ministry, Bucharest, 2 July 1940. In his diary, Carol spoke of closer collaboration with Germany 'through an alliance'. Fabricius's account of the conversation refers to 'closer collaboration with Germany in all fields, guaranteed by political treaties'.
6. Horia Sima, *Sfârşitul unei domnii sângeroase*, Timişoara, 1995, pp. 147–9; Walter Hagen (pseudonym for Dr Höttl, the former leader of SD Intelligence Services in South-East Europe), *Die Geheime Front. Organisation, Personen und Aktionen des Deutschen Geheimdienstes*, Linz and Vienna, 1950, p. 284.
7. DGFP, D, 10, Doc. nr 161, Legation in Romania to the Foreign Ministry, Bucharest, 13 July 1940, signed Fabricius.
8. MAE, 71/Germania, Vol. 79, pp. 186–90, To His Excellency Marshal Göring from the President of the Council of Ministers of the Romanian Kingdom, Bucharest, 16 July 1940; DGFP, D, 10, Doc. nr 196, Memorandum by an Official of the Political Department, Berlin, 20 July 1940, signed Kramarz.
9. Jürgen Förster, 'Zur Bündnispolitik Rumäniens vor und während des Zweiten Weltkrieges', in (eds) Manfred Messerschmidt, Klaus A. Maier, Werner Rahn and Bruno Thoss, *Militärgeschichte, Probleme- Thesen- Wege. Im Auftrag des Militärgeschichtlichen Forschungsamtes aus Anlass seines 25 jährigen Bestehens*, Stuttgart, 1983, pp. 294–310 (297).
10. PA, Büro des Staatssekretärs, Rumänien, Vol. 2, 2.40–7.40, Note, Berlin, 5 July 1940, signed Heinburg. Manoilescu's brother, Grigore, was director of the Iron Guard newspaper, *Buna Vestire*. Gigurtu was also favourable to the Iron Guard: Sima, *Sfârşitul unei domnii sângeroase*, p. 150.

11 For Crainic's ideological links with the Iron Guard, see Armin Heinen, *Die Legion 'Erzengel Michael' in Rumänien. Soziale Bewegung und politische Organisation*, Munich, 1986, pp. 140, 171, 183–7, 251–2.
12 Mihail Manoilescu, *Dictatul de la Viena. Memorii iulie–august 1940*, (ed.) Valeriu Dinu, Bucharest, 1991, p. 61.
13 On 27 July Manoilescu and Gigurtu visited Rome. Count Ciano described the Romanians as 'simply disgusting. They open their mouths only to exude honeyed compliments. They have become anti-French, anti-English, and anti-League of Nations. They talk with contempt of the diktat of Versailles – too honeyed.' For this information, see Galeazzo Ciano, *The Ciano Diaries, 1939–1943*, (ed.) Hugh Gibson, New York, 1946, 27 July 1940, p. 279.
14 MAE, 71/Germania, Vol. 79, p. 97, Creation of the new government under the Presidency of I. Gigurtu. Declaration of the Government, 4 July 1940.
15 MAE, 71/România, Vol. 353, pp. 274–5, *Neamul Românesc*, 9 July 1940, 'The government programme. An explanation by I. Gigurtu, President of the Council of Ministers'; ibid, p. 281, *Berliner Börsenzeitung*, 6 July 1940, Interview with I. Gigurtu, 'Policy of Reality'.
16 MAE, 71/Germania, Vol. 79, p. 153, Declaration of Minister Manoilescu made at Bucharest to representatives of DNB Agency on 14 July 1940 on the occasion of Romania's departure from the League of Nations.
17 MAE, 71/Germania, Vol. 79, pp. 139–46, 13 July 1940, Report submitted to the Führer by Minister von Killinger regarding the meetings in Bucharest on 26–27 June 1940.
18 MAE, 71/Germania, Vol. 79, p. 93, To the Romanian Legation in Berlin, Tel. nr 40024, 2 July 1940, signed Argetoianu.
19 Arh. St., Însemnări Zilnice, Carol II, roll 22, Vol. 11a, Tuesday 9 July 1940, p. 296.
20 MAE, 71/Germania, Vol. 79, p. 264, To the Legation in Berlin, Tel. nr 41893, 10 July 1940, signed Manoilescu.
21 Arh. St., Însemnări Zilnice, Carol II, roll 22, Vol. 11a, Wednesday 10 July 1940, p. 297; MAE, 71/Germania, Vol. 79, p. 180, To the Legation in Berlin, Tel. nr 43668, 16 July 1940, signed Manoilescu.
22 MAE, 71/Germania, Vol. 79, p. 203, From the President of the Council of Ministers and the Minister for Foreign Affairs, Bucharest, 18 July 1940.
23 MAE, 71/Germania, Vol. 79, p. 266, To the Legation in Berlin, Tel. nr 45024, 23 July 1940, signed Manoilescu.
24 DGFP, D, 10, Doc. nr 104, Foreign Minister to the Legation in Romania, For Fabricius, 4 July 1940.
25 Förster, 'Zur Bündnispolitik Rumäniens vor und während des Zweiten Weltkrieges', p. 296; MAE, 71/Germania, Vol. 79, pp. 81–2, Document dated 29 June 1940, signed Gigurtu.
26 Arh. St., Însemnări Zilnice, Carol II, roll 22, Vol. 11a, Saturday 6 July 1940, p. 293; DGFP, D, 10, Doc. nr 123, Minister in Romania to the Foreign Ministry, For Ribbentrop, Bucharest, 6 July 1940.
27 MAE, 71/Germania, Vol. 79, pp. 158–62, Adolf Hitler to King Carol II of Romania, Führer Headquarters, 15 July 1940.
28 MAE, 71/Germania, Vol. 79, pp. 164–67, Response by King Carol to Hitler's letter of 15 July 1940, sent to the Führer through Gigurtu, President of the

Council of Ministers, on 26 July 1940 on the occasion of the talks at Berchtesgaden.
29 For what follows on the meeting at the Berghof, see MAE, 71/Germania, Vol. 79, pp. 242–6, Résumé of conversations at the Berghof on 26 July 1940, unsigned. The German document is rather more revealing: DGFP, D, 10, Doc. nr 234, Unsigned Memorandum. Record of the conversation between the Führer and Romanian Minister President Gigurtu, in the presence of the Reich Foreign Minister, Romanian Foreign Minister Manoilescu, Minister Fabricius, and the Romanian Minister in Berlin, at the Berghof, on 26 July 1940. See also Manoilescu's account of the meeting. This was, however, written after the Second World War. See, Mihail Manoilescu, *Dictatul de la Viena*, pp. 108–12.
30 MAE, 71/Germania, Vol. 79, pp. 242–6, Résumé of conversations at the Berghof on 26 July 1940, unsigned; DGFP, D, 10, Doc. nr 234, Unsigned memorandum. Record of the conversation between the Führer and Romanian Minister President Gigurtu, in the presence of the Reich Foreign Minister, Romanian Foreign Minister Manoilescu, Minister Fabricius, and the Romanian Minister in Berlin, at the Berghof, on 26 July 1940.
31 DGFP, D, 10, Doc. nr 233, Memorandum by an Official of the Foreign Minister's Secretariat. Record of conversation between the Reich Foreign Minister and Romanian Minister President Gigurtu, in the presence of the Romanian Foreign Minister, at Fuschl, 26 July 1940.
32 DGFP, D, 10, Doc. nr 253, Foreign Minister to the State Secretary, 29 July 1940.
33 DGFP, D, 10, Doc. nr 262, Minister in Romania to the Foreign Ministry, Bucharest, 31 July 1940.
34 MAE, 71/Germania, Vol. 79, pp. 271–3, Note of a conversation held on 31 July 1940 by Mihail Manoilescu and Fabricius, German Minister, at the Foreign Ministry.
35 Mihail Manoilescu, *Dictatul de la Viena*, pp. 175–7.
36 MAE, 71/Germania, Vol. 80, p. 48, Legation in Berlin to the Foreign Minister, Tel. nr 40381, 9 August 1940, signed Romalo; ibid, p. 57, Legation in Berlin to the Foreign Ministry, Tel. nr 40385, 10 August 1940, signed Romalo.
37 DGFP, D, 10, Doc. nr 305, Memorandum by the State Secretary, Berlin, 7 August 1940.
38 For the negotiations at Turnu-Severin see, Cristian Troncotă, 'August 1940: Din culisele marii nedreptăți istorice', *Magazin istoric*, serie nouă, 25, nr 1 (286), (January 1991), pp. 18–22; Mihail Manoilescu, *Dictatul de la Viena*, pp. 152–64; Valer Pop, *Bătălia Pentru Ardeal*, no place of publication, no date, pp. 93–9, 101–17, 121–37. See also, A. Simion, *Dictatul de la Viena*, Cluj, 1972, pp. 159–78.
39 MAE, 71/Germania, Vol. 80, pp. 72–3, Minister Manoilescu and Fabricius at the Foreign Ministry, Monday 19 August 1940; DGFP, D, 10, Doc. nr 376, Memorandum by the Director of the Political Department, Berlin, 21 August 1940. According to Ulrich von Hassell, 'Hitler shudders at the prospect of having to act as umpire between Hungary and Romania': *Vom Andern Deutschland. Aus den Nachgelassenen Tagebüchern, 1938–1944*, Zürich, 1947, 10 August 1940, p. 161.
40 MAE, 71/Germania, Vol. 80, pp. 96–8, Note of a conversation of 25 August, 11 am, Minister Mihail Manoilescu and Fabricius at the Foreign Ministry; ibid, pp. 117–18, To the Legation in Berlin, Tel. nr 52812, 26 August 1940,

signed Manoilescu; ibid, pp. 108–11, To the Romanian Legation in Berlin, Tel. no nr, 26 August 1940, signed Manoilescu
41 MAE, 71/Germania, Vol. 80, pp. 129–34, Letter addressed to His Excellency Ribbentrop, Reich Foreign Minister, by the Prime Minister, I. Gigurtu, on 27 August 1940.
42 MAE, 71/1920–1944, Transylvania, Vol. 42, pp. 143–4, From Minister Manoilescu in Vienna to the Foreign Ministry, Tel. nr 1, 29 August 1940; ibid, pp. 152–4, From Minister Manoilescu in Vienna to the Foreign Ministry, Tel. nr 5, 29 August 1940; DGFP, D, 10, Doc. nr 408, Memorandum by an Official of the Foreign Minister's Secretariat, Vienna, 31 August 1940. Record of the conversation between the Reich Foreign Minister and Romanian Foreign Minister Manoilescu, in the presence of Count Ciano, at the Hotel Imperial in Vienna, on 29 August 1940. Valer Pop also accompanied Manoilescu to Vienna. See his account of his conversation with Ribbentrop and Ciano in *Bătălia Pentru Ardeal*, pp. 168–72. It should not be imagined, however, that the Hungarians were treated any more lightly in their discussions with Ribbentrop on 29 August. Ribbentrop pointed out that Germany would not tolerate damage to Germany's 'vital interests' i.e. Romanian petroleum, during the war in the West. He also stressed that Hungary had not always treated the Reich with respect, such as being unwilling to allow the Germans use of Hungarian railways during the war against Poland, and their complaints following the First Vienna Award in 1938. Hungary was also to accept the arbitration unconditionally. For this information, see DGFP, D, 10, Doc. nr 410, Memorandum by an Official of the Foreign Minister's Secretariat, Vienna, 31 August 1940. Record of the conversation between the Reich Foreign Minister and the Hungarian Foreign Minister, Count Csáky, in the presence of Count Ciano and the Hungarian Minister President, Count Teleki, at the Hotel Imperial in Vienna, on 29 August 1940. Ciano noted in his diary with regard to the conversations with both the Romanians and Hungarians on 29 August: 'Ribbentrop assails the Hungarians... he accuses Hungary of having engaged in anti-German policy on more than one occasion... The conversation with the Romanians is less violent.' See, Ciano, *The Ciano Diaries, 1939–1943*, p. 288.
43 MAE, 71/1920–1944, Transylvania, Vol. 42, pp. 148–9, From Minister Manoilescu in Vienna, Tel. nr 3, 29 August 1940.
44 MAE, 71/1920–1944, Transylvania, Vol. 42, pp.189–211, Debates of the Crown Council under the Presidency of His Majesty, held on Friday, 30 August 1940.
45 MAE, 71/1920–1944, Transylvania, Vol 42, p. 166, To Minister Manoilescu in Vienna, Tel. nr 53660, 30 August 1940, signed Gigurtu.
46 Macartney notes that the population figures for the area given to Hungary under the Vienna Award were:

	1930 Romanian Census	1941 Hungarian Census
Magyar	911,550	1,347,012
Romanian	1,176,433	1,066,353
German	68,694	47,501
Jews	138,885	(Yiddish) 45,593
Others	99,585	70,832
Total	2,395,147	2,577,291

See, C. A. Macartney, *October Fifteenth: A History of Modern Hungary, 1929–1945*, Part 1, Edinburgh, 1956, pp. 422–3. Note, however, that between the imposition of the Vienna Award in 1940 and the 1941 Hungarian census there was substantial population movement of Hungarians from the Romanian-controlled area of Transylvania to Hungarian northern Transylvania and vice-versa for the Romanians.

47 For the full text of the Vienna Award, see DGFP, D, 10, Doc. nr 413, Documents on the Second Vienna Award, Vienna, 30 August 1940. The area gained by the Hungarians was less than their original demand at Turnu Severin. Nevertheless, according to Ciano, who witnessed the signature ceremony, 'the Hungarians cannot contain their joy when they see the map. Then we hear a loud thud. It was Manoilescu, who fainted on the table': Ciano, *The Ciano Diaries, 1939–1940*, 30 August 1940, p. 289.

48 See, for example, Mircea Muşat, who describes the arbitration as 'one of the most odious, criminal and dirty acts of fascism': *1940. Drama României Mari*, Bucharest, 1992, p. 179. See, likewise, Ion Calafeteanu 'L'isolement international de la Roumanie et le Diktat de Vienne', *Revue roumaine d'études internationales*, 15, 1 (51), (1981), pp. 45–54 (esp. p. 53), and A. Simion's discussion of the proceedings at Vienna, in which he claims that the Reich was punishing Romania for her anti-Axis policy: *Dictatul de la Viena*, Cluj, 1972, p. 181.

49 Mihail Manoilescu, *Dictatul de la Viena*, pp. 183–8; Pop, *Bătălia pentru Ardeal*, pp. 156–8 and 168–72.

50 Pop, *Bătălia pentru Ardeal*, pp. 90–3, 163–4; Mihail Manoilescu, *Dictatul de la Viena*, pp. 136–9, 175, 182. The Treaty of Craiova was signed with Bulgaria on 7 September 1940.

51 Grigore Gafencu, *Jurnal, iunie 1940–iulie 1942*, (eds) Ion Ardeleanu and Vasile Arimia, Bucharest, no date, p. 33.

52 DGFP, D, 10, Doc. nr 407, Memorandum by an Official of the Foreign Minister's Secretariat, Vienna, 28 August 1940. Record of the conversation between the Führer, and Count Ciano, in the presence of Foreign Minister v. Ribbentrop, Ambassadors v. Mackensen and Alfieri, and Counsellor of Legation Hewel, at Obersalzburg, on 28 August 1940.

53 Stephen Fischer-Galaţi, 'The Great Powers and the Fate of Transylvania Between the Two World Wars', in (ed.) John F. Cadzow, *Transylvania: The Roots of Ethnic Conflict*, Ohio, 1983, pp. 180–9 (187).

54 DGFP, D, 10, Doc. nr 393, Minister in Hungary to the Foreign Ministry, Budapest, 26 August 1940.

55 DGFP, D, 10, Doc. nr 396, Minister in Romania to the Foreign Ministry, Bucharest, 26 August 1940; Nicolae Jurcă (ed.), 'Wilhelm Fabricius: "Dictatul de la Viena a fost un act desgustător"', *Magazin istoric*, serie nouă, 25, nr 12 (297), (December 1991), pp. 45–9 (48).

56 Gafencu, *Jurnal*, p. 33.

57 H. W. Koch, 'Hitler's "Programme" and the Genesis of Operation Barbarossa', in (ed.) H. W. Koch, *Aspects of the Third Reich*, London, 1985, pp. 285–322 (esp. 291–300).

58 Gerhard L. Weinberg, *Germany and the Soviet Union, 1939–1941*, Leiden, 1954, pp. 114–29.

59 DGFP, D, 9, Doc. nr 21, Ambassador in the Soviet Union to the Foreign Ministry, Moscow, 26 June 1940.

60 DGFP, D, 10, Doc. nr 130, Embassy in the Soviet Union to the Foreign Ministry, Moscow, 8 July 1940, signed Schulenburg.
61 Andreas Hillgruber, *Hitler, König Carol und Marschall Antonescu. Die deutsch–rumänischen Beziehungen, 1938–1944*, Wiesbaden, 1965, pp. 78–9.
62 DGFP, D, 10, Doc. nr 119, Minister in Hungary to the Foreign Ministry, Budapest, 5 July 1940.
63 DGFP, D, 10, Doc. nr 129, Memorandum by an official of the Foreign Minister's Secretariat, Berlin, 8 July 1940. Record of the conversation between the Führer and Count Ciano in the presence of the Reich Foreign Minister, 7 July 1940.
64 DGFP, D, 10, Doc. nr 384, Minister in Hungary to the Foreign Ministry, Budapest, 24 August 1940.
65 Generaloberst Halder, *Kriegstagebuch*, (ed.) Hans-Adolf Jacobsen with Alfred Philippi, Vol. 2, Stuttgart, 1962, 26 August 1940, pp. 77–8.
66 DGFP, D, 10, Doc. nr 393, Minister in Hungary to the Foreign Ministry, Budapest, 26 August 1940.
67 DGFP, D, 10, Doc. nr 400, The Director of the Political Department to the Foreign Minister, Berlin, 27 August 1940.
68 Fischer-Galați, 'The Great Powers and the Fate of Transylvania between the Two World Wars', p. 187; DGFP, D, 10, Doc. nr 389, Memorandum by an Official of the Foreign Ministry, Berlin, 25 August 1940, signed Overbeck.
69 Hillgruber, *Hitler, König Carol und Marschall Antonescu*, p. 29; Mihail Manoilescu, *Dictatul de la Viena*, p. 240.
70 DGFP, D, 10, Doc. nr 406, The Ambassador in the Soviet Union to the Foreign Ministry, Moscow, 28 August 1940.
71 MAE, 71/1920–1944, Transylvania, Vol. 42, p. 186, 30 August 1940, General Dombrowsky's meeting with Hermann Neubacher. For a discussion of Hungarian links with the Soviets, see Stephen Fischer-Galați, 'The Great Powers and the Fate of Transylvania Between the Two World Wars'; see also Mihail Manoilescu, *Dictatul de la Viena*, pp. 247–65, and Raoul Bossy, *Amintiri din viața diplomatică (1918–1940)*, (ed.) Stelian Neagoe, Vol. 2, Bucharest, 1993, pp. 287–8.
72 DGFP, D, 10, pp. 549–50, Editor's Note. Draft of entries by Helmuth Greiner in the War Diary of the Wehrmacht Operations Staff (1 August 1940–30 November 1940) for 26 August.
73 Mihail Manoilescu, *Dictatul de la Viena*, pp. 252–3.
74 DGFP, D, 10, Doc. nr 407, Memorandum by an Official of the Foreign Minister's Secretariat, Vienna, 28 August 1940. Record of the conversation between the Führer and Count Ciano, in the presence of the Foreign Minister v. Ribbentrop, Ambassadors v. Mackensen and Alfieri, and Councillor of Legation Hewel, at Obersalzburg, on 28 August 1940.
75 On 28 August, following the meeting with Hitler, Ciano recorded that the Führer had left the solution of the Hungarian–Romanian question to himself and Ribbentrop. 'The only thing (Hitler) has at heart is that peace be preserved there and that Romanian oil continues to flow to his reservoirs': Ciano, *The Ciano Diaries, 1939–1943*, p. 288.
76 Ion Gheorghe, *Rumäniens Weg zum Satelliten-Staat*, Heidelberg, 1952, pp. 71–2; Bossy, *Amintiri din viața diplomatică*, Vol. 2, p. 289. On 10 September 1940, Hitler informed the Hungarian minister to Berlin that the decisive factor in

the decision regarding the new Hungarian–Romanian border in Transylvania had been the need to ensure the safety of the Romanian oilfields: Report from the Hungarian Ambassador in Berlin, Sztójay, to Foreign Minister Csáky, Berlin, 10 September 1940, (ed.) Lajos Kerekes, *Allianz Hitler–Horthy–Mussolini. Dokumente zur Ungarischen Aussenpolitik (1933–1944)*, Budapest, 1966, Doc. nr 92, pp. 282–8.

77 Grigore Gafencu, *Prelude to the Russian Campaign: From the Moscow Pact (August 21st 1939) to the Opening of Hostilities in Russia (June 22nd 1941)*, translated by Fletcher-Allen, London, 1945, p. 56.

78 Halder, *Kriegstagebuch*, Vol. 2, 31 August 1940, p. 83.

79 Hillgruber, *Hitler, König Carol und Marschall Antonescu*, p. 93.

80 Petre Ilie, 'Relațiile dintre Garda de Fier și Germania nazistă', in *Împotriva fascismului. Sesiunea științifica privind analiza critică și desmascarea fascismului în România, București, 4–5 martie, 1971*, Bucharest, 1971, pp. 83–95; Dinu C. Giurescu, *Illustrated History of the Romanian People*, Bucharest, 1981, p. 555; typically also, see (ed.) Andrei Oțetea, *A Concise History of Romania*, translated by Andrew Mackenzie, London, 1985, p. 477.

81 DGFP, D, 11, Doc. nr 17, The Minister in Romania to the Foreign Ministry, Bucharest, 5 September 1940.

82 'Carol was dethroned not by Germany... but by the Romanian people': Pavel Pavel, *How Romania Failed*, London, no date, p. 234.

83 For Germany's negligible role in the creation of the National Legionary State, see Rebecca Haynes, 'Germany and the Establishment of the Romanian National Legionary State, September 1940', in *Slavonic and East European Review*, Vol. 77, nr 4, October 1999, pp. 700–25.

84 Antonescu repeated Carol's request for a German military mission to Romania on 7 September. The mission arrived in Bucharest on 14 October. See, Jürgen Förster, 'Rumäniens Weg in die deutsche Abhängigkeit. Zur Rolle der deutschen Militärmission 1940–41', *Militärgeschichtliche Mitteilungen*, 25–26, nr 1, 1979, pp. 47–78 (58).

Conclusion

The aim of all Romanian foreign-policy makers during the inter-war period was to maintain the territorial integrity of Greater Romania. Although Romania had almost doubled in size as a result of the Paris peace treaties, she remained vulnerable to revisionist attacks by her Bulgarian, Hungarian and Soviet neighbours.

During the 1920s and early 1930s, the Romanian foreign ministry responded to these potential threats by integrating the country into the French-backed collective security system. Romania was a member of the League of Nations and was incorporated into the French security system in Eastern Europe by her Treaty of Friendship with France of 1926. Romania and Britain had no formal alliance, but Britain's role as a guarantor of the League of Nations ensured that good relations existed between the two countries. Romania was also protected by a number of regional alliances. The treaty with Poland of 1921 protected Romania against attack by the Soviet Union, while the Little Entente and Balkan Entente protected Romania against Hungary and Bulgaria respectively. Relations with Germany, which had been strong before the First World War, were relatively neglected. Germany was now ranged with the revisionist powers and backed Hungarian claims on Transylvania, while Romania was included amongst the anti-revisionist countries.

Nicolae Titulescu, during his 1932 to 1936 foreign ministry, sought to strengthen Romania's position within the collective security system by incorporating Romania into the Franco-Soviet alliance system. Titulescu's policy, however, was opposed by the majority of Romania's anti-bolshevik ruling class. In addition, Titulescu was unable to secure Soviet acknowledgement of Romania's sovereign rights over Bessarabia. At the same time as Titulescu's pro-Soviet policy was alienating Romanian politicians, the French-backed collective security system was beginning to crumble.

The League of Nations had already suffered a blow to its prestige on account of its failure to solve the Manchurian crisis in 1932. The League's imposition of sanctions against Italy in 1935 created resentment in Romania, which exported petroleum to Italy. At the same time, France's 1935 alliance with the Soviet Union alienated even the more francophile members of the Romanian government. More importantly, France was largely passive in the face of Germany's re-emergence as a Great Power in the mid-1930s. France's failure to respond at all to Hitler's remilitarisation of the Rhineland in March 1936 signalled the decline of French prestige in Eastern Europe. The victory of the socialist Popular Front in the French elections of May 1936 was regarded as a victory for bolshevism by Romanians and further damaged French prestige in their eyes. In addition, French economic influence was declining in Eastern Europe as a result of France's inability to help the agrarian countries of Eastern Europe during the Depression. It was Germany which was fast becoming the most important economic influence in the region.

A shift away from the strictly pro-French line in Romania's foreign policy was signalled by the dismissal of Titulescu as foreign minister at the end of August 1936. He had made himself repugnant to King Carol and the majority of Romanian politicians by his support for a mutual assistance pact with the Soviets. Titulescu's pro-Soviet and pro-French policies had also alienated Germany.

From 1936 onwards King Carol and his foreign ministers sought to achieve a position of informal neutrality between the Great Powers. The king and his ministers attempted to accommodate Romania to the gradual re-establishment of German influence in Eastern Europe. At the same time they sought to retain Romania's traditional alliances and links with the West. Increasingly Britain, rather than France, came to be regarded as the most important of the western powers. Neutrality between the powers, however, necessarily required that greater emphasis be put on the relationship with Germany, since she had been the Great Power most neglected by the Romanians since the First World War.

Three factors in particular prompted the Romanians to seek the friendship of the Reich. These remained central to the Romanian–German relationship throughout the period 1936 to 1940. First, the economic relationship was of paramount importance. Beginning with the economic treaty of March 1935, Germany was well on the way to re-establishing the economic hegemony in Romania which she had held before the First World War. Germany alone was capable and willing to absorb Romania's agricultural surpluses and raw materials in return for industrial goods. With the inauguration of the German Four Year Plan in 1936, Romania's petroleum acquired a particular importance to the Germans. In subsequent years, and as the international situation intensified, Romanian petroleum was frequently bartered against armaments from Germany. Both the German foreign ministry and the Romanian government believed that strong political relations between the two countries would eventually arise out of economic collaboration.

The second factor which necessitated the creation of good links with Germany was the question of Hungarian revisionism. As German influence began to reassert itself in Central Europe in the mid-1930s, Romanian leaders feared that Germany would be disposed to back Hungarian revisionist claims against Romania. The Romanians hoped that by earning German goodwill, the Reich would no longer support Hungarian claims. The Romanians were encouraged in this hope by declarations made by Nazi leaders to the effect that Germany would guarantee Romania's territorial integrity. In return, Nazi leaders asked the Romanian government not to extend any of its alliances against Germany, or to enter any anti-German coalitions. In addition, Romania was not to conclude an alliance with the Soviet Union or to allow right of passage through Romania to the Red Army. Hermann Göring was particularly active in attempting to convince the Romanians that neutrality towards the Reich would be rewarded by a German guarantee. His position as Commissioner for the Four Year Plan, and the importance of Romanian petroleum and agricultural produce to German war plans, explains his efforts to convince Romanian leaders to take a benevolent attitude towards the Reich. The Romanians were confused by the discrepancies between the promises made by Nazi leaders, and the German foreign ministry's guarded support for Hungarian revisionism. Nevertheless, the Romanian government continued to believe that by maintaining neutrality, and showing goodwill towards the Reich in foreign policy, the Germans would not allow Hungary to threaten Romania.

The third factor which served to bring Romania closer to Germany after 1936 was Romania's fear of the Soviet Union. The anti-Soviet and anti-bolshevik feelings of Romania's ruling-class contributed to the downfall of Foreign Minister Nicolae Titulescu in August 1936. The Soviet Union was not only perceived as an ideological threat to the Romanian monarchy, but also as a military threat to Bessarabia. With the Soviet Union's re-emergence as an actor in international affairs, many Romanian politicians were inclined to see friendship with Germany as a necessary counter-balance to the Soviet Union. As the 1930s progressed, Romanians increasingly saw Germany as their only protection against a Soviet reoccupation of Bessarabia.

The period of Victor Antonescu's foreign ministry, which endured from late August 1936 to December 1937, was marked by the attempt to achieve neutrality between the Great Powers and, at the same time, to establish strong links with the Reich. A series of foreign-policy debates were held in parliament and the press in the winter and spring of 1936–37. These debates showed evidence of an increasing desire among politicians of all political persuasions to reach a position of informal neutrality between the Great Powers for Romania, while simultaneously improving relations with the Reich. Neutrality was to be achieved by Romania refusing to extend her foreign-policy obligations, even towards her traditional allies. A foundation for future political links with Germany was to develop out of increasing economic collaboration. Foremost amongst the exponents of this thinking was Gheorghe Brătianu who stood close to King Carol and was frequently used by the king as an unofficial emissary to Germany. Brătianu was influenced by Belgium's declaration of neutrality in the autumn of 1936.

Victor Antonescu's ministry quickly demonstrated its resolve to maintain German goodwill by pursuing a neutral course between the Great Powers. Romanian diplomats gave the Reich frequent assurances of Romania's resolve not to enter an alliance with the Soviets. The Romanians also informed German officials that their government would not allow the Red Army rights of passage through Romania, which would be necessary if the Soviets needed to come to the assistance of their Czechoslovak ally. In their desire to achieve neutrality towards the Reich, Romanian foreign-policy makers were increasingly at odds with their Little Entente ally, Czechoslovakia. The Czechoslovaks had entered into an alliance with the Soviet Union in 1935 and hoped to secure the support of Romania in the event of a German attack. In September 1936, Romania, together with Yugoslavia, prevented the extension of the Little Entente's commitments into a full pact of mutual assistance. Such a pact would have forced Romania and Yugoslavia to fight for Czechoslovakia in the event of a German attack. To prevent their countries becoming involved in hostilities against Germany, Romanian and Yugoslavian leaders also stalled the plans for a Franco-Little Entente mutual assistance pact in the spring of 1937.

The policy of pursuing neutrality between the powers was continued under the brief Goga–Cuza government which held power from late December 1937 to February 1938. Although both Octavian Goga and A. C. Cuza were overt germanophiles, their period in government did not see a pronounced shift towards Germany. With the installation of the royal dictatorship in February 1938, the policy of unofficial neutrality was continued. The Anschluss prompted a curb on the activities of the Iron Guard, which the government feared might be used by the Reich to promote a pro-German government. In the wake of the Anschluss, the government also sought to prevent Romania's economic conventions with the former Austrian state being incorporated into her agreements with Germany. Despite these bids to restrict German influence in Romania, the government continued to give the Germans assurances of its neutrality. This was particularly apparent as the Sudeten crisis gathered pace during the course of 1938.

Romanian historians have frequently asserted that Romania alone remained loyal to Czechoslovakia in 1938. In reality, the Romanian foreign ministry under Nicolae Petrescu-Comnen sought to avoid its obligations towards the Czechoslovaks in order to maintain its neutrality towards the Reich. The Romanian government allowed the flight of Soviet aircraft bound for Czechoslovakia to fly over Romanian air space. At the same time, though, the Romanians gave frequent assurances to the Germans that they would not give the Red Army right of passage through Romania to help the Czechoslovaks. Under their Little Entente obligations, the Romanians were obliged to help the Czechoslovaks in the event of a Hungarian attack upon her. The Romanians made frequent requests to the German government to prevent Hungary becoming involved in any potential conflict so that Romania would not find herself at war with Germany. They also requested that any German attack on Czechoslovakia should not be launched from Hungarian soil, which could also have forced the Romanian army to fight. Throughout 1938, the Romanians frequently exhorted the Czechoslovak government to come to an agreement with the Sudeten Germans which was agreeable to the German government.

The Munich agreement posed further problems for the Romanian government. Munich reflected the unwillingness of Britain and France to maintain the Paris peace settlement. At the same time, the Anschluss and Munich gave the Reich a dominant economic and strategic position within Central and South-East Europe. The annexation of the Sudetenland by the Reich and the subsequent award of southern Slovakia to Hungary in November 1938 were evidence that revision of the Paris settlement was now accepted by the Great Powers. It became all the more important for the Romanians to secure German goodwill in order to prevent the Reich backing Hungarian claims to Transylvania. Romania and Hungary were now competitors for German support. Moreover, the discussions regarding the passage of Soviet troops through Romania which had taken place during the course of 1938, led to renewed

Romanian fears regarding Soviet involvement in European affairs. The Soviets, in particular, had never fully acknowledged Romania's sovereignty over Bessarabia.

In the immediate aftermath of Munich, King Carol and Foreign Minister Comnen continued to seek good relations with all the Great Powers. In keeping with this policy, Carol visited Britain, France and Germany in November. In economic terms, however, it was now clear that Germany was the biggest player. German control of the Sudetenland, and the Reich's effective stranglehold over the Czechoslovak economy, ensured that Germany was now Romania's main trading partner and supplier of armaments. Only one day after the Munich agreement, King Carol had requested greater economic collaboration with the Reich. The king additionally wished to build up the Romanian armaments industry and airforce with German help.

The growing importance of Germany for Romania in the weeks after Munich was reflected in attempts to prevent Hungarian revisionism against Czechoslovakia. In particular, the Romanian government feared that if Hungary were awarded the whole of Slovakia, it would signal the beginning of attempts to reacquire Transylvania. Foreign Minister Comnen justified his requests to the Reich on the grounds that Romania had shown her goodwill and wish for neutrality towards Germany during the Sudeten crisis. Such justifications were frequently used over the following years by Romanian diplomats when they requested the Reich's intercession with Hungary. Following the award of southern Slovakia to Hungary under the terms of the Vienna Award of 2 November 1938, the Romanians sought to ensure Czechoslovakia's retention of Ruthenia. During his discussion with Hitler in November, King Carol stressed the importance for Romania of Ruthenia not falling under Hungarian control. The direct route through Ruthenia and Czechoslovakia, argued the king, was important for trading links with the Reich.

The murder of the pro-German Iron Guard leader, Corneliu Zelea Codreanu, prompted a deterioration of relations with Germany. Since the murder took place only days after Carol's meeting with Hitler, the Führer was angered by the implication that he had agreed with the murder. Romanian–German relations entered into a highly tense period.

In late December 1938, King Carol appointed Grigore Gafencu as foreign minister. Gafencu aimed to maintain neutrality, or 'equilibrium' as he put it, between the Great Powers. Nevertheless, Romania's relationship with Germany was taking on ever greater significance as a result of Germany's geo-political hegemony in Central and South-East Europe. To this longer-standing factor which prompted Romania to seek

Germany's friendship, was added the immediate need to conciliate Germany following the murder of Codreanu. The measures used by Gafencu to conciliate Germany had already been foreseen during the course of 1938. Plans for economic collaboration had been discussed by King Carol during his trip to Germany in November. Gafencu's task was to speed up the process of cooperation.

At the heart of Gafencu's policy towards Germany lay the question of a territorial guarantee for Romania. Gafencu sought to make concrete the declarations made by German leaders over the years, in which Romania would receive a territorial guarantee against Hungarian revisionism in exchange for neutrality towards Germany. Not all members of the Romanian political establishment followed Gafencu's line on Germany. The 'Tilea affair' is explicable in terms of the divisions created within the Romanian government by Gafencu's apparent 'pro-German' policy. Both Tilea and senior members of government such as interior minister, Armand Călinescu, feared that receipt of a German guarantee in return for Romanian economic concessions would bind Romania too firmly into the German camp. Romania would thereby lose the support and sympathy of the western powers.

The first three months of 1939 appear to represent a strong shift in Romanian foreign policy in favour of Germany due to Gafencu's conciliatory measures. The signing of the March 1939 economic accord represented a further step towards Romania's economic dependency on Germany. Nevertheless, the accord was welcomed even by pro-western ministers such as Călinescu. The accord included plans for German help in building up Romania's industrial and agricultural sectors, as well as development of her armaments industry and airforce. Nevertheless, Gafencu successfully retained a neutral position for Romania. Despite the embarrassment caused by the 'Tilea affair', Gafencu and King Carol's plea to the western powers to take an active role in the affairs of Central and South-East Europe following Germany's invasion of Czechoslovakia on 15 March, did not fall on deaf ears.

By late March 1939, negotiations were already in progress with the British government. These led to the Anglo-French guarantee of Romania of 13 April 1939. During the negotiations, Gafencu sought to preserve Romania's position of 'equilibrium' between the West and Germany. He rejected any reciprocal pledges which could have obliged Romania to help the western powers fight Germany. He also refused to transform Romania's alliance with Poland, which existed for mutual defence against a Soviet attack, into an *erga omnes* agreement. Gafencu believed this would be construed as an anti-German move and bring both

Romania and Poland into conflict with the Reich. The Anglo-French guarantee was, as Gafencu wished, a unilateral guarantee of Romania's borders by Britain and France. The guarantee did not oblige Romania to fight for the western powers. In theory, therefore, Romania remained free to treat with Germany. Gafencu now hoped to use receipt of the western guarantee to force the Germans to guarantee Romania. Although Gafencu failed to get a German guarantee during his trip to Berlin in April 1939, he continued to make the request during the summer of 1939.

Gafencu's main task in the spring and summer of 1939 was to prevent Romania being drawn into the various British plans to create an anti-German bloc in Eastern Europe. Gafencu refused to have Romania mentioned in any of the British negotiations conducted with the Soviet Union during the summer of 1939. He believed any Romanian association with the Soviet Union would destroy Romania's relations with Germany. In the same manner, he sought to prevent any mention of Romania or the Balkan Entente in the negotiations which culminated in the Anglo-Turkish Treaty of October 1939. In this way Gafencu's policy of 'equilibrium' was maintained during the summer of 1939. Nevertheless, the Romanians were finding it increasingly difficult to remain neutral between Britain and Germany as relations between these two countries faltered during the course of 1939. German criticism that Romania was party to Britain's policy of 'encirclement' of Germany made Gafencu ever more ready to comply with German wishes.

By the autumn of 1939, Gafencu's policy of equilibrium was becoming increasingly difficult to maintain. The Nazi–Soviet Pact of 23 August 1939 increased the sense of political and military isolation within Romania. The fear now was that Germany had consented to the Soviet seizure of Bessarabia as the price of Soviet friendship. The opening of the European war and the Soviet Union's invasion of Poland on 19 September 1939 demonstrated Romania's isolation from the West. Under these conditions, Germany alone appeared as a potential mediator between Romania and the Soviet Union and began to take central place in Romania's Great Power relationships.

On 6 September, Romania declared her official neutrality in the war. Gafencu continued his attempts to retain equilibrium between the powers. His plans for a 'Balkan bloc' and a 'bloc of neutrals' aimed not only to prove to the Germans the sincerity of Romanian neutrality but also to act as a bulwark to possible Soviet expansion in the area. Despite these attempts by Gafencu to retain equilibrium and freedom of action in foreign policy, the growing threat of Soviet involvement in the Balkans made a shift towards Germany expedient.

In November 1939, King Carol sought to mediate peace between Germany and the West. His hope was that the Reich and the western powers would join forces against the Soviet Union. By now, the Soviet Union was regarded by politicians of all persuasions as of far greater danger to Romania than Germany. The Soviet Union's potential for aggression was again made clear to the Romanians following the outbreak of the Winter War in November. Increasing contacts between Moscow, Budapest and Sofia in the winter of 1939–40 led to fears of a territorial amputation of Romania. Under these circumstances, Gafencu sought to exploit previous conversations with German officials in which common German–Romanian anti-bolshevism, fear of pan-slavism and the importance of Greater Romania as an anti-communist bulwark on the Danube, had been expressed. He also repeated Romania's past loyalty and neutrality towards the Reich as justification for German mediation with the Soviets. The importance of Germany for Romanian security became all the more crucial as the Romanians were made aware during the autumn of 1939 that the Anglo-French guarantee would not operate against the Soviet Union.

The autumn and winter of 1939–40 witnessed important economic concessions to the Germans by the Romanian government. The exchange of large quantities of Romanian petroleum for arms captured in Poland was a major feature of these agreements, which culminated in the May 1940 'Oil for Arms' pact. During this period, the Romanian government also began collaboration with the German Abwehr against British sabotage of petroleum deliveries bound for Germany. King Carol began a process of rapprochement with the Romanian- and German-based Iron Guard. He hoped thereby not only to stabilise his own regime, by co-opting the country's most popular nationalist movement, but also to increase his standing in the Reich.

Hence by the spring of 1940, Gafencu's policy of equilibrium was already beginning to unravel. On 28 May 1940 neutral Belgium, which had provided the model for Romania's own neutrality policy, capitulated. On the following day, the Romanian government declared its wish for closer collaboration with the Reich 'in all domains'. Gafencu, who continued to argue that Romania should pursue a neutral course because the outcome of the war was not yet clear, resigned on 1 June. The following month saw the Soviet annexation of Bessarabia and the northern Bukovina. In early July, fearing further annexations by the Soviets, and possible attack by Hungary and Bulgaria, King Carol turned to Germany, requesting a full-scale alliance and the sending of a German military mission to Romania. The Anglo-French guarantee was abrogated and Romania left the League of Nations. Pro-German Iron Guardists entered the government. The price of German protection, however, was that Romania should resolve her territorial disputes by entering into negotiations with Bulgaria and Hungary. Under the Vienna Award of August 1940, Romania lost northern Transylvania to Hungary but received a territorial guarantee by the Axis of rump Romania. The loss of northern Transylvania proved too much for Carol's regime. Popular protests and Iron Guard risings in early September forced Carol to abdicate in favour of a regime led by General Antonescu.

The foundations of General Antonescu's alliance with Germany were laid by King Carol in the summer of 1940 in response to the Soviet annexation of Bessarabia and the northern Bukovina. Antonescu's regime did not represent a break in Romania's foreign-policy orientation. Even the Iron Guard, which governed briefly with Antonescu, had originally entered the government in the summer of 1940 as Carol sought to build up his pro-German credentials. Direct German involvement in the establishment of the Antonescu regime in the autumn of 1940 has almost certainly been exaggerated.

The gradual shift towards Germany in the late 1930s was a result of Romania's geo-political situation. Caught between Germany and the Soviet Union, Romania's links with the West became increasingly difficult to maintain as German and Soviet influence in the affairs of Eastern Europe grew. The western powers recognised Romania's strategic importance. They recognised also the importance of her economy to the Reich's war effort. With the opening of the European war, however, military support became increasingly difficult. In these circumstances, it was the Soviet threat, rather than a potential German threat, which Romanian foreign-policy makers headed by King Carol regarded as greatest. Romania had no direct territorial disputes with the Reich. Foreign-policy neutrality towards Germany and economic concessions offered the possibility that the Reich would prevent Hungary laying claim to Transylvania. With the Soviets, however, Romania had a direct territorial quarrel. In addition, it was feared that a Soviet occupation of Romania would lead to the destruction of the Romanian monarchy and ruling class.

Given that Romania's shift towards Germany in the late 1930s was motivated by fear of communism, it can be seen as partly ideological as well as geo-political. In the mid-1930s it was only the Iron Guard and individual pro-German politicians such as Octavian Goga who repeatedly stressed the ideological links between Romania and the Nazi Reich: namely, common anti-bolshevism, antisemitism and fear of pan-slavism. By 1939–40 these arguments were in regular use by

Romanian diplomats as they attempted to win German support against the Soviets. Likewise, the ethnic principle, which the Nazis supported at least in theory, acquired increasing importance to Romanian politicians. Ethnic criteria had long been used by Romanian historians to justify Romania's borders. Among politicians, however, it was the Iron Guard which argued in the mid-1930s that Romania's borders were not justified by the Paris peace treaties but according to the national principle. In other words, Greater Romania existed because it comprised the Romanian nation and not because its borders had received the approval of the Great Powers. The effect of the 1938 Anschluss and Munich agreement was to destroy the validity of the Paris peace treaties. It became clear to Romanian politicians that their country's borders could no longer be justified by the treaties. Mainstream Romanian politicians now sought to justify Greater Romania's borders on ethnic grounds. Armand Călinescu stated in February 1939 that 'the border of the Romanian state is the border of the Romanian area of settlement. It is not the result of any treaty, it is the product of history and natural rights.'[1] In like manner, Gheorghe Brătianu justified the existence of Greater Romania: 'Romania is not based on the peace treaties or on the decision of the Great Powers but on the reality of...national unity.'[2]

Nevertheless, despite these nationalist affinities, Romania's move towards alliance with Germany remained primarily pragmatic and was driven by fear of the Soviet Union. In April 1940 Minister Fabricius in Bucharest informed Berlin that the Romanians recognised that protection against the Soviets could only be achieved by alignment with Germany. He added that 'for the most part this line of policy is dictated by the head and not by the heart'. Fabricius concluded that alignment with Germany could only be sustained 'as long as faith in the victory of German arms, or at least in the maintenance of German hegemony in Europe lasts'.[3] This pragmatic approach also lay at the heart of General Antonescu's alliance with the Germans. In a letter to Iuliu Maniu written in February 1941 Antonescu justified his alliance with the Reich. 'Could we remain with out old alignments when the great democratic powers could not even assure their own existence?...In the political space in which we find ourselves, the single genuine forces at present remain Germany and Russia...However, a political alignment with Russia is a moral and factual impossibility...As a result, I have adopted from the beginning, without hesitation, a precise foreign-policy orientation....'. Hermann Neubacher later reported that '...Antonescu's fear of Soviet Russia provided the only political basis on which [Germany and Romania] could work together'.[4]

178 *Conclusion*

The pragmatic nature of the move towards Germany, opens up the question as to the extent to which the Romanian government misread German policy towards Eastern Europe. Three specific issues are important here. First, the oft-repeated promise of a German guarantee did not become a reality until Romania had already been truncated in the summer of 1940. Secondly, the supposedly irreconcilable nature of the Nazi and bolshevik regimes was disproved by the Nazi–Soviet Pact. Thirdly, the Romanian belief that the Germans would arbitrate on the Transylvanian issue on the ethnic principle was quickly dashed by the Vienna Award which was primarily territorially based.

With regard to the issue of a guarantee, the Romanian government was well aware of the conflicts between different foreign-policy organisations within the Reich. They were fully aware that Göring's claims that the Reich did not support Hungarian revisionism were in direct contradiction to the foreign ministry's line. Nevertheless, the fact remained that the Reich alone, as the regional Great Power, could offer Romania adequate support against Hungarian revisionism. By the outbreak of war in 1939, it was quite clear that the Anglo-French guarantee was useless. Acceptance of support from the Soviet Union against Hungary was not perceived as an alternative. Moreover, as we have seen, it is highly likely that a guarantee was offered by Germany in March 1939 but that the Romanians regarded the price as too high. Thereafter, as the international situation worsened, even the remote possibility of German support against Hungary or the Soviets made a policy of goodwill towards Germany essential. Romania's economic assets, especially petroleum, could always be used as a bargaining tool.

Concerning the Nazi–Soviet Pact and the loss of northern Transylvania, the Romanian government was perhaps unaware of the extent to which Nazi leaders were prepared temporarily to jettison long-term ideological goals regarding the Soviet Union in order to gain short-term advantage. The alliance with the Soviets was a product of Foreign Minister Ribbentrop's foreign-policy plan in which Germany and the Soviets were to unite against the British Empire. His policy thus conflicted with Hitler's goal of war against the Soviet Union and the Lebensraum ideology. Nonetheless, Hitler was prepared to use Ribbentrop's policy as a temporary measure in order to prevent Germany finding herself at war on two fronts.[5] Similarly, the truncation of Transylvania was not, as Romanian historians often maintain, part of a deeply laid plot against Romania. The truncation of Transylvania was a strategic response by Germany to the threat of Soviet incursion into the Balkans. As such, the Second Vienna Award was part of Germany's preparations for war against an increasingly aggressive Soviet Union. Reactions regarding the Transylvanian issue highlight the inability of many Romanian historians to look at their country's history in a broader context. While Romania was of strategic and economic importance to Germany, she was also part of a wider foreign policy and changing international context which of necessity led to frequent foreign-policy adjustments.

The pragmatic nature of Romania's commitment to Germany meant that Romanian war aims in the Second World War remained primarily those of recreating Greater Romania. Wider German war aims did not win large-scale support within the Romanian government or army. Since Romanian support for Germany was of the 'head rather than the heart', it was relatively easy for the Romanian government to consider leaving the German camp as the tide of war turned against the Reich in 1944.

Finally, the Romanian government's attempt to maintain neutrality between the Great Powers in the 1930s should be placed in its historical context. Historically, the success of Romanian diplomacy could be characterised as an ability to maintain neutrality, or 'equilibrium', between the European powers, together with an astute sense of the appropriate moment in which to tie Romania's colours to one or another power or power bloc.

The autonomous existence of the Romanian Principalities during the period of Ottoman hegemony in South-East Europe depended in large measure on the ability of Romanian rulers to steer a course between the Porte on the one hand, and foreign Christian rulers on the other. Constantin Brâncoveanu, for instance, who ruled Wallachia between 1688 and 1714 successfully trod a path between the Ottoman, Russian and Habsburg empires which enabled Wallachia to retain her autonomy.[6] In the nineteenth century, it was the ability of Romanian leaders to exploit the tensions between the declining Ottoman empire and the expanding Russian empire, together with winning the goodwill of the western powers, which created the foundations for the creation of the Romanian kingdom in 1881.

In 1883 Romania committed herself to an alliance with Germany, Austria-Hungary and Italy. Romanian politicians continued, nevertheless, to watch 'closely for changes in the political atmosphere of Europe and in the balance between competing alliance systems'.[7] Having declared formal neutrality in 1914, Romania entered the First World War on the allied side in 1916. It was by now clear that Romania's territorial claims would only be met following the defeat of the central powers and with the support of the Entente. Romania's timely re-entry into the war on the allied side in the autumn of 1918 enabled her to sit

180 Conclusion

at Versailles as a victor power, despite having made a separate peace with the central powers earlier that year.

Likewise, Romania entered the Axis camp in the autumn of 1940 when it was clear that this was her sole protection against further Soviet aggression. Although Romania had lost territory at Axis hands, it was clear that only with Axis support against the Soviet Union and by vying with Hungary for Axis goodwill, could she ever hope to re-establish her territorial integrity. In the same manner, when the tide of war had clearly turned against Germany, Romania once again jumped ship into the allied camp. Although the loss of Bessarabia to the Soviet Union was to be permanent, collaboration with the Soviets brought Romania the return of the whole of Transylvania at the end of the war. Romania played her diplomatic cards with astuteness during the first half of the twentieth century. Although there were times when her foreign-policy options were severely limited, as in the summer of 1940, she was never a mere pawn of the Great Powers.

Notes

1. Armand Călinescu, *Das Neue Rumänien. Ergebnisse einer Königlichen und Nationalen Revolution*, Bucharest, 1939, p. 48.
2. Gheorghe Brătianu, 'Rumänien zwischen Deutschland und dem Balkan', *Deutsches Wollen* (April 1939), pp. 9–13 (11).
3. DGFP, D, 9, Doc. nr 33, Legation in Romania to the Foreign Ministry, Bucharest, 1 April 1940, signed Clodius, Fabricius.
4. Quoted by Larry L. Watts in 'Antonescu and the German Alliance', *Romanian Civilization*, 1, nr 1 (Summer 1992), pp. 61–76, (63–4).
5. Wolfgang Michalka, *Ribbentrop und die Deutsche Weltpolitik 1933–1940. Aussenpolitische Konzeptionen und Entscheidungsprozesse im Dritten Reich*, Munich, 1980, esp. pp. 278–306.
6. See Ştefan Ionescu, 'The European Scope of the Great Prince's Policy', in *Romania: Pages of History*, 13, nr 3 (1988), pp. 131–64.
7. For Romania's pre-1918 foreign policy, see Keith Hitchins, *Rumania, 1866–1947*, Oxford, 1994, pp. 136–54 (143) and pp. 251–91.

Bibliography

Bibliographies and reference works

American Historical Association, 'Recently Published Articles', Vol. 1, nr 1, February 1976–Vol. 15, nr 3, Autumn 1990.
Anuarul statistic al României, 1939 și 1940, Bucharest, 1940.
Bibliografia istorică a României, 7 vols, Bucharest, 1970–1990.
Deletant, Andrea and Dennis, *Romania*, World Bibliographic Series, Oxford, 1985.
Grothusen, Klaus-Detlev (ed.), *Südosteuropa Handbuch*, Vol. 2, Göttingen, 1977.
Hillgruber, Andreas (ed.), *Südost-Europa im zweiten Weltkrieg. Literaturbericht und Bibliographie*, Frankfurt, 1962.
Ionescu, Șerban N., *Who was Who in Twentieth Century Romania*, Boulder and New York, 1994.
Kimmich, Christoph M. (ed.), *German Foreign Policy 1918–1945: A Guide to Research and Research Materials*, Delaware, 1981.
Ministerul Regal al Afacerilor Străine, *Anuar diplomatic și consular al Regatului României 1942*, Bucharest, 1942.
Politics and Political Parties in Rumania, International Reference Library, London, 1936.
Recker, M. L. (ed.), *Enzyklopädie deutscher Geschichte*, Vol. 8, Munich, 1990.
Scheider, Th. (ed.), *Handbuch der europäischen Geschichte*, Vol. 7, Stuttgart, 1979.
Volkmann, Hans-Erich, *Wirtschaft im Dritten Reich*, 2 vols, Koblenz, 1984.

Unpublished primary sources

Arhiva Ministerului Afacerilor Externe (Archive of the Ministry for Foreign Affairs, Bucharest)

Fond 71/Anglia: volume 10
Fond 71/1920–1944, Dosare Speciale:
  Anul 1938, volume 356 G-14.d
  Anul 1939, volume 398
  Austria A1, volume 270
  Anschluss, volume 272
  Cehoslovacia C7, volumes 300–303
  Cehoslovacia C7b, volumes 308, 313
  România R3, volume 482
  România R6, volume 487
  România R7, volume 376/1
  România R25, volumes 394, 395
  România R29, volume 487
Fond 71/1939 E9: volumes 1, 2, 90, 92, 116
Fond 71/Francia
Fond 71/Germania: volumes 74–82, 97

Fond Înțelegerea Balcanică: volumes 7, 20
Fond Mica Înțelegere: volumes 15–19, 29, 52
Fond 71/România: volumes 3–9, 82, 103, 353, 357, 357/1, 382, 383, 402, 415 bis, 433, 434, 503, 504
Fond 71/1920–1944, Transylvania: volumes 42, 43
Fond 71/Turcia: volume 61
(Miscellaneous) 2 Conv. G.19

Arhivele Statului (State Archives, Bucharest)
Fond Casa Regală
Fond Constantin Argetoianu, Însemnări Zilnice
Fond Ministerul Propagandei Naționale
Fond Președinția Consiliului de Miniștri

Microfilm collections:
Portugalia I-021-85-21, roll 21,
Portugalia I-021-85-22, roll 22,
Academia Portugheză de Istorie,
Donația Monique Urdăreanu:
Însemnări Zilnice, Carol II, 1937–1951

Statele Unite ale Americii (S.U.A.), roll 39
(German diplomatic records microfilmed at Alexandria, VA)

Biblioteca Academiei Române, Arhiva Istorică (Romanian Academy Library, Historical Archive)
Fond nrs 10–14
(copies of German documents from the former Zentralarchiv, Potsdam now located in the Bundesarchiv, Berlin)

Biblioteca Națională (National Library, Special Collections Section, Bucharest)
Fond St. Georges

Bundesarchiv, Berlin
NS 10 – Persönliche Adjutantur des Führers und Reichskanzlers: 17, 18, 35, 37, 62, 89
NS 19 – Persönlicher Stab des Reichsführers SS: 809, 1649, 2292, 3888
NS 43 – Aussenpolitisches Amt der NSDAP: 43/19, 43/49, 43/52, 43/60
R 43 – Reichskanzlei: II/1419a, II/1486a – Auswärtige Angelegenheiten, Rumänien (1919–1944)

Bundesarchiv, Koblenz
Kl. Erw. 101 F – Korrespondenz von Andreas Hillgruber mit deutschen Diplomaten und Militärs zur Vorbereitung seiner Dissertation 'Deutschland und Rumänien 1939–1944' (1952–1953)

Politisches Archiv des Auswärtigen Amtes, Bonn
Büro des Chef des Auslandsorganisation (A.O.):
Rumänien, Vol. 114 (1937–1940)
Büro des Staatssekretärs:
Rumänien, Vols 1–5 (11.1938–3.1941)
Büro des Unterstaatssekretärs:
Militärmission, Rumänien (9.1940–1.1941)
Deutsche Gesandschaft, Ankara:
Pol 3, Rumänien, Vol. 3 (1939)
Deutsche Gesandschaft, Bukarest:
H, Handelsattaché Konradi, (1938–1939)
IA 3, Beziehungen Rumänien und Deutschland, Vols 1–4 (1932–1939)
IA 4, Rumänien, aussenpolitisch, Vols 1–6 (1932–1940)
IA 5, Rumänien, innenpolitisch, Vols 5–9 (1936–1940)
IA 5a, Rumänien, innenpolitisch, Einzelmappe, Jahresberichte, Vol. 1 (1935–1939)
IA 5b, Rumänien, innenpolitisch, Einzelmappe, Prozess Codreanu, Vol. 1 (1938)
IA 28, Balkan – gemeinschaftliches, Vols 1– 3, (1932–1940)
II A2, Dr Wilhelm Fabricius, Vols 1–3 (1936–1939)
  Alfred Gerstenberg (1938–1939)
  Dr Gerhard Stelzer (1938–1939)
ID 1, Personalia des rumänischen Königshauses, Vols 1–2 (1923–1940)
II D2, Konsulat, Kronstadt, Vols 1–3 (1923–1940)
Handelspolitische Abteilung:
Handakten Carl August Clodius, Rumänien, Vols 2–7 (11.1938–3.1941)
Handakten Emil Wiehl, Rumänien, Vols 13–14 (3.1940–7.1941)
Ha Pol IV b Rumänien, Handel 12, Rumänien/Tschechoslowakei, Vol. 1 (5.1936–5.1939)
Inland A/B:
82–12, Rumänien, Sdh. I – Eiserne Garde (1940)
Inland II geheim:
Berichte und Meldungen zur Lage in und über Rumänien, Vols 422–424 (1937–1942);
Rumänische Persönlichkeiten und deutsche Politiker, Vol. 428 (1940–1941)
Politische Abteilung IV:
Po 1, Rumänien, allgemeine auswärtige Politik, Vol. 1 (5.1938–7.1940)
Po 2, Rumänien, politische Beziehungen Rumäniens zu Deutschland, Vols 1–2 (5.1936–2.1939)
Po 3, Rumänien, politische Beziehungen zwischen Rumänien und Ungarn, Vol. 1 (8.1936–7.1939)
Po 5, Rumänien, innere Politik, Parlaments und Parteiwesen, Vols 1–5 (5.1936–6.1940)
Po 7, Rumänien, Ministerien, Vol. 1 (7.1936–12.1939)
Po 8, Rumänien, diplomatische und konsularische Vertretungen Rumäniens im Ausland, Vol. 1 (6.1936–12.1940)

Public Record Office, London

Foreign Office Records
FO 371: Political correspondence of the Foreign Office

Published collections of documents

Arimia, Vasile, Ardeleanu, Ion and Lache, Ştefan, (eds), *Antonescu-Hitler. Corespondenţa şi întîlniri inedite (1940–1944)*, Vol. 1, Bucharest, 1991.
Boberach, Heinz (ed.), *Meldungen aus dem Reich. Die geheimen Lageberichte des Sicherheitsdienstes der SS 1938–1945*, 18 vols, Herrsching, 1984–5.
Ciucă, Marcel-Dumitru (ed.), *Procesul Mareşalului Antonescu. Documente*, 2 vols, Bucharest, 1995.
Codreanu, C. Z., *Circulările Căpitanului, 1934–1937*, no place of publication, 1937.
Documents on British Foreign Policy, 1919–1939. Third Series: 1938–39, 9 vols, London, 1949–1955.
Documents on German Foreign Policy, Series C: 1933–1937, 6 vols, Washington, D.C. and London, 1957–1983; Series D: 1937–45, 14 vols, Washington, D.C., London and Arlington, Virginia, 1949–1976.
Documente privind situaţia internaţională şi politică a României, 1939, Institutul de studii istorice şi social-politice, Buletin informativ, Vol. 3, Bucharest, 1967, Mimeo.
Emessen, T. R. (ed.), *Aus Görings Schreibtisch. Ein Dokumentenfund*, Berlin, 1947.
Foreign Relations of the United States, Diplomatic Papers 1939, 5 vols, Washington, D.C., 1956–1957.
Kerekes, Lajos, (ed.), *Allianz Hitler–Horthy–Mussolini. Dokumente zur ungarischen Aussenpolitik (1933–1944)*, Budapest, 1966.
Les archives secrètes de la Wilhelmstrasse, Vols 1–9.2, Paris, 1950–1961.
Michalka, Wolfgang (ed.), *Das Dritte Reich. Dokumente zur Innen- und Aussenpolitik*, 2 vols, Munich, 1985.
Plămădeală, A., *Contribuţii istorice privind perioada 1918–1939. Elie Miron Cristea, documente şi însemnări corespondenţe*, Sibiu, 1987.
Schumann, Wolfgang (ed.), *Griff nach Südosteuropa. Neue Dokumente über die Politik des deutschen Imperialismus und Militarismus gegenüber Südosteuropa im zweiten Weltkrieg*, Berlin, 1973.
Treptow, Kurt W. and Buzatu, Gheorghe (eds), *Corneliu Zelea Codreanu în faţa istoriei, Vol. 1, 'Procesul' lui Corneliu Zelea Codreanu (mai 1938)*, Iaşi, 1994.
Trial of the Major War Criminals before the International Military Tribunal, 42 vols, Nuremberg, 1947–1949.

Other sources, including diaries and memoirs

Adamthwaite, Anthony, *France and the Coming of the Second World War, 1936–1939*, London, 1977.
Antip, Constantin, 'Führerul. Antonescu singurul capabil să călăuzească destinele României', *Magazin istoric*, serie nouă, 25, nr 1 (286), (January 1991), pp. 33–6.
Antonescu, Mihai A., *Politica externă a României*, Bucharest, 1937.
—— *Pro-Germania*, Bucharest, 1941.

Argetoianu, Constantin, *Orientări generale pentru alcătuirea unui plan economic pe un termen mai lung*, no place of publication, 1938.
Aster, Sidney, *1939: The Making of the Second World War*, London, 1973.
Avramovski, Zivko, 'Attempt to Form a Neutral Bloc in the Balkans (September–December 1939)', *Studia Balcanica*, 4, (1971), pp. 123–52.
Axworthy, Mark, *Third Axis Fourth Ally: Romanian Armed Forces in the European War, 1941–1945*, London, 1995.
Bade, Klaus J. (ed.), *Deutsche im Ausland – Fremde in Deutschland. Migration in Geschichte und Gegenwart*, Munich, 1992.
Banea, Ion, *Rânduri către generația noastră*, no place of publication, 1940.
Barbu, Zev, 'Romania' in *Fascism in Europe*, edited by S. J. Woolf, London, 1968, pp. 146–66.
Barbul, Gheorghe, *Memorial Antonescu. Al treilea om al Axei*, Iași, 1992.
Barker, Elisabeth, *British Policy in South-East Europe in the Second World War*, London, 1976.
Basch, Antonin, *The Danube Basin and the German Economic Sphere*, London, 1944.
Beck, Jozef, *Final Report*, New York, 1957.
Bell, P. M. H., *The Origins of the Second World War in Europe*, London, 1986.
Benditer, J., 'Anschlussul și unele consecințe ale lui asupra politicii externe a României', *Studii și cercetari științifice istorie*, filiala Iași, 7, fasc. 2, (1956), pp. 135–56.
—— 'Atitudinea guvernului român fața de Cehoslovacia în lunile premergătoare München-ului (mai–septembrie 1938)', *Studii revistă de istorie*, 9, nr 5, (1956), pp. 7–20.
Bentley, Michael and Stevenson, John (eds), *High and Low Politics in Modern Britain: Ten Studies*, Oxford, 1983.
Berend, Tibor Iván, and Ránki, György, 'German–Hungarian Relations Following Hitler's Rise to Power (1933–1934)', *Acta Historica*, 8, (1961), pp. 313–46.
Bibescu, Martha, *Jurnal politic, ianuarie 1939–ianuarie 1941*, edited and translated by Cristian Popișteanu and Nicolae Minei, Bucharest, 1979.
Böhm, Johann, *Das nationalsozialistische Deutschland und die deutsche Volksgruppe in Rumänien 1936–1944*, Frankfurt, 1985.
Boia, Eugene, *Romania's Diplomatic Relations with Yugoslavia in the Interwar Period, 1919–1941*, Boulder and New York, 1993.
Bolitho, Hector, *Romania under King Carol*, London, 1939.
Borejska, Jerzy W., 'Die Rivalität zwischen Faschismus und Nationalsozialismus in Ostmitteleuropa, *Vierteljahreshefte für Zeitgeschichte*, 29, (1981), pp. 579–614.
Bossy, Raoul, *Amintiri din viața diplomatică (1918–1940)*, edited by Stelian Neagoe, 2 vols, Bucharest, 1993.
Botescu, Dan, 'România și problema Dunării în preajma izbucnirii celui de-al doilea război mondial, *Danubius*, 5, (1971), pp. 225–50.
—— 'Problema Dunării în cadrul relațiilor româno-germane în anii celui de al doilea război mondial', *Analele științifice ale universității 'Al. I. Cuza' din Iași*, serie nouă, secțiunea 3, istorie-filozofie, 21, (1975), pp. 45–50.
Bracher, Karl Dietrich, Funke, Manfred, and Jacobsen, Hans-Adolf, (eds), *Deutschland 1933–1945. Neue Studien zur nationalsozialistischen Herrschaft*, Düsseldorf, 1992.
Brătianu, Georges I., *La Roumanie et la crise du système politique européen*, Bucharest, 1936.

Brătianu, Gheorghe, *Problemele politicii noastre externe*, Bucharest, 1934.
—— 'Rumänien zwischen Deutschland und dem Balkan', *Deutsches Wollen*, (April 1939), pp. 9–13.
—— 'Rumänische Neutralität', *Europäische Revue*, (February 1940), pp. 78–82.
—— *Zweite Denkschrift über die Rumänische Frage 1940. Aufteilung Rumäniens oder Gebiets- und Bevölkerungs-clearing im Südost Europas*, Bucharest, 1941.
Brestoiu, H., 'România – ţintă a expansiuni hitleriste', *Magazin istoric*, 21, nr 10, (247), (October 1987), pp. 12–16.
Broszat Martin, 'Die Eiserne Garde und das Dritte Reich', *Politische Studien*, 9, (1958), pp. 628–36.
—— 'Faschismus und Kollaboration in Ostmitteleuropa zwischen den Weltkriegen', *Vierteljahreshefte für Zeitgeschichte*, 14, nr 3, (1966), pp. 225–51.
—— 'Deutschland-Ungarn-Rumänien. Entwicklung und Grundfaktoren nationalsozialistischer Hegemonial und Bundnispolitik, 1938–1941', *Historische Zeitschrift*, 206, (1968), pp. 45–96.
—— 'Soziale Motivation und Führer-bindung des Nationalsozialismus', in *Nationalsozialistische Aussenpolitik*, edited by Wolfgang Michalka, Darmstadt, 1978, pp. 92–116.
Bruchis, Michael, *One Step Back, Two Steps Forward: On the Language Policy of the Communist Party of the Soviet Union in the National Republics. (Moldavian: A Look Back, A Survey, and Perspectives 1924–1980)*, Boulder and New York, 1982.
Bunescu, Tr., 'Manifestări ale maselor populare din Transilvania împotriva Dictatului de la Viena', *Analele institutului de studii istorice şi social-politice de pe lîngă C. C. al P.C.R.*, 12, nr 5, (1966), pp. 93–103.
—— 'Dictatul de la Viena – încălcare brutală a independenţei şi suveranităţii României', *Analele institutului de studii istorice şi social-politice de pe lîngă C. C. al P.C.R.*, 14, nr 1, (1968), pp. 69–85.
—— 'Unele consideraţii privind politica externă a României în perioada dictaturii regale', *Studii de filozofie şi socialism ştiinţific*, Universitatea din Timişoara, 2, (1975), pp. 327–42.
Buzatu, Gheorghe, *Dosare ale războiului mondial*, Iaşi, 1979.
—— *Din istoria secretă a celui de-al doilea război mondial*, Bucharest, 1988.
—— *Mareşalul Antonescu în faţa istoriei*, Vol. 1, Iaşi, 1990.
Calafeteanu, Ion, 'România şi blocul neutrilor (octombrie–decembrie 1939)', *Revista română de studii internaţionale*, 6, nos 2–3, (16–17), (1972), pp. 267–300.
—— 'Proclamarea oficială a neutralităţii României la începutul celui de al doilea război mondial (6 septembrie 1939)', *Revista română de studii internaţionale*, 7, nr 4, (1973), pp. 167–89.
—— 'Eforturile diplomaţiei româneşti în vederea realizării unităţii de acţiune a statelor din sud-estul Europei în faţa expansiunii fasciste (martie 1938–iulie 1939)', in *Probleme de politică externă a României, 1918–1940. Culegere de studii*, edited by Viorica Moisuc, Bucharest, 1977, pp. 326–76.
—— 'The Last Conference of the Balkan Entente and the Problem of Territorial Status Quo in South-East Europe', *Revue roumaine d'histoire*, 19, nos 2–3, (April–September 1980), pp. 229–45.
—— *Diplomaţia românească în sud-estul Europiei (martie 1938–martie 1940)*, Bucharest, 1980.
—— 'L'isolement international de la Roumanie et le Diktat de Vienne', *Revue roumaine d'études internationales*, 15, nr 1 (51), (1981), pp. 45–54.

—— Revizionismul Ungar și România, Bucharest, 1995.
Călinescu, Armand, Das neue Rumänien. Ergebnisse einer Königlichen und nationalen Revolution, Bucharest, 1939.
—— and Gafencu, Grigore, Rumänien und die Mitteleuropäische Krise, Bucharest, 1939.
—— Însemnări politice, 1916–1939, edited by Al. Gh. Savu, Bucharest, 1990.
—— Discursuri parlamentare 1934–1937, Vol. 2, Bucharest, 1993.
Călinescu, Barbu, 'Scrisoare din Cambridge. Cifrul lui Armand Călinescu', Magazin istoric, 21, nr 10 (247), (October 1987), pp. 16–17.
Campus, Eliza, 'Poziția României în timpul primei faze a celui de al doilea război mondial (septembrie 1939–aprilie 1940)', Studii și articole de istorie, 2, (1957), pp. 577–609.
—— 'Criză politică a Dictaturii Regale (1940)', Studii și articole de istorie, 4, (1962), pp. 349–79.
—— 'Poziția Micii Înțelegeri și a Întelegerii Balcanice față de Germania nazistă', Analele institutului de studii istorice și social-politice de pe lîngă C. C. al P.C.R, 12, nr 5, (1966), pp. 65–72.
—— Mica Înțelegere, Bucharest, 1968.
—— Înțelegere Balcanică, Bucharest, 1972.
—— 'Poziția României fața de politica de revanșă și agresiune a marilor puteri fasciste din Europe', in Probleme de politică externă a României, 1918–1940. Culegere de studii, edited by Viorica Moisuc, Bucharest, 1977, pp. 163.
—— Din politica externă a României, 1913–1947, Bucharest, 1980.
Carol II, În zodia Satanei. Reflexiuni asupra politicii internaționale, no place of publication, 1994.
Castellan, Georges, 'The Germans in Romania', Journal of Contemporary History, 6, nr 1, (1971), pp. 52–75.
Ceaușescu, Ilie (ed.), Istoria militară a poporului român, Vol. 6, Bucharest, 1989.
Chanady, A. and Jensen, J., 'Germany, Romania and the British Guarantee of March–April 1939', Australian Journal of Politics and History, 16, nr 2, (1970), pp. 201–17.
Charlé, Klaus, Die Eiserne Garde. Eine Darstellung der völkischen Erneuerungsbewegung in Rumänien, Berlin and Vienna, 1939.
Childers, Thomas and Caplan, Jane (eds), Reevaluating the Third Reich, New York, 1993.
Chiper, Ioan, 'Relațiile româno-germane in 1933', Studii revistă de istorie, 21, nr 4, (1968), pp. 715–35.
—— and Constantiniu, Fl., 'Din nou despre cauzele înlăturării din guvern a lui Nicolae Titulescu (29 august 1936)', Revista română de studii internaționale, 2 (6), (1969), pp. 37–53.
—— 'Efortul de refacere a integrității teritoriale a României', Memoriile secției de științe istorice, series 4, 15, (1990), pp. 87–94.
Ciano, Galeazzo, The Ciano Diaries 1939–1943, edited by Hugh Gibson, New York, 1946.
—— Ciano's Diary, 1937–1938, translated by Andreas Mayor, London, 1952.
Cine a fost Armand Călinescu. Mărturii, no editor, Bucharest, 1992.
Cine este Zelinsky-Codreanu? Cum a înșelat el țara timpule 15 ani. Uneltiri cu organizațiunile străine. Sustragerea de acte din arhiva secretă a statului, no editor, Bucharest, 1938.

Ciobanu, El., 'În legătură cu poziția României față de Cehoslovacia în perioada Münchenului', *Analele institutului studii istorice și social-politice de pe lîngă C. C. al P.C.R.*, 12, nr 1, (1966), pp. 99–100.
Ciobanu, Mircea, *Convorbiri cu Mihai I al României*, Bucharest, 1991.
Comnen, N. P., *Das internationale Statut Rumäniens und seine geschichtlichen Voraussetzungen*, Jena, 1933.
—— 'Asigurările celui de-al III-lea Reich = Vorbe goale', edited by Ion Pătroiu, *Magazin istoric*, 17, nr 10 (199), (October 1983), pp. 22–8.
Comnène, N. P., *Anarchie, dictature ou organisation internationale?* Geneva, 1946.
—— *Preludi del grande dramma. (Ricordi e documenti di un diplomatico)*, Rome, 1947.
—— *I Responsabili*, Verona, 1949.
Constantiniu, Florin, *Între Hitler și Stalin. România și Pactul Ribbentrop–Molotov*, Bucharest, 1991.
—— 'Dictatul de la Moscova (26–28 iunie 1940) și relațiile sovieto-germane', *Revista istorică*, serie nouă, 3, nr 1–2, (1992), pp. 11–22.
Cretzianu, Alexander, 'The Soviet Ultimatum to Romania (26 June 1940)', *Journal of Central European Affairs*, 9, nr 4, (January 1950), pp. 396–403.
Cretzianu, Alexandre, *The Lost Opportunity*, London, 1957.
—— (ed. Sherman David Spector), 'Relapse into Bondage, 1918–1947: The Political Memoirs of Alexandre Cretzianu, Free Romania's Last World Diplomatist': Chapter 1: 'The Fall of Titulescu', *Southeastern Europe*, 11, nr 2, (1984), pp. 237–50; ibid, Chapter 2: 'Titulescu's Policy without Titulescu', *Southeastern Europe*, 12, nr 1 (1985), pp. 103–24; ibid, Chapter 3: 'The Last Throes of Peace', *Southeastern Europe*, 12, nr 2, (1985), pp. 243–59; ibid, Chapter 4: 'Royal Dictatorship', *Southeastern Europe*, 15, Parts 1–2, (1988), pp. 99–113; ibid, Chapter 5: 'The Sinking of the Little Entente', *Southeastern Europe*, 15, Parts 1–2, (1988), pp. 114–27; ibid, Chapter 6: 'Crisis with Germany', *Southeastern Europe*, 15, Parts 1–2, (1988), pp. 128–36.
Creveld, Martin L. van, *Hitler's Strategy 1940–1941: The Balkan Clue*, Cambridge, 1973.
Dandara, Livia, *Romania în vîltoarea anului 1939*, Bucharest, 1985.
Deletant, Dennis, 'A Shuttlecock of History: Bessarabia', *South Slav Journal*, 10, nr 4, (1987–8), pp. 1–14.
Dima, Nicholas, *Bessarabia and Bukovina: The Soviet–Romanian Territorial Dispute*, Boulder and New York, 1982.
Dobrinescu, Valeriu Florin, 'Betrachtungen über die Aussenpolitik Rumäniens (1919–1940)', *Extras din Anuarul institutului de istorie și arheologie 'A. D. Xenopol'*, 17, (1980), pp. 91–104.
—— 'Some Considerations on Romanian–English Relations (1919–1940)', *Anuarul institutului de istorie și arheologie 'A. D. Xenopol'*, 18, (1981), pp. 69–86.
—— *Bătălia diplomatică pentru Basarabia*, 1918–1940, Iași, 1991.
—— and Ion Pătroiu, *Anglia și România între anii 1939–1947*, Bucharest, 1992.
—— and Gh. Nicolescu, *Plata și răsplata istoriei Ion Antonescu, militar și diplomat (1914–1940)*, Iași, 1994.
Dragan, Josif Constantin, *Antonescu. Mareșalul României și războaiele de reîntregire*, no place of publication, 1991.
Drăgoi, Ovidiu, *Relațiunile economice ale României cu Germania 1934–1938*, Bucharest, 1939, with an introduction by Mihail Manoilescu.

Eichholtz, Dietrich, *Geschichte der Deutschen Kriegswirtschaft 1939–1945*, Berlin, 1969.
—— and Patzold, Kurt (eds), *Der Weg in den Krieg*, Berlin, 1989.
Fabry, Philipp Walter, *Balkan-Wirren 1940–1941. Diplomatische und militärische Vorbereitung des deutschen Donauüberganges*, Darmstadt, 1966.
Fătu, Mihai, and Spălățelu, Ion, *Garda de Fier, organizație teroristă de tip fascist*, Bucharest, 1980.
—— *Contribuții la studierea regimului politic din România (septembrie 1940–august 1944)*, Bucharest, 1984.
—— and Mușat, Mircea, *Horthyist-Fascist Terror in Northwestern Romania, September 1940–October 1944*, Bucharest, 1986.
—— 'Dictatul fascist de la Viena din august 1940 și consecințele sale', *Crisia complexul muzeal județean Bihor, Oradea*, 17, (1987), pp. 229–41.
—— *Cu pumnii strînși. Octavian Goga în viața politică a României (1918–1938)*, Bucharest, 1993.
Fenyo, Mario D., *Hitler, Horthy and Hungary: German–Hungarian Relations 1941–1944*, New Haven, 1972.
Fest, Joachim C., *The Face of the Third Reich*, London, 1970.
Fischer, Fritz, *From Kaiserreich to Third Reich: Elements of Continuity in German History, 1871–1945*, London, 1986.
Fischer-Galați, Stephen, 'The Great Powers and the Fate of Transylvania between the Two World Wars', in *Transylvania: The Roots of Ethnic Conflict*, edited by John F. Cadzow, Ohio, 1983, pp. 180–9.
—— 'Smokescreen and Iron Curtain: A Reassessment of Territorial Revisionism vis-à-vis Romania since World War One', *East European Quarterly*, 22, nr 1, (March 1988), pp. 37–53.
Focas, Spiridon G., *The Lower Danube River in the Southeastern European Political and Economic Complex from Antiquity to the Conference of Belgrade of 1948*, Boulder and New York, 1987.
Forndran, Erhard, Golczewski, Frank, and Riesenberger, Dieter (eds), *Innen- und Aussenpolitik unter nationalsozialistischer Bedrohung. Determinanten internationaler Beziehungen in historischen Fallstudien*, Opladen, 1977.
Förster, Jürgen, 'Rumäniens Weg in die deutsche Abhängigkeit. Zur Rolle der deutsche Militärmission 1940/41', *Militärgeschichtliche Mitteilungen*, 25–26, nr 1, 1979, pp. 47–78.
—— 'Zur Bundnispolitik Rumäniens vor und während des zweiten Weltkrieges' in *Militärgeschichte, Probleme – Thesen – Wege. Im Auftrag des Militärgeschichtlichen Forschungsamtes aus Anlass seines 25jährigen Bestehens*, edited by Manfred Messerschmidt, Klaus A. Maier, Werner Rahn, and Bruno Thoss, Stuttgart, 1982, pp. 294–310.
—— 'Hitler Turns East – German War Policy in 1940 and 1941', in *From Peace to War. Germany, Soviet Russia and the World, 1939–1941*, edited by Bernd Wegner, Providence and Oxford, 1997, pp. 115–34.
Forstmeier, Friedrich and Volkmann, Hans-Erich (eds), *Kriegswirtschaft und Rüstung, 1939–1945*, Düsseldorf, 1977.
Fox, Barry Crosby, 'German Relations with Romania 1933–1944', unpublished PhD thesis, Dept of History, Western Reserve University, September 1964.
Funderburk, David Britton, *Politica Marii Britanii față de România 1938–1940. Studiu asupra stratagiei economice și politice*, Bucharest, 1983.

Bibliography

Funke, Manfred (ed.), *Hitler, Deutschland und die Mächte. Materialien zur Aussenpolitik des Dritten Reiches*, Düsseldorf, 1976.

Gafencu, Grigore, *L'Entente Balkanique du 9 février 1939 au 8 février 1940*, no place of publication, 1940.

—— *Politica externă a României 1939. Cinci cuvântări*, no place of publication, no date.

—— *Prelude to the Russian Campaign: From the Moscow Pact (August 21st 1939) to the Opening of Hostilities in Russia (June 22nd 1941)*, translated by Fletcher-Allen, London, 1945.

—— *The Last Days of Europe: A Diplomatic Journey in 1939*, translated by Fletcher-Allen, London, 1947.

—— *Însemnări politice, 1929–1939*, edited by Stelian Neagoe, Bucharest, 1991.

—— *Jurnal, iunie 1940–iulie 1942*, edited by Ion Ardeleanu and Vasile Arimia, Bucharest, no date.

Georgescu, Vlad, *The Romanians: A History*, London, 1991.

Gheorghe, Ion, *Rumäniens Weg zum Satelliten-Staat*, Heidelberg, 1952.

Ghyka, Matila, *The World Mine Oyster: The Memoirs of Matila Ghyka*, London, 1961.

Gigurtu, I. P., *Discurs rostit cu ocazia discuţiei generale a adresei de răspuns la mesajul tronului in şedinţa Camerei Deputaţilor din 23 iunie 1939*, Bucharest, 1939.

Gilbert, Martin and Gott, Richard, *The Appeasers*, London, 1967.

Goebbels, Joseph, *Die Tagebücher von Joseph Goebbels. Sämtliche Fragmente*, edited by Elke Fröhlich, 15 vols, Munich, 1987–1995.

Gold, Jack, 'Bessarabia: The Thorny "Non-Existent" Problem', *East European Quarterly*, 8, nr 1, (1979), pp. 47–74.

Göring, Hermann, *The Political Testament of Hermann Göring*, translated by H. W. Blood-Ryan, London, no date.

Grenzebach, William S., *Germany's Informal Empire in East-Central Europe: German Economic Policy toward Yugoslavia and Romania, 1933–1939*, Stuttgart, 1988.

Gritzbach, Erich, *Hermann Goering: The Man and his Work*, translated by Gerald Griffin, Georgia, 1980.

Gruchmann, Lothar, *Nationalsozialistische Grossraumordnung. Die Konstruktion einer 'deutschen Monroe-Doktrin'*, Stuttgart, 1962.

Hacman, M., 'Werden und Wesen der rumänisch-deutschen Freundschaftsbeziehungen', *Monatshefte für Auswärtige Politik*, 8, (1942), pp. 716–22.

Hagen, Walter, *Die Geheime Front. Organisation, Personen und Aktionen des Deutschen Geheimdienstes*, Linz and Vienna, 1950.

Haigh, R. H., Morris, D. S., and Peters, A. R. (eds), *The Years of Triumph? German Diplomatic and Military Policy, 1933–1941*, Aldershot, 1986.

Halder, Generaloberst, *Kriegstagebuch*, edited by Hans-Adolf Jacobsen with Alfred Philippi, 3 vols, Stuttgart, 1962.

Hassell, Ulrich von, *Vom Andern Deutschland. Aus den Nachgelassenen Tagebücher 1938–1944 von Ulrich von Hassell*, Zürich, 1947.

Haynes, Rebecca, 'German Historians and the Romanian National Legionary State, 1940–41', *Slavonic and East European Review*, 71, nr 4, (October 1993), pp. 676–83.

—— (ed.) *Occasional Papers in Romanian Studies*, nr 2, London, 1998.

—— 'Germany and the Establishment of the Romanian National Legionary State, September 1940', *Slavonic and East European Review*, 77, nr 4, October 1999, pp. 700–725.

Hegemann, Margot 'Cîteva date privind așanumitul pact al petrolului (mai 1940)', *Studii revistă de istorie*, 17, nr 1, (1964), pp. 45–9.
Heiber, Helmut (ed.), *Reichsführer!... Briefe an und von Himmler*, Stuttgart, 1968.
Heinen, Armin, *Die Legion 'Erzengel Michael' in Rumänien. Soziale Bewegung und politische Organisation*, Munich, 1986.
—— 'Die Hitler–Stalin Pact und Rumänien', in *Hitler–Stalin Pakt 1939. Das Ende Ostmitteleuropas?*, edited by Erwin Oberländer, Frankfurt, 1989, pp. 98–113.
Hibbeln, Ewald, *Codreanu und die Eiserne Garde*, no place of publication, 1984.
Hildebrand, Klaus, *The Third Reich*, London, 1984.
Hill, Leonidas E., 'The Wilhelmstrasse in the Nazi Era', *Political Science Quarterly*, 82, (1967), pp. 546–70.
—— 'Three Crises 1938–1939', *Journal of Contemporary History*, 3, nr 1 (1968), pp. 113–42.
Hillgruber, Andreas, 'Deutschland und Ungarn 1933–1944. Ein Überblick über die politischen und militärischen Beziehungen im Rahman der europäischen Politik', *Wehrwissenschaftliche Rundschau*, 9, (1959), pp. 651–76.
—— *Hitler,König Carol und Marschall Antonescu. Die deutsch–rumänischen Beziehungen 1938–1944*, Wiesbaden, 1965.
—— *Hitlers Strategie, Politik und Kriegführung, 1940–1941*, Frankfurt,1965.
—— (ed.), *Staatsmänner und Diplomaten bei Hitler. Vertrauliche Aufzeichnungen über Unterredungen mit Vertretern des Auslandes 1939–1941*, Frankfurt, 1967.
—— *Germany and the Two World Wars*, translated by William C. Kirby, Cambridge, Mass., 1981.
Hitchens, Marilyn J. G., *Germany, Russia and the Balkans: Prelude to the Nazi–Soviet Non-Aggression Pact April–August 1939*, Boulder and New York, 1983.
Hitchins, Keith, *Rumania, 1866–1947*, Oxford, 1994.
Höhne, Heinz, *Canaris*, London, 1979.
Hoisington, William A. Jr., 'The Struggle for Economic Influence in Southeastern Europe: the French Failure in Romania, 1940', *Journal of Modern History*, 43, nr 3, (September 1971), pp. 468–82.
Hollingworth, Clare, *There's a German Just Behind Me*, London, 1942.
Höpfner, Hans-Paul, *Deutsche Südosteuropapolitik in der Weimarer Republik*, Frankfurt, 1983.
Hoppe, H-J., 'Die Balkanstaaten Rumänien, Jugoslawien, Bulgarien – Nationale Gegensätze und NS-Grossraumpolitik', in *Innen- und Aussenpolitik unter nationalsozialistischer Bedrohung. Determinanten internationaler Beziehungen in historischen Fallstudien*, edited by Erhard Forndran, Frank Golczewski, Dieter Riesenberger, Opladen, 1977, pp. 161–75.
—— *Bulgarien – Hitlers eigenwilliger Verbündeter. Eine Fallstudie zur nationalsozialistischen Südosteuropapolitik*, Stuttgart, 1979.
Hoptner, J. B., *Yugoslavia in Crisis 1934–1941*, New York, 1962.
Ilie, Petre, 'Relațiile dintre Garda de Fier și Germania nazistă', in *Împotriva fascismului. Sesiunea științifică privind analiza critică și demascarea fascismului în România, București, 4–5 martie 1971*, Bucharest, 1971, pp. 83–95.
Illyés, Elemér, *National Minorities in Romania: Change in Transylvania*, Boulder and New York, 1982.
Împotriva fascismului. Sesiunea științifică privind analiza critică și desmascarea fascismului în România, București, 4–5 martie 1971, no editor, Bucharest, 1971.

192 Bibliography

Ionescu, Ştefan, 'The European Scope of the Great Prince's Policy', *Romania: Pages of History*, 13, nr 3, (1988), pp. 131–64.

Irving, David, (ed.), *Breach of Security: The German Secret Intelligence File on Events leading to the Second World War*, London, 1968.

—— *Hitler's War, 1939–1942*, London, 1977.

—— *The War Path: Hitler's Germany, 1933–1939*, London, 1978.

—— *Göring: A Biography*, London, 1991.

Jäckel, Eberhard, *Hitler's Weltanschauung: A Blueprint for Power*, translated by Herbert Arnold, Middletown, Connecticut, 1972.

Jacobsen, Hans-Adolf, *Nationalsozialistische Aussenpolitik, 1933–1938*, Frankfurt, 1968.

—— *Misstrauische Nachbarn. Deutsche Ostpolitik, 1919/1970*, Düsseldorf, 1970.

—— Löser, Jochen, Proektor, Daniel and Slutsch, Sergej (eds), *Deutsch–russische Zeitenwende. Krieg und Frieden, 1941–1995*, Baden-Baden, 1995.

Jordan, Nicole, *The Popular Front and Central Europe: The Dilemma of French Impotence, 1918–1940*, Cambridge, 1992.

Kaiser, David E., *Economic Diplomacy and the Origins of the Second World War: Germany, Britain, France and Eastern Europe, 1930–1939*, Princeton, 1980.

—— 'Hitler and the Coming of the War', in *Modern Germany Reconsidered, 1870–1945*, edited by Gordon Martel, London, 1992, pp. 178–97.

Kalbe, E., 'Zu den Etappen der Balkanpolitik des faschistischen deutschen Imperialismus', *Revue des études sud-est européenes*,13, nr 3, (1975), pp. 347–51.

Kershaw, Ian, *The Nazi Dictatorship: Problems and Perspectives of Interpretation*, London, 1989.

Kiszling, R., 'Die militärischen Vereinbarungen der Kleinen Entente (1929–1937)', *Südost-Forschungen*, 18, nr 1, (1959), pp. 122–69.

Klein, Burton, H., *Germany's Economic Preparations for War*, Harvard, 1959.

Koch, H. W., 'Hitler's "Programme" and the Genesis of Operation Barbarossa', in *Aspects of the Third Reich*, edited by H. W. Koch, London, 1985, pp. 285–322.

—— 'Operation Barbarossa – The Current State of the Debate', *The Historical Journal*, 31, nr 2, (1988), pp. 377–90.

Komjathy, Anthony Tihamer, *The Crises of France's East Central European Diplomacy, 1933–1938*, Boulder and New York, 1976.

—— 'The First Vienna Award (November 2, 1938)', *Austrian History Yearbook*, 15–16, (1978–80), pp. 131–56.

—— and Rebecca Stockwell, *German Minorities and the Third Reich: Ethnic Germans of East Central Europe between the Wars*, New York, 1980.

Kordt, Erich, *Wahn und Wirklichkeit. Die Aussenpolitik des Dritten Reiches. Versuch einer Darstellung*, Stuttgart, 1948.

—— *Nicht aus den Akten. Die Wilhemstrasse in Frieden und Krieg. Erlebnisse, Begegnungen und Eindrücke, 1928–1945*, Stuttgart, 1950.

Kövics, Emma, 'Ungarn und Deutschland zwischen den beiden Weltkriegen. (Das erste Kolloquium der bundesdeutschen und ungarischen Historiker)', *Acta Historica Academiae Scientiarum Hungaricae*, 30, nos 3–4, (1984), pp. 381–87.

Kozeński, J., 'South-Eastern Europe in Nazi Expansionist Plans', *Polish Western Affairs*, 21, nr 1, (1980), pp. 47–58.

Kube, Alfred, *Pour le mérite und Hakenkreuz. Hermann Göring im Dritten Reich*, Munich, 1986.

Kuhn, Axel, *Hitlers aussenpolitisches Programm. Entstehung und Entwicklung, 1919–1939*, Stuttgart, 1970.
Kuusisto, Seppo, *Alfred Rosenberg in der nationalsozialistischen Aussenpolitik, 1933–1939*, Helsinki, 1984.
Laeuen, Harald, *Marschall Antonescu*, Essen, 1943.
Laffan, R. G. D., *Survey of International Affairs 1938*, Vols 2 and 3, London, 1951 and 1953.
Lazea, Alvina, 'Probleme ale cooperării militare româno-franceze în anul 1936', *Studii revistă de istorie*, 22, nr 1, (1969), pp. 105–27.
Lecca, Radu, *Eu i-am salvat pe evreii din România*, Bucharest, 1994.
Lee, Asher, *Goering: Air Leader*, London, 1972.
Lee, Marshall M., and Michalka, Wolfgang, *German Foreign Policy, 1917–1933: Continuity or Break?*, Leamington Spa, 1987.
Liveanu, Vasile, 'Condițiile instaurării dictaturii Legionare-Antonesciene', in *Împotriva fascismului. Sesiunea științifică privind analiza critică și demascarea fascismului în România, București, 4–5 martie 1971*, Bucharest, 1971, pp. 164–82.
Lukacs, John A., *The Great Powers and Eastern Europe*, New York, 1953.
Lukes, Igor, *Czechoslovakia between Stalin and Hitler: The Diplomacy of Edvard Beneš in the 1930s*, New York, 1996.
Lumans, Valdis O., *Himmler's Auxiliaries: The Volksdeutsche Mittelstelle and the German National Minorities of Europe, 1933–1945*, Chapel Hill and London, 1993.
Lungu, Dov B., 'The European Crisis of March–April 1939: The Romanian Dimension', *International History Review*, 7, (1985), pp. 390–414.
—— *Romania and the Great Powers 1933–1940*, Durham and London, 1989.
Macartney, C. A., *Hungary and her Successors: The Treaty of Trianon and its Consequences, 1919–1937*, Oxford, 1937.
—— *October Fifteenth: a History of Modern Hungary, 1939–1945*, Parts 1 and 2, Edinburgh, 1956 and 1957.
—— and Palmer, A. W., *Independent Eastern Europe*, London, 1962.
Machray, Robert, *The Struggle for the Danube and the Little Entente, 1929–1938*, London, 1938.
Madgearu, Virgil N., *Evoluția economiei românești după războiul mondial*, Bucharest, 1940.
Malița, Mircea, *Romanian Diplomacy: A Historical Survey*, Bucharest, 1970.
Maniu, Juliu and Brătianu, Constantin M., *How Romania was Surrendered*, London, 1941.
Manoilescu, Mihail, *Mussolini, Hitler, Kemal*, Brăila, 1934.
—— *Generația nouă și politica veche. Discurs ținut în Senat la 27 noemvrie 1936 de Mihail Manoilescu*, Bucharest, 1936.
—— 'Idea de plan economic național', *Asociația generală a inginerilor din România*, nr 81, 1938.
—— 'Solidaritatea economică a estului european', *Extras din Revista cursurilor și conferințelor universitare*, nos 3–4, (May–June 1939).
—— *Dictatul de la Viena. Memorii, iulie–august 1940*, edited by Valeriu Dinu, Bucharest, 1991.
—— *Memorii*, edited by Valeriu Dinu, 2 vols, Bucharest, 1993.
Marguerat, Philippe, *Le IIIe Reich et la pétrole roumain, 1938–1940*, Leiden, 1977.
Martel, Gordon, (ed.), *Modern Germany Reconsidered, 1870–1945*, London, 1992.

Martens, Stefan, *Hermann Göring*. *'Erster Paladin des Führers' und 'Zweiter Mann im Reich'*, Paderborn, 1985.

Marzari, Frank, 'Some Factors Making for Neutrality in the Balkans in August–September 1939', *East European Quarterly*, 3, nr 2, (1969), pp. 179–99.

—— 'The Bessarabian Microcosm: September 1939–February 1940', *Canadian Slavonic Papers* 12, nr 2, (1970), pp. 128–41.

—— 'Projects for an Italian-Led Balkan Bloc of Neutrals, September–December 1939', *The Historical Journal*, 13, nr 4, (1970), pp. 767–88.

Matei, Gh., 'Solidaritatea poporului român cu poporul cehoslovac împotriva agresiunii hitleriste', *Analele institutului de studii istorice și social-politice de pe lîngă C. C. al P.C.R.*, 12, nr 5, pp. 69–72.

McKenzie, Vernon, *Here Lies Goebbels!*, London, 1940.

Mendelsohn, Ezra, *The Jews of East Central Europe Between the World Wars*, Bloomington, 1983.

Meyer, Henry Cord, *Mitteleuropa in German Thought and Action, 1815–1945*, The Hague, 1955.

Mezincescu, Eduard, *Mareșalul Antonescu și catastrofa României*, Bucharest, 1993.

Michalka, Wolfgang (ed.), *Nationalsozialistische Aussenpolitik*, Darmstadt, 1978.

—— 'Vom Antikominternpakt zum euro-asiatischen Kontinental-block. Ribbentrops Alternativ-konzeption zu Hitlers aussenpolitischem "Program" ', in *Nationalsozialistiche Aussenpolitik*, edited by Wolfgang Michalka, Darmstadt, 1978, pp. 471–92.

—— *Ribbentrop und die deutsche Weltpolitik, 1933–1940. Aussenpolitische Konzeptionen und Entscheidungsprozesse im Dritten Reich*, Munich, 1980.

Miege, Wolfgang, *Das Dritte Reich und die deutsche Volksgruppe in Rumänien, 1933–38*, Frankfurt, 1972.

Militärgeschichtlichen Forschungsamt (ed.), *Das Deutsche Reich und der zweite Weltkrieg*, 6 vols, Stuttgart, 1979–1990.

Milward, Alan S., *War, Economy and Society, 1939–1945*, London, 1987.

Minei, Nicolae, 'Amintirile unui fost ministru de externe. România și "criza cehoslovacă" ', *Magazin istoric*, 14, nr 4 (157), (April 1980), pp. 43–7.

Moisuc, Viorica, 'Acțiuni diplomatice desfășurate după Anschluss de România împotriva expansiunii Germaniei hitleriste spre sud-estul Europei', *Studii revistă de istorie*, 19, nr 4, (1966), pp. 707–22.

—— 'Tratatul economic româno-german din 23 martie 1939 și semnificația sa', *Analele institutului de studii istorice și social-politice de pe lîngă C. C. al P.C.R.*, 13, nr 4, (1967), pp. 130–46.

—— 'Ofensiva Germaniei hitleriste pentru acapararea economiei României în perioada ianuarie 1938–mai 1940', *Revista română de studii internaționale*, 5, nr 4 (14), (1971), pp. 113–35.

—— *Diplomația României și problema apărării suveranității și independenței naționale în perioada martie 1938–mai 1940*, Bucharest, 1971.

—— *Probleme de politică externă a României, 1919–1939. Culegere de studii*, Bucharest, 1971.

—— *Probleme de politică externă a României, 1918–1940. Culegere de studii*, Bucharest, 1977.

—— *Probleme de politică externă a României, 1918–1940*, Vol. 3, Bucharest, 1988.

—— *Premisele izolării politice a României, 1919–1940*, Bucharest, 1991.

Mommsen, Hans, 'National Socialism: Continuity and Change' in *Fascism: A Reader's Guide*, edited by Walter Laqueur, London, 1976, pp. 179–210.
—— 'Reflections on the Position of Hitler and Göring in the Third Reich', in *Reevalutating the Third Reich*, edited by Thomas Childers and Jane Caplan, New York, 1993.
Mosse, George L. (ed.), *International Fascism: New Thoughts and New Approaches*, London, 1979.
Moța, Ion, I., *Cranii de Lemn. Articole 1922–1936*, Sibiu, 1936.
Mușat, Mircea, and Ardeleanu, Ion, *România după Marea Unire*, Vol. 2, Part II-a, noiembrie 1933–septembrie 1940, Bucharest, 1988.
—— *1940. Drama României Mari*, Bucharest, 1992.
Nagy, Nicholas M. Talavera, *The Green Shirts and the Others: A History of Fascism in Hungary and Romania*, Stanford, 1970.
Nanu, Frederic C., *Politica externă a României, 1918–1933*, Iași, 1993.
Nedelcu, Florea, 'Étude concernant le rôle de l'Allemagne Hitlérienne dans l'evolution des organisations fascistes de Roumanie dans la période 1933–1937', *Revue roumaine d'histoire*, 10, nr 6, (1971), pp. 991–1011.
—— 'Unele considerații privind politica externă a României în perioada septembrie 1936–decembrie 1937', *Revista română de studii internaționale*, 5, nr 1 (II), (1971), pp. 83–97.
—— 'Cu privire la politica externă a României în perioada guvernării Goga–Cuza', *Probleme de politică externă a României, 1919–1939. Culegere de studii*, edited by Viorica Moisuc, Bucharest, 1971, pp. 259–96.
—— 'Date noi privind legăturile Gărzii de Fier cu nazismul', *Revista de istorie*, 32, nr 7, (1979), pp. 1351–4.
—— *De la restaurație la Dictatura Regală. Din viața politică a României, 1930–1938*, Cluj-Napoca, 1981.
Neubacher, Hermann, *Sonderauftrag Südost 1940–1945. Bericht ein fliegenden Diplomaten*, Göttingen, 1957.
Newman, Simon, *March 1939: The British Guarantee to Poland*, Oxford, 1976.
Niri, A., *Istoricul unui tratat înrobitor. (Tratatul economic româno-german din martie 1939)*, Bucharest, 1965.
Oberländer, Erwin (ed.), *Hitler–Stalin Pakt 1939. Das Ende Ostmitteleuropas?*, Frankfurt, 1989.
Oldson, William O., 'Romania and the Munich Crisis, August–September 1938', *East European Quarterly*, 11, nr 2, (1977), pp. 177–90.
Olshausen, Klaus, *Zwischenspiel auf dem Balkan. Die deutsch Politik gegenüber Jugoslawien und Griechenland von März bis Juli 1941*, Stuttgart, 1973.
—— 'Die deutsche Balkan-Politik, 1940–1941', in *Hitler, Deutchland und die Mächte. Materialien zur Aussenpolitik des Dritten Reiches*, edited by Manfred Funke, Düsseldorf, 1976. pp. 707–27.
Oprea, Ion M., *Nicolae Titulescu's Diplomatic Activity*, translated by Andrei Bantaș, Bucharest, 1968.
Orlow, Dietrich, *The Nazis in the Balkans*, Pittsburgh, 1968.
Overy, R. J., *The Nazi Economic Recovery, 1932–1938*, London, 1982.
—— *Goering: The 'Iron Man '*, London, 1984.
—— *War and Economy in the Third Reich*, Oxford, 1994.
Palaghița, Ștefan, *Garda de Fier. Spre reînvierea României*, Bucharest, 1993.
Papen, Franz von, *Memoirs*, translated by Brian Connell, London, 1952.

Patrașcanu, Lucrețiu, *Sub trei dictaturi*, no place of publication, no date.
Paul of Hohenzollern-Romania, Prince, *King Carol II: A Life of my Grandfather*, London, 1988.
Pavel, Pavel, *How Romania Failed*, London, no date.
Pearton, Maurice, *Oil and the Romanian State*, Oxford, 1971.
——'British Policy towards Romania 1939–41', in *Occasional Papers in Romanian Studies*, nr 2, edited by Rebecca Haynes, London, 1998, pp. 59–92.
Petrașcu, N. N., *Evoluția politică a României în ultimii douăzeci de ani (1918–1938)*, Bucharest, 1939.
Polihroniade, Mihail, 'Tineretul și politica externă', *Rânduiala*, nr 3, (1937).
Pop, Gheorghe T., *Caracterul antinațional și antipopular al activității Partidului Național Creștin*, Cluj-Napoca, 1978.
Pop, Valer, *Bătălia pentru Ardeal*, no place of publication, no date.
Popescu-Puțuri, Ion, 'România în timpul celui de-al doilea război mondial', *Analele institutului de studii istorice și social-politice de pe lîngă C. C. al P.C.R.*, 12, nr 5, (1966), pp. 35–68.
Popișteanu, Cristian, *România și Antanta Balcanică*, Bucharest, 1968.
——'Diplomatic Actions Carried out by Romania in the Spring and Summer of 1939', *Studia Balcanica*, 7, (1973), Sofia, pp. 253–6.
Porter, Ivor, *Operation Autonomous: With S.O.E. in Wartime Romania*, London, 1989.
Potra, George G., '28–29 august 1936 în culisele "cazului" Titulescu', *Magazin istoric*, 3, nr 9 (30), (September 1969), pp. 50–4.
——'Proiectele diplomației hitleriste vizează România', *Magazin istoric*, 13, nr 4 (145), (April 1979), pp. 36–41.
Preda, Eugen, 'Octombrie 1940. Wehrmachtul pătrunde în România', *Magazin istoric*, 19, nr 11 (224), (November 1985), pp. 21–7.
——'Octombrie 1940. Wehrmachtul pătrunde în România (II)', *Magazin istoric*, 19, nr 12 (225), (December 1985), pp. 22–6.
——'1939: The Road Towards War. Historiography and Reality: A Contribution to Reappraisal – 50 Years On', *Revue roumaine d'histoire*, 27, nr 3 (1989), pp. 165–87.
Presseisen, E. L., 'Prelude to "Barbarossa": Germany and the Balkans 1940–1941', *Journal of Modern History*, 32, (1960), pp. 359–70.
Prost, H., *Destin de la Roumanie, 1918–1954*, Paris, 1954.
Quinlan, Paul D., *Clash over Romania: British and American Policies Towards Romania, 1938–1947*, Los Angeles, 1977.
——'The Tilea Affair: A Further Inquiry', *Balkan Studies*, 19, (1978), pp. 147–57.
——*The Playboy King: Carol II of Romania*, Westport, Connecticut, 1995.
Randa, Alexandru M., *Revoluția național-socialistă*, Bucharest, 1937.
——*Statul fascist*, Bucharest, 1935.
Ránki, György, *Economy and Foreign Policy: The Struggle of the Great Powers for Hegemony in the Danube Valley, 1919–1939*, Boulder and New York, 1983.
Read, Anthony and Fischer, David, *The Deadly Embrace: Hitler, Stalin and the Nazi–Soviet Pact 1939–1941*, New York, 1988.
Recker, Marie-Luise, 'Vom Revisionismus zur Grossmachtstellung deutsche Aussenpolitik 1933 bis 1945', in *Deutschland 1933–1945. Neue Studien zur nationalsozialistischen Herrschaft*, edited by Karl Dietrich Bracher, Manfred Funke and Hans-Adolf Jacobsen, Düsseldorf, 1992. pp. 315–32.

Reichert, Günter, *Das Scheitern der Kleine Entente, 1933–1938*, Munich, 1971.
Ribbentrop, Joachim von, *The Ribbentrop Memoirs*, translated by Oliver Watson, London, 1954.
Rich, Norman, *Hitler's War Aims: Ideology, The Nazi State, and the Course of Expansion*, London, 1973.
Roberts, Henry L., *Rumania: Political Problems of an Agrarian State*, New Haven, 1951.
Roman, Viorel, *Rumänien im Spannungsfeld der Grossmächte, 1878–1944. Von der okzidentlischen Peripherie zum orientalischen Sozialismus*, Offenbach, 1989.
Rosenberg, Alfred, *Memoirs*, translated by Eric Passelt, Chicago, 1949.
——*Das politische Tagebuch Alfred Rosenbergs aus den Jahren 1934/5 und 1939/40*, Göttingen, 1956.
Rosetti, Radu, R., *Pagini de jurnal*, edited by Cristian Popișteanu, Marian Ștefan, and Ioana Ursu, Bucharest, 1993.
Roucek, J. S., *The Politics of the Balkans*, New York, 1939.
Sakmyster, Thomas L., *Hungary, the Great Powers and the Danubian Crisis 1936–1939*, Athens GA, 1980.
Savu, Al. Gh., 'Aspecte ale politicii externe a României în preajma declanșării celui de-al doilea război mondial', *Analele institutului de studii istorice și social-politice de pe lîngă C. C. al P.C.R.*, 12, nr 1, (1966), pp. 66–84.
——*Dictatura Regală (1938–1940)*, Bucharest, 1970.
——*Sistemul partidelor politice din România, 1919–1940*, Bucharest,1976.
Schmidt, Paul, *Statist auf diplomatischer Bühne 1923–1945*, Bonn, 1949.
Schröder, Hans-Jürgen, 'Südosteuropa als "Informal Empire" Deutschlands 1933–1939. Das Beispiel Jugoslawien', *Jahrbücher für Geschichte Osteuropas*, 23, (1975), pp. 70–96.
——'Deutsche Südosteuropapolitik, 1929–1936. Zur Kontinuität deutscher Aussenpolitik in der Weltwirtsachft', *Geschichte und Gesellschaft*, 2, nr 1, (1976), pp. 5–32.
——'Der Aufbau der deutschen Hegemonialstellung in Südosteuropa, 1933–1936', in *Hitler, Deutschland und die Mächte. Materialien zur Aussenpolitik des Dritten Reiches*, edited by Manfred Funke, Düsseldorf, 1976, pp. 757–73.
Scurtu, Ioan, *Istoria Partidului Național Țărănesc*, Bucharest, 1994.
Sergej, Slutsch, 'Deutschland und die UdSSR 1918–1939. Motive und Folgen aussenpolitischer Entscheidungen', in *Deutsch–russischer Zeitenwende. Krieg und Frieden 1941–1995*, edited by Hans-Adolf Jacobsen, Jochen Löser, Daniel Proektor and Sergej Slutsch, Baden-Baden, 1995, pp. 28–90.
Seton-Watson, H., *Eastern Europe between the Wars 1919–1941*, Cambridge, 1946.
Shapiro, Paul A., 'Prelude to Dictatorship in Romania: The National Christian Party in Power, December 1937–February 1938', *Canadian-American Slavic Studies*, 8, nr 1, (Spring 1974), pp. 45–88.
Sima, Horia, *Histoire du mouvement Légionnaire*, Rio de Janeiro, 1972.
——*Sfârșitul unei domnii sângeroase*, Timișoara, 1995.
——*Era libertății. Statul Național Legionar*, 2 vols, Timișoara, 1995.
Simion. A., *Dictatul de la Viena*, Cluj, 1972.
——'Musafiri nedoriți', *Magazin istoric*, 8, nr 1 (82), (January 1974), pp. 50–5.
Sonea, Gavrila, *Viața economică și politică a României, 1933–1938*, Bucharest, 1978.
Spălățelu, Ion, '20.000.000 mărci pentru Garda de Fier', *Magazin istoric*, 16, nr 11 (188), (November 1982), pp. 33–5.

Stanciu, Ion, 'Situația internă și externă a României în perioada septembrie 1940–decembrie 1941 în noi surse documentare străine', *Revista de istorie*, 38, nr 4, (April 1985), pp. 335–51.

Stoica, Adrian and Mureșan, Camil, 'Cu privire la politica de aservire a țării față de Germania hitleristă dusă de burghezo-moșierimea română în anii 1938–1939', *Studia Universitatis Babeș-Bolyai*, series 4, fascicul 1, historia (Cluj), (1961), pp. 181–7.

Sturdza, Michel, *The Suicide of Europe: Memoirs of Prince Michel Sturdza, Former Foreign Minister of Romania*, Boston, 1968.

Talpeș, Ioan, *Diplomație și apărare, 1933–1939. Coordonate ale politicii externe românești*, Bucharest, 1988.

——'Coordonate ale politicii militare românești (1935–1939)', in *Probleme de politică externă a României, 1918–1940*, Vol. 3, edited by Viorica Moisuc, Bucharest, 1988, pp. 112–76.

Tașcă, Gheorghe, *Directivele politicei externe a României. Axele Paris–Londra și Roma–Berlin*, Bucharest, 1938.

Tătărescu, Gheorghe, *Patru ani de guvernare, noembrie 1933–noembrie 1937*, Bucharest, 1937.

——*Evacuarea Basarabiei și a Bucovinei de nord*, Craiova, no date.

——*Mărturii pentru istorie*, edited by Sanda Tătărescu-Negropontes, Bucharest, 1996.

Tharaud, Jérome and Jean, *L'Envoyé de l'Archange*, Paris, 1939.

Tilea, V. V., *Envoy Extraordinary: Memoirs of a Romanian Diplomat*, edited by Ileana Tilea, London, 1998.

Titulescu, Nicolae, *Politică externă a României (1937)*, (eds) George G. Potra, Constantin I. Turcu and Ion M. Oprea, Bucharest, 1994.

Tonch, Hans, *Wirtschaft und Politik auf dem Balkan: Untersuchung zu den deutschrumänischen Beziehungen in der Weimarer Republik unter besonderer Berücksichtigung der Weltwirtschaftkrise*, Frankfurt, 1984.

Toynbee, Arnold J., (ed.), *Survey of International Affairs 1937*, Vol. 1, London, 1938.

——(ed.), *Survey of International Affairs 1939–1946: The World in March 1939*, London, 1952.

——(ed.), *Survey of International Affairs 1939–1946: Hitler's Europe*, London, 1954.

——and Toynbee, Veronica M., (eds), *Survey of International Affairs 1939–1946: The Eve of War, 1939*, London, 1958.

——(eds), *Survey of International Affairs 1939–1946: The Initial Triumph of the Axis*, London, 1958.

Treue, Wilhelm, 'Das Dritte Reich und die Westmächte auf dem Balkan', *Vierteljahreshefte für Zeitgeschichte*, 1, (1953), pp. 45–64.

Troncotă, Cristian, 'August 1940. Din culisele marii nedreptăți istorice', *Magazin istoric*, serie nouă, 25, nr 1 (286), (January 1991), pp. 18–22.

——'Din istoria serviciilor secrete. S. S. I.–Abwehr 1937–1940', *Magazin istoric*, serie nouă, (July 1994), pp. 13–17; ibid, (August 1994), pp. 73–77; ibid, (September 1994), pp. 28–32.

——*Eugen Cristescu. Asul serviciilor secrete românești*, Bucharest, 1994.

Tuțu, Dumitru, 'Alianțe militare ale României (1921–1939)', in *Probleme de Politică Externă a României, 1918–1940. Culegere de studii*, edited by Viorica Moisuc, Bucharest, 1977, pp. 108–49.

Udrea, Traian, 'La politique exterieure de la dictature legionnaire antonescienne (septembrie 1940–janvier 1941)', *Revue roumaine d'histoire*, 10, nr 6, (1971), pp. 971–90.

Ueberschär, Gerd R., 'Hitlers Entschluss zum "Lebensraum" – Krieg im Osten. Programmatsiches Ziel oder militärstrategisches Kalkül?', in *'Unternehmen Barbarossa'. Der deutsche Überfall auf die Sowjetunion 1941*, edited by Gerd R. Ueberschär and Wolfram Wette, Paderborn, 1984, pp. 83–110.

Vago, Bela, *The Shadow of the Swastika: The Rise of Fascism and Anti-Semitism in the Danube Basin, 1936–1939*, London, 1975.

Veiga, Francisco, *Istoria Gărzii de Fier, 1919–1941. Mistica ultranaționalismului*, Bucharest, 1993.

Volovici, Leon, *Nationalist Ideology and Anti-Semitism: The Case of Romanian Intellectuals in the 1930s*, Oxford, 1991.

Waldeck, R. G., *Athene Palace Bucharest: Hitler's 'New Order' Comes to Romania*, London, 1943.

Wandycz, Piotr, 'The Little Entente Sixty Years Later', *Slavonic and East European Review*, 59, nr 4, (1981), pp. 548–64.

Watt, Donald Cameron, 'Misinformation, Misconception, Mistrust: Episodes in British Policy and the Approach of War, 1938–1939', in Michael Bentley and John Stevenson (eds), *High and Low Politics in Modern Britain: Ten Studies*, Oxford, 1983, pp. 214–55.

—— *How War Came: The Immediate Origins of the Second World War, 1938–1939*, London, 1989.

Watts, Larry L., *In serviciul Mareșalului*, 2 vols, Munich, 1985.

——'Antonescu and the German Alliance', *Romanian Civilization*, 1, nr 1, (Summer 1992), pp. 61–76.

——*Romanian Cassandra: Ion Antonescu and the Struggle for Reform, 1916–1941*, Boulder and New York, 1993.

——'Carol and Antonescu: Attitudes Towards the Use of Violence in Politics', *Romanian Civilization*, 2, nr 2, (Fall-Winter 1993), pp. 3–23.

Weber, Eugen, 'Romania', in *The European Right: An Historical Profile*, edited by Eugen Weber and Hans Rogger, Berkeley, 1965, pp. 501–73.

——'The Men of the Archangel', in George L. Mosse (ed.), *International Fascism: New Thoughts and New Approaches*, London, 1979, pp. 317–45.

Wegner, Bernd (ed.), *From Peace to War. Germany, Soviet Russia and the World, 1939–1941*, Providence and Oxford, 1997.

Weinberg, Gerhard L., *Germany and the Soviet Union, 1939–1941*, Leiden, 1954.

——*The Foreign Policy of Hitler's Germany: Diplomatic Revolution in Europe, 1933–1936*, Chicago, 1970.

——*The Foreign Policy of Hitler's Germany: Starting World War Two, 1937–1939*, Chicago, 1980.

——*Germany, Hitler and World War Two: Essays in Modern German and World History*, Cambridge, 1995.

Weizsäcker, Ernst von, *Die Weizsäcker-Papiere, 1933–1950*, edited by Leonidas E. Hill, Berlin, 1974.

Wendt, Bernd Jürgen, *Economic Appeasement. Handel und Finanz in der britischen Deutschland-Politik, 1933–1939*, Düsseldorf, 1971.

Young, R. J., *In Command of France: French Foreign Policy and Military Planning, 1933–1940*, Harvard, 1978.

Zaharia, Gh., 'Cu privire la politica externă a României în prima etapă a celui de-al doilea război mondial', *Analele institutului de studii istorice și social-politice de pe lîngă C. C. al P.C.R.*, 12, nr 5, (1966), pp. 73–5.

——'România în preajma și la începutul celui de-al doilea război mondial', in *Probleme de politică externă a României, 1918–1940. Culegere de studii*, edited by Viorica Moisuc, Bucharest, 1977, pp. 388–426.

——and Calafeteanu, Ion, 'The International Situation and Romania's Foreign Policy between 1938 and 1940', *Revue roumaine d'histoire*, 18, nr 1, (1979), pp. 83–105.

——and Botoran, Constantin, *Politică de apărare națională a României în contextul European interbelic, 1919–1939*, Bucharest, 1981.

Živkova, Ljudmila, 'The Economic Policy of Germany and Britain in South-Eastern Europe on the Eve of the Second World War', *Études Balkaniques*, 5, (1969), pp. 36–54.

Index

Anglo-Franco-Turkish treaty   103–6, 115, 123, 174
Anglo-French guarantee   90, 99, 101–4, 107, 112, 113, 123–4, 126, 146, 159, 173–4, 175
Anglo-Turkish declaration   103–4
Antonescu, Ion   1, 2, 44, 46, 61, 85, 159, 166, 176, 177
Antonescu, Victor   13, 19, 20, 21, 22, 24, 25, 27, 30, 32, 34, 35, 44, 170
Argetoianu, Constanin   10, 36, 41, 44, 55–6, 57, 58–9, 80, 84, 85, 111, 117, 136, 145, 160
Austria   47–8, 171
Austria-Hungary   3, 28, 179

Balkan bloc   119, 120–1, 174
Balkan Entente   3, 4, 6, 34, 89–90, 98, 100, 103–5, 138, 167, 174
   see also Balkan bloc; Bloc of neutrals
Belgium   22, 23, 38, 120, 132, 145, 175
Bessarabia   2, 3, 4, 52, 59, 66, 71, 103, 106, 107, 124, 125, 127, 145, 149, 155, 167, 169, 174, *and*
   German attitude towards   106, 125, 133, 143
   Soviet ultimatum over   134–7, 144, 180
Bloc of neutrals   34, 42, 119, 120–3, 138, 174
Brătianu, Gheorghe   22–3, 27, 28, 29, 34, 37, 41, 51, 58–9, 69, 79, 177
Britain   48, 51, 73, 171, *and*
   Carol II's November 1938 visit to London   56, 57, 69, 172
   relations with: Romania   3, 8, 20, 57, 65, 75–6, 77–8, 81, 90, 96, 99–101, 110, 113, 121, 126–7, 129, 137, 155
   see also Anglo-French guarantee; Anglo-Turkish declaration;
   Anglo-Franco-Turkish treaty; Balkan Entente; Greece; Romania relations with: Britain; Tilea, V.V.; Turkey
Bujoiu, Ion   74, 81, 83, 84
Bukovina   2, 71, 135, 136, 143, 144, 145, 149, 155, 157, 144
Bulgaria   2, 3, 34, 74, 107, 145, 167, 175, *and*
   negotiations with Romania regarding southern Dobruja   148–51, 154, 164
   see also Balkan bloc; Balkan Entente; Bloc of neutrals

Cadrilater   *see* Dobruja, southern
Călinescu, Armand   44, 46, 49, 60, 80–1, 83, 84, 88, 103, 106, 109–11, 116, 173, 177
Carol II   1–6, 10, 23, 25, 28, 44, 45, 48, 51, 56, 69, 76, 84, 89, 94, 105, 116, 121, 129, 130, 132, 168, 176, *and*
   Anglo-French guarantee   99, 113, 146
   his antibolshevism   4, 23
   Bessarabian ultimatum   135–6
   France   6–7, 23, 35
   German guarantee, desire for   102
   Germany   7, 56, 57, 73, 74, 81, 85, 86, 90, 119–20, 133, 142, 145, 146, 147–8, 175
   Göring, Hermann   11, 40; meeting with in November 1938   57, 70, 72
   Hitler, Adolf   7, 148, 149; meeting with in November 1938   57, 58, 172
   Iron Guard   32–3, 49, 50
   Ribbentrop, Joachim von   59
   Soviet Union   4, 26, 59, 103, 119–20, 129
   Sudeten crisis   52, 53, 55
   Tilea affair   78

Carol II – *continued*
  Titulescu, Nicolae 4–7, 13
  Transylvania, Romanian-Hungarian negotiations regarding 148, 151
Carpatho-Ukraine *see* Ruthenia
Chamberlain, Neville 57, 120
Ciano, Count Galeazzo 123, 152, 156, 157–8
Clodius, Carl 74–5, 112
Codreanu, Corneliu Zelea 33, 41, 49, 50, 51, 59, 63, 172
Comnen, Nicolae Petrescu- 8, 10, 15, 20, 25, 29–31, 32, 39, 40, 43, 47, 48, 53, 54, 55, 58, 68, 116, 171, 172
Crainic, Nichifor 147, 161
Cretzianu, Alexandru 31, 40, 112
Crutzescu, Radu 55, 69, 123
Cuza, A.C. 10, 28, 35, 43, 45, 46, 50, 170
Czechoslovakia
  relations with: *Little Entente* 3, 23–6, 170; *Romania* (armament supplies to 20, 35, 54, 55, 56, 58, 82, 85–6; economic 8, 21, 85; pressure for National Peasant Party government 35; purchase of Soviet aircraft 54); *Soviet Union* 4, 24, 54, 170
  Sudeten crisis 51–5

Djuvara, Radu 52, 53, 54
Dobruja, southern 2–3, 150–1, 154, 156

European Danube Commission, Germany's entry into 70, 72–3, 92

Fabricius, Wilhelm 40, 51, 80, 95, 120, 155, 159
Four Year Plan 11–12, 20–1, 169
France 5, 15, 18, 21, 48, 73, 100, 113, 118, 127, 134–5, 145, 168, *and*
  relations with: *Little Entente*, proposed alliance with 24–6, 35, 38; *Romania* 51, 35, 100, 110, 171 (armaments 8, 20, 35, 54–5; economic 3, 6–8, 48, 56, 57, 75, 85, 86, 96, 168); *Soviet Union* 3, 4, 5, 23, 24, 103, 168
  Sudeten crisis 53, 54
  see also Anglo-French guarantee; Anglo-Turkish declaration; Anglo-Franco-Turkish treaty

Gafencu, Grigore 91, 154, 155, 172–5, *and*
  Anglo-Turkish treaty 103–6
  Balkan bloc and bloc of neutrals 34, 120–3
  Balkan Entente 89–90
  Britain, visit to 103
  equilibrium, theory of 69
  European Danube Commission 72–3, 92
  German-Romanian economic treaty reaction to 87
Germans, 'ethnic', of Transylvania 72
Germany: economic collaboration 73, 74, 81, 85–6; guarantee 68, 70, 79–80, 90, 93, 99–102, 113, 173
  Hitler, meeting with 102
  Nazi-Soviet pact 106–7
  Polish-Romanian treaty 100–1
  Polish refugees 111–12
  Romanian neutrality 107, 129–30, 132–3
  Ruthenia 88–9
  Soviet Union 100, 101, 102–3, 114, 124–5, 129, 174; and Ukraine as German-backed buffer-state against 109
  Tilea affair, reaction to 77–8, 82
  see also Anglo-French guarantee
German guarantee 10–12, 29–30, 53, 54, 59, 68, 70, 79–81, 90, 93, 99–102, 110, 113, 152, 153, 169, 173, 178
German-Romanian economic treaty (1939), *and*
  implementation of 85–6, 97

Index 203

German-Romanian economic treaty (1939) – *continued*
 negotiations for 74–6, 81
 origins of 21, 67–8, 74, 90, 93
 proposed German-Romanian non-aggression pact 95
 provisions of 86, 95
 reactions to 87–8
Germans, 'ethnic', of Transylvania 49, 67, 70–2, 149–50
Germany, *and*
 Anglo-Franco-Turkish Treaty, reactions to 121–2
 Balkans, general economic relations with 16
 Bessarabia, attitude towards 106, 125, 133, 143
 French security system in Eastern Europe 8, 9–10
 relations with: *Czechoslovakia* 11, 48, 76, 81, 173; *Hungary* 8–9, 11, 12, 22, 23, 29–30, 41, 45, 48, 53, 58, 59, 66, 77, 79, 98, 102, 103, 108, 169, 176, 178 (and Romanian-Hungarian Transylvanian dispute 148–59, 162, 163, 165, 169); *Romania* 8, 9–12, 20, 29, 31–3, 46–7, 49–51, 54, 56, 57, 70, 73, 76, 77–8, 97, 107, 109–12, 116, 120–2, 126–31, 138, 146, 148–59, 165, 166, 169; *Soviet Union* 143, 155–8, 178–9 (*see also* Bessarabia, German attitude towards; Nazi-Soviet Pact); *Yugoslavia* 8–9, 11, 23, 30, 40, 41, 48, 53, 59
Gerstenberg, Alfred 74, 79, 107
Gigurtu, Ion 44, 60, 84, 87–8, 107–8, 109, 126, 133, 135, 136, 145, 145–50, 160, 161
Goga, Octavian 10, 13, 27–8, 35–6, 43, 44–5, 71, 170, 176
Göring, Hermann 10–12, 20, 29–31, 40, 53, 55, 57, 59, 70, 79, 80, 85, 97, 102, 169
Greece 3, 6, 77, 99, 100, 104, 106, 113, 120

Halifax, Edward, Lord 57, 77
Hedrich, Hans 71–2, 110
Himmler, Heinrich 110
Hitler, Adolf 5, 7, 57, 58, 59, 145, 148, 149, 172, *and*
 Anglo-French guarantee, attitude towards Romanian receipt of 102, 145
 Bulgaria, decision to award southern Dobruja to 150
 Carol II, letters from Hitler: 29 June 1940 145; 15 July 1940 149
 Codreanu, Corneliu Zelea, reaction to murder of 60
 Goga-Cuza government 43
 guarantee to Romania 53, 54, 79
 guarantee to Yugoslavia 40
 Hungarian revisionism, attitude towards 11, 23, 29, 31, 57, 58, 102, 114, 154
 Manoilescu and Gigurtu, meeting with in July 1940 149–50
 peace proposals of September 1939 120, 137
 Vienna Award August 1940, background to, and Hitler's fears of Soviet intervention in Transylvania 155–8, 165
 Germans, ethnic, of Transylvania 149–50
Hoare, Sir Reginald 78, 83
Hungary 2, 3, 8, 24, 52, 58, 68, 70, 74, 76, 81, 88, 108, 145, 149, 156–7, 171, 175, 180
 see also Balkan bloc; Bloc of neutrals; Germany relations with: Hungary; Romania relations with: Hungary; Ruthenia; Slovakia; Transylvania

Iorga, Nicolae 42, 51
Iron Guard 12, 31–3, 46, 49–51, 85, 110–11, 131–2, 134–5, 147, 176, 177
Italy 6, 34, 73, 137, 144, 156, 157–8, 168
 see also Balkan bloc; Bloc of neutrals; Ciano, Count Galeazzo;

Italy – *continued*
  Mussolini, Benito; Romania relations with: Italy

Jews, Goga-Cuza government's measures against   45–6

Killinger, Manfred von   128, 132–3, 135–6, 141, 147
Konradi, Arthur   50, 63

League of Nations   3, 6, 26, 44, 45, 53, 147, 161, 167, 176
Legion of the Archangel Michael   *see* Iron Guard
Little Entente   3, 4, 9, 23–6, 28, 52–3, 112, 167, *and*
  relations with: Romania   23–6, 29

Malaxa, Nicolae   84–5, 110
Maniu, Iuliu   33, 35, 41, 50, 177
Manoilescu, Mihail   87, 97, 146–8, 161, *and*
  Hitler, meeting with   149–50
  Vienna Award, August 1940   152–4
Marin, Vasile   31, 49
Marinescu, Gabriel   110
Micescu, Istrate   44
Michael of Romania, Prince and King   7, 60
Mihalache, Ion   21–2, 27, 28
Moldovanu, Victor, and proposed alliance with Germany   147–8
Molotov, Vyacheslav   135, 156, 157
Moruzov, Mihail   110, 128, 132–3, 147
Munich conference   55–6, 57
Mussolini, Benito   121, 122

National Christian Party   10, 27
National Liberal Party   35, 41, 87
National Peasant Party   21, 27, 33, 35
National Renaissance Front   72, 128, 134–5
Nazi-Soviet Pact   106, 115, 174, 178
Neubacher, Hermann   128, 129, 131, 141
Neurath, Constantin von   11, 29, 32, 43
Noveanu, Vasile   131, 147

oil   *see* petroleum

Papen, Franz von   104, 105, 122
Paris treaties   2, 3, 167, 177
Petrescu-Comnen, Nicolae   *see* Comnen, Nicolae, Petrescu-
petroleum   10, 11, 20, 54–5, 73, 109–10, 126–9, 130, 140, 146, 155–6, 157–8, 165, 169, *and*
  'Oil for Arms' Pact (provisional), March 1940   129
  'Oil for Arms' Pact, May 1940   109–10, 131, 175
Poland   20, 22, 23, 45, 77, 99, 100, *and*
  Soviet Union and attitude towards Soviet right of passage   5, 25, 26, 53, 100
  see also Romania relations with: Poland
Pop, Valer   151, 153–4

Ribbentrop, Joachim von   59, 66, 70, 79, 102, 111, 150, 152, 156, 157–8, 178
Romalo, Al.   131, 134, 141, 150–1
Romania, *and*
  anti-bolshevism of   4, 5, 167
  neutrality declaration of   107–8, 116, 117
  relations with: *Britain*   13, 44, 48–9, 55–7, 65, 69, 75–8, 81–2, 86, 90, 99–101, 104, 107, 114, 122, 127, 128–30, 140, 167, 174–5; *Bulgaria*, regarding southern Dobruja   148–51, 154, 164; *Czechoslovakia*   8, 25, 38, 44 (and Sudeten crisis 51–5, 171); *France*   2–6, 13, 19, 21, 23, 26, 27, 28, 44, 54, 56, 61, 69, 76–7, 80, 82, 100–1, 161, 167–8, 172; *Germany*: as counterweight and protector against Soviet Union   4–5, 13–14, 15, 18, 22, 26, 37, 59, 81, 85, 106–7, 108, 109, 111, 115, 117, 119, 125, 126, 129–30, 132, 133, 139, 142, 145,

Romania – *continued*
146, 159, 169, 170, 176, 177, 180; as support against Hungarian revisionism 22–3, 57–8, 68, 88–9, 103, 148–59; economic 20–2, 36, 48, 54–5, 56, 87, 88, 109–11, 168–9, 172 (*see also* German-Romanian economic treaty); Romania as bulwark for Germany against communism 23, 107, 108, 133–7; *Hungary* 28, 52–3, 58, 139, 148–50, 151–3, 164, 169, 172, 178; *Italy* 6, 13, 44, 146, 160; *Poland* 13, 24, 44, 107, 111–12, 116, 118 (Polish-Romanian alliance 3, 5, 23, 26, 54, 100–1, 108–9, 112, 167, 173–4); *Soviet Union* 1, 4–5, 22–3, 24, 25, 33, 34, 43, 108–9, 116, 119–20, 124, 125, 128, 133, 169, 175–8 (and Soviet right of passage through Romania 26, 29, 31, 38, 52–4, 171–2); *Turkey* 103, 104; *Yugoslavia* 20, 22, 23–6, 30, 40, 44, 45, 54, 59
Rosenberg, Alfred 10, 23, 27, 30, 50, 51, 72
Russia 2, 13, 160, 179
see also Soviet Union
Ruthenia 57, 58, 66, 68, 76, 81, 88–9, 172

Sima, Horia 110, 131–2, 134–5, 136, 146, 147
Slovakia 52, 57, 58, 88, 154, 171, 172
Soviet-Finnish 'winter war', effects on Romanian policy 122, 127, 129
Soviet Union, *and*
Bessarabia 2–3, 4, 59, 66, 103, 106, 127; ultimatum over 134–7, 137, 167, 172, 175, 180

relations with: *Czechoslovakia* 4, 52; *Romania* 46, 124, 146, 153, 155–7, 175

Tătărescu, Gheorghe 20, 21, 32, 36, 37, 47, 49, 69, 74, 76, 78, 105, 116, 125ff
Tilea, Viorel V. 69, 76–8, 81, 82–3, 95, 173
Titulescu, Nicolae 2, 3–7, 12–13, 36, 41, 62, 167, 169
Transylvania 2, 3, 58, 71, 83, 88, 95, 148–59, 167, 176
Tripartite Pact 2, 147, 159
Triple Alliance 3, 146, 179
Turkey 3, 6, 77, 99, 100, 102, 103–6, 121–2, 123

Ukraine, as German-backed bufferstate between Romania and Soviet Union 109
United States of America 3, 96
Urdăreanu, Ernest 84, 85, 110, 111, 130, 131, 132, 148

Vaida-Voevod, Alexandru 10, 117, 128, 136
Vienna Award
November 1938 58, 88, 154, 172
August 1940 153, 163, 176, 178

Weizsäcker, Ernst von 46, 47, 49, 50, 52, 123
Wohlthat, Helmut 21, 37, 74–5, 79–80, 81

Yugoslavia 3, 5, 6, 8–9, 23–6, 34, 44, 77, 99, 100, 104, 108, 170
see also Balkan bloc; Bloc of neutrals